Henry Harrison Brown Collection Vol 1:
(4 Books)
How to control fate through suggestion,
Concentration, the road to success,
Man's Greatest Discovery,
New Thought Primer

2017 by McAllister Editions (MCALLISTEREDITIONS@GMAIL.COM). This book is a classic, and a product of its time. It does not reflect the same views on race, gender, sexuality, ethnicity, and interpersonal relations as it would if it was written today.

CONTENTS

- ABOUT THIS BOOK 1
- INTRODUCTION 2
- PART I 4
- THE SCIENCE AND PHILOSOPHY OF LIFE 4
- INTRODUCTION TO PART II. 25
- PART II 26
- SUGGESTION: ITS PLACE AND POWER 26
- SUPPLEMENT TO THE FIFTH EDITION. 37
- BOOK TWO 44
- CONCENTRATION, THE ROAD TO SUCCESS 44
- INTRODUCTION 44
- WHAT IS SUCCESS? 44
- SECTION I. 47
- THE "WHY" OF THE BOOK. 47
- SECTION II. 50
- CONCENTRATION IS NATURAL. 50
- SECTION III. 54
- PAYING ATTENTION. 54
- SECTION IV. 59
- SOME CHANNELS OF WASTE. 59
- SECTION V. 63
- "I AM LIFE". 63
- SECTION VI. 66
- HOW SHALL I CONCENTRATE. 66
- SECTION VII. 69
- THE WILL. 69
- SECTION VIII. 72
- HABITS. 72
- SECTION IX. 76
- "IN THE SILENCE" 76
- SECTION X. 81
- COMPENSATION OF CONCENTRATION'. 81

SECTION XI	86
WITH EYES, SEE NOT.	86
SECTION XII.	90
THE IDEAL.	90
SECTION XIII.	97
PEAYER.	97
SECTION XIV.	101
DESIRE VERSUS WISH.	101
SECTION XV.	106
MENTAL POISE.	106
SECTION XVI.	108
METHODS OF CONCENTRATION.	108
SECTION XVII.	112
DIRECTIONS FOR PRACTICE.	112
SECTION XVIII.	116
HOW TO DO IT.	116
SECTION XIX.	119
SOME PRACTICAL SUGGESTIONS.	119
SECTION XX.	124
SELF-STUDY AND THE LAW OF LIFE.	124
SECTION XXI.	128
SPECIAL DESIRES VS. PRINCIPLE.	128
SECTION XXII.	133
MY ONE RULE—AGREEMENT.	133
SECTION XXIII.	137
LOVE.	137
SECTION XXIV.	141
OPINIONS AND METHODS OF OTHERS.	141
THE PARTING WORD.	145
BOOK THREE	146
MAN'S GREATEST DISCOVERY.	146
SIX SOUL CULTURE ESSAYS.	146
MAN'S GREATEST DISCOVERY	146
SIX SOUL CULTURE ESSAYS.	146
FOREWORD	147

1	151
THOUGHT AS POWER.	151
AN EXPLANATION AND A PROPHECY	151
2	156
TELEPATHY	156
THE MISSING LINK	156
3	162
THE ULTIMATE OF POWER.	162
4	167
LIFE: ITS POTENTIAL AND ITS CONSERVATION	167
5	174
VIBRATIONS	174
6	179
THE VICTORY OVER DEATHS	179
LEVITATION, MATERIALIZATION, AND DE-MATERIALIZATION	179
BOOK FOUR	193
NEW THOUGHT PRIMER	193
ORIGIN, HISTORY AND PRINCIPLES OF NEW THOUGHT TO THE MEMORY AND OMNIPRESENCE OF	193
FOREWORD	193
ORIGIN, HISTORY AND PRINCIPLES OF NEW THOUGHT	195
LITERATURE OF NEW THOUGHT	223
SOUL CULTURE AND "NOW" PHILOSOPHY, EXPLAINED AND DEFINED.	229

ABOUT THIS BOOK

This little book is attracting much attention. The author's long experience along these lines enables him to write only -what he has demonstrated as Truth. It should be used as a text-book by every thinking person. It teaches the science and philosophy of life and explains the place and power of Suggestion in a simple and practical manner. It gives the key to Success and Health. Ella Wheeler Wilcox, in her article in the Hearst papers, .says: "It is worth many dollars to anyone who will live its philosophy."'

INTRODUCTION

Some of the matter of these Essays has appeared in various journals and more especially in the Suggester and Thinker. It is here collected, revised, extended, improved, and put into a permanent shape for study. In its previous form, it attracted considerable attention and won much appreciation.

This volume contains the most important knowledge man can possess, i. e., knowledge of the Power to control his own Destiny. In his own life and that of many others, the author has seen the demonstration of this Power. The reader has but to follow the instructions herein laid down to reach that condition of realization which Jesus knew when he affirmed: "I and my Father are ONE."

The way is easy. Its principle is Truth. Its incentive is Love. Its result is Life "more abundantly." That there may be understanding, in Part I. the philosophy of Unity has been elucidated and verified by the Law of Vibration.

That this Principle of Unity and the Law of Vibration may be applied to daily thinking and living, in Part II the Principle of Suggestion is unfolded. This is an ever-present and an ever-active Principle. He who accepts, understands and applies it, attains mastery over all conditions. This principle is the basis of the many metaphysical movements of the day and, when intelligently obeyed, gives one all the power that any "healer" possesses.

That the reader may attain this power, methods of thinking and affirming are scattered through these pages. At the close, are affirmations for practice that all may, through a trained Will, learn "The Art of Living." The end and aim of the book is to help the reader to Self-Control. No perception of Truth ever gave man such Power as does this of Self-Suggestion, or, as we will term it, AFFIRMATION. It is the discovery that Thought is Force and that man can control, in its objective expression, this Infinite Sub-Conscious Life, which is the Real Man—the Ego— and thus control Fate.

All the mystery of the ancient and modern schools is cleared away from the subject and all the misconceptions of theology are avoided. As Darwin investigated, and as Spencer reasoned, upon objective phenomena, the effects, so have I tried to investigate and reason upon the Cause, the Subjective man. The Spirit that has inspired me is that of the Affirmation, ALL IS GOOD. I have tried to let it manifest in me under that New Commandment, "That ye love one another."

SAN FRANCISCO, CAL. Nov. 1, 1901.

PART I

THE SCIENCE AND PHILOSOPHY OF LIFE

Unity.

Unity Of nature is now the basic thought in science and in the new Philosophy. The ancient and child-man thought duality. This conception, which from earliest times has dominated the conceptions of man, has passed from the mind of the present thinker. With it must pass all the old conceptions of man and nature. With these conceptions, must also ultimately pass the customs, laws and theologies based upon the unscientific, primitive conception of nature as duality.

This conception of unity, as opposed to that of duality, is destined by evolution to work a revolution whose import it is now impossible to overestimate.

Half Science

Our science has not been half science, even since Darwin and Spencer gave it the key to all the knowledge which comes to the soul from the external consciousness by observation and reasoning. Darwin gave man his first true conception of the world without himself. The survival, in greater or less degree, of the idea of dualism in the scientific mind and in philosophic speculation, has so colored investigation that constantly there has arisen from it the idea of limitation, division, antagonism, contest, struggle, etc. This conception of duality has either been present or has been introduced as explanation in much scientific reasoning and, in the most independent minds, it has at least been recognized as a fact of nature. This conception is so false that the New and Coming Philosophy will bear the same relation to the old as the child does to the man.

Revolution.

It is safe to say that this conception of an all-pervading Unity is destined to work a change in thought and life greater than that wrought by Copernicus when he "changed the front of the universe," or by Jesus, when he lifted philosophy from Force to Love. Darwin and his coworkers not only threw miracle and supernatural into law, but they did more; they destroyed duality and, though this thought has been constantly permeating the common mind, it has been overlooked by philosophers. But common sense has joined unconsciously with the demonstrations of science and made mind and matter into one unity. The result of this can be only dimly foreseen. But this I prophesy:—in future, man will look within himself and not without, as now, for knowledge and direction—will find the universe in himself and not, as now, himself in the universe. This is the greatest change of front man has ever made. It is revolution, but until he makes it he is neither true nor free.

Tendency of Thought.

This tendency of thought is seen in every new work in philosophy and in every new deduction of science. Few are there who dare to follow out to the end logical conclusions, or are free to give to the world the clearest light of their reasoning. Professor W. J. Powell, of the government ethnological bureau, has recently published a work which is destined to rank high in the future for its insight and its reasoning on the Oneness of nature. Professor McGee, in reviewing the book-in The Forum, says of Prof. Powell: "Accepting the observed unity of matter and motion, Powell is able to escape that besetting dualism that has clung to the human mind ever since the sylvan savage first noticed front and rear, this side and that side." "This observed unity" is the basis of reasoning and of life in Soul Culture. Soul Culture is, therefore, that coming thing which is neither religion nor science, but is the union of the two, Soul being the religious side, and Culture being the scientific side of the thought. Its first affirmation is Unity. This affirmation is constantly repeated until it becomes the instinctive thought, to solve all problems of life.

One Something.

All is One—Something! The name is of no consequence. I would not quarrel with one who would say Brahm, God, Force, or any other term that to him meant Unity. I find it more acceptable to say,—All is Spirit. What Spirit is, can be answered only by saying: Spirit is All and All is to consciousness only differing manifestations of Spirit.

Duality.

There are not two forces, two antagonistic somethings, warring in nature for mastery. These two things have heretofore been in the mind balanced. Some of these warring mental twins arc God and Devil, angels and demons, men and women, spirit and body, mind and matter, matter and motion, matter and spirit, good and evil, health and disease, life and death—as separate entities. These are two only to the child-man, who reasons from appearances, but to him who looks at cause they will ever be manifestations of the One. There are no double standards. One reigns forever, and that one is Mind or Spirit— omnipotent, omniscient and omnipresent. Cause being One, there can be only harmony. There can be no antagonism; no struggle; no contest; no evil; no wrong; no progress. There can be only manifestation of the One in harmony and in purpose, or it would be self-destructive and there would in time be not even One.

Cause.

The One manifests in many million ways, but they are all harmony, all good and right, or they are all discord, and evil and wrong. Cause—the One—these names are not given, but they are names man gives to effects. They are very readily transferable and are transferred so constantly that no standard as to good, etc., has ever been found permanent among any people, and never one for the- race. The only one ever held in theory is the one in all theologies, which is the belief that the Supreme Power can do no wrong. But this has rarely descended to practical application. Yet its evidences how dimly man has seen, but how truly he has ever felt, the fact which science to-day demonstrates, that the Universe is one energy. Thus, in the New Philosophy, these terms mean nothing when applied to nature, but are significant when applied to man himself. They mean in him effects of the one Cause. They are names for his convenience alone. They mean nothing as to Cause itself.

Fate.

Man is thus his own Fate, inasmuch as he has power to choose, to use and to name, and, as fast as he learns his power, to control the manifestations of the One, he shall decide how and when this power shall in manifestation serve him. Thus, in future, man, instead of being slave, or creature, to an outside power as in all the past, shall BE that power, and manifest as he chooses; shall make all other manifestations obey him instead of obeying, as now. He shall no longer fear a god outside himself, but reverence himself as a manifestation of the Indivisible God.

He shall not only choose how he shall himself manifest, but he shall decide how all other manifestations shall affect him, or whether they shall affect him at all. And he shall control all manifestations of a less pitch in vibration than his own, be they manifestations known as heat or human thought. He will, by choice, adapt manifestations to himself, or himself to vibrations, until he finds his ideal of happiness, or, what is the same, until every manifestation of the One gives him pleasure.

Man.

All reasoning will hereafter be from Man, and from Man as center of the universe, and from the universe only as the circumference of Man. It is with Man alone, then, that Soul Culture deals. Man is to us the representative of All. In him we find All; and in studying him, we study All. If science wants to use the term Force, let it be understood that it is the same to Soul Culture as the term I use—Spirit. Not yet has Spirit to science the same meaning as Force. Therefore, Spirit is used here. Both are terms for THAT WHICH IS THE I AM THAT I AM. For Truth knows only unity—"The one that inhabiteth eternity." Man is, therefore all the rest is. Without the ear, no sound; without the eye, no light; without the nerve, no sensation. Hence without Man, no anything. Without Man, no God—no One. Man is All.

Logic

This is logic. Dare we accept it and live it? Soul Culture says: Yes. Can we demonstrate our logic to be the truth? Soul Culture does. Hence the "about face" that must come in science. Where it now looks outside Man to vibration, it will look within and declare Sensation to be All. For, despite learned libraries, all that is known is Sensation. When man is wise, he will study only Sensation, for Sensation is to Man—All. Where man now knows only in part, all will then be opened to him. Where he "now sees through a glass darkly," he will then, as Spirit, see Cause face to face. How? By recognizing faculties in himself that allay him with Cause, by recognizing himself as part of the indivisible One. In fact, through his recognition of oneness with Spirit, he will declare himself Spirit, and hence regard himself as Cause. Nothing comes except by evolution. And, as the faculties we now manifest have been gradually developed because the Soul pushed them out and then they have been cultivated, so have the psychic faculties by which we take hold on Cause instinctively made themselves manifest. Now we have to be only equally wise in cultivating them. As our ancestors have been cultivating eye and hand, so must we cultivate these psychic faculties and by thus becoming a conscious factor in our own evolution, become soon consciously one with Unity.

Matter.

This intellectual position ignores entirely the thought of physical Man. Since matter and motion are one, Man cannot be two; i. e., matter and motion. If matter is, then physical Man is. If motion is, then Man is motion. Therefore, let us be logical and say:—All is matter, hence Man is matter— or, say all is motion, hence Man is motion —Spirit. Both physical and spiritual, Man cannot be. Science has decided this forever. There is only motion. Matter is only a form of motion; so is heat; so are the other so-called physical forces. By telepathy, thought and emotion have been demonstrated to be motion; therefore, no longer can Man be thought of as a physical being.

Evolution.

Here is the key to the coming evolution. This Man of unity explains the vagaries, sophistries, mysticisms of "Christian Science," Theosophy, and kindred movements. Their teachers perceive this truth dimly, but, lacking the scientific spirit, they have become blinded by the excess of light. Science will explain the manifestations of all these, as it has explained those with which it has already dealt and will find the One Force behind all. That force Man can know and master. Gods, angels, mahatmas, spirits, if they exist, are either human or of human creation. Above Man, there can be nothing; for, beyond "Spirit conscious of its own existence," (Hegel's definition of Man), nothing is possible. Man may manifest to infinity. Some man well developed may show himself to one less developed, and he who sees may say, "God," "Mahatma," etc., But what of that? What he is, I am.

Not Eddyism

To declare that Man is not physical, is as far from the Eddy folly of saying, "You have no body," as it would have been, when Copernicus said, 'The sun stands still," to have said, "There is no earth." We have body, as we have thought, and even the most strenuous Eddyite will think. Both body and thought are manifestations of force and only differ as heat and light differ—in pitch, (length and speed of vibration). To this conception of nature, are all these various systems of "Divine Science," "Christian Science," and other more or less true philosophies, bringing the common mind. They are Johns, some of them not clad even in the skins and camel's hair of truth, but all crying in a wilderness of materialistic thinking, "Prepare ye the way." And lo, here comes the Messiah of Science, saying; — "I am Unity,"

Sensation

Sound, light, heat, electricity, magnetism, phosphoresence, X-ray, chemical affinity, and other known forms of force are now known to be one, differing only in rates of vibration. Therefore must we, in this thought of unity, now study man and regard not only body, but thought, love, hate, sorrow, sexual passion, and all other emotions as forms of the one energy, differing only in the rate of vibration. That is, we have to study only the effect of vibration upon self—that is, study Sensation,

Force

As force and as a manifestation of force, Man can be as intelligently studied as have been the recognized forces of science and their effects. And, as Man has learned to control those for his benefit, so can he learn to control this force which is himself. He as force, manifests as thought, emotion, and psychic power. As he has interrogated nature and, by experiment, learned to weigh, measure and control what he calls physical force, he can, by experiment, learn to consciously use and control this force called psychic or spiritual. He is now almost entirely unconscious of it and it uses him instinctively as once did electricity. As he now uses one and is master, he can use the other and be MASTER OF SELF.

Intelligent Use.

To learn to do voluntarily and consciously what he is now doing involuntarily and unconsciously, i. e., manifesting life, is now the field of human achievement. I predict that when once man has found the way, he will have no use for all the present cumbrous machinery called science, nor for much of the present mechanical or motive powers. Occult manifestations of the One power will do all that is now done and more, with less labor, cost of friction than is possible even with liquid air. "Chalk marks don't draw cars," once said a railroad man. But we are much nearer to the time when some manifestation of force less tangible than chalk marks will draw cars, than was the possibility of lightning drawing them when Franklin drew it from the clouds, or we then were to the possibility of wireless telegraphy. Chinese used powder in play centuries before Christian nations used it to kill; so Hindoo jugglers use occult forces to-day, but the Anglo-Saxon will use them in work. I believe the Anglo-Saxon is "the coming man" who will not only conquer the world, but will also conquer the near, but unseen, realm of psychic power.

Spirit.

As spirit, to be e-du-coed (drawn out, educated) is man in the New Thought—Man is Spirit with unlimited power of manifestation. As the recognition of Man as soul and body has led to the present development, until now he finds himself limited in manifestation by this dual conception of Man and Nature, even so by this idea of unity of Nature and of Man as Spirit, will he be freed. He can then manifest without limitation and will thus usher in the new civilization waiting just ahead of us.

We are What All that has, in this thought of duality, We Think* been affirmed of Man is false when he is considered in this thought of unity. Facts will not change, but our mental attitudes respecting them do change. This will virtually change to us all things, for facts are to us what we think them to be. This applies even to the one fact that makes all other facts possible—that one fact is ourselves. We are in manifestation what we think we are. Therefore, if we think we are body and mind, we shall manifest as body and mind; if we think we are worms of the dust, we shall live dust; if we think we are gods (as we are), we shall live as gods. Thus will this thought of the universe and of Man as Unity—as Spirit—work a greater revolution in life's manifestation than was ever wrought before by any discovery, invention, or philosophy.

Preparation.

He who would take up the study of Man as Spirit must be willing to lay aside all preconceived opinions of Man and Nature, forget all science has said except this thought of unity, for unity is the only fact, except the law by which it manifests,— evolution,—that is of any practical benefit to him. In this study of Man, he is to ignore all present thought of body, thinking of it as only a manifestation of Spirit —as the materialized clothing of Spirit. In this thought, all I have said and may say is true; under the old thought of duality, all I have said or may say is false. This mental attitude is the one indispensable requisite. One may obtain facts in the supposed realm of matter while he is repugnant to them; but, in the psychic realm, to recognize facts, one must be receptive, otherwise he is like the blind man seeking to be convinced of color.

Vibration.

To the Soul Culturist, all thought of duality of essence has passed away, as have the myths of the middle ages, and he recognizes only a duality of manifestation, as Cause and Effect. To him in his relation to the Without (the external universe), there is only one Cause,— VIBRATION. This vibration is the only possible manifestation of Unity. In himself, he knows but one Effect,— SENSATION. Sensation is the only possible manifestation of Unity in him. This manifestation we call LIFE,

Sensation.

As the rates of vibration vary, so do the sensations vary. As the possible number of different vibrations is infinite, so the possible number of sensations is infinite. Man, then, is infinite in possibility here and now. He has only to develop his power to recognize sensations and of the many million vibrations that are constantly impinging upon him to choose those to which he will respond, and those which he will harness to do his work. Emerson's favorite saying may yet be true in mechanics: "Hitch your wagon to a star." Man will learn to recognize, to reproduce, and to enjoy those sensations he chooses; and will learn to ignore those which are to him unpleasant. He will thus become his own Fate and Destiny.

The New Man.

The New Man will have no senses, but he will be sensation. He will not be limited to five senses, but will constantly increase his recognition of sensation, and, thus becoming more sensitive, he will, in the ages to come, find himself responsive to every vibration in space. Then he will know ALL. A textbook on Physics, "up-to-date," now in use in our colleges, gives this definition of heat: "Heat is either a sensation, or that which produces a sensation." This is a definition that could be given of everything that man feels and of every feeling. It is true; the author told more than he intended. Everything external to man "is that which produces a sensation," and everything within him "is a sensation,"

Definition by Physics.

This is all the definition Physics gives of the phenomena of nature. We can say of air, water, electricity, light, etc., etc., they are sensations in man, and they are that which produces these sensations. But, really, the author could have said: "Heat is in man a sensation made by vibrations of a certain wave length and speed." This would also be true of everything else. He would have to go farther yet and give the length and speed of the wave. This would help the intellect to grasp an idea of heat, but the man knows by feeling what is beyond every possible definition. Heat is sensation. The child knows it by feeling, and the scientist knows no more. Where is the place to study heat, in stove or in man? Without man, there is no heat. To one under proper Suggestion, there is none. Again, the hypnotic subject under Suggestion is burned to a blister by a cold coin. Where is. heat? We answer,—in sensation. Thought can as well produce sensation as can those vibrations which science recognizes, for Thought is also a vibration. Now let science revise her definitions and her conclusions.

Finer Vibrations.

Not with the ordinary vibrations caught by science does Soul Culture deal. It deals with those which science has not yet caught; with those that can burn with cold steel; with those that enable the surgeon to amputate without either anesthesia, or pain, or blood, or inflammation; with those that carry messages from mind to mind without wire or battery; and with those that enable lovers to enjoy a communion, each with each, though they are at antipodes. These vibrations produce sensations as palpable to the one able to recognize them as are those of heat and cold.

All Knowledge Possible.

Thus is it that all knowledge is open to Man, not by the development of new senses, but by learning to recognize sensation as all of life to him, and by distinguishing those beyond the limit of the five senses. He will thus come to the fulfillment of the prophecy of the Psalmist and have "conscious dominion over all things." This is now seen in possibility. It is the object of Soul Culture to lead Man intelligently to this,—his own.

Race Sensitiveness.

The Anglo-Saxon race is growing more sensitive, and, as a result, is manifesting psychic powers to a marked degree. Inspiration is poured out in all directions as never before during the historic period. Invention, discovery, research, are in evidence, while literature of all kinds comes in floods, and from pulpit and platform the divine afflatus pours in tremendous streams. Everybody feels able to write or declaim. It is the developing power of man to feel the finer vibrations, and, though he does not know the reason and does not understand the power, yet, as he has instinctively obeyed the coarser ones, so is he instinctively obeying these. We thus account for the medium, the healer, and the psychic. It is thus we have our geniuses and our abnormalities, like Blind Tom. They are all acting as aspen leaves act in the wind, under the finer vibrations of Unity.

Diseases and Survival.

Because of this sensitiveness, there is an increase of disease and diseases, especially nervous diseases. They will increase until we learn how to control these finer forces. The "struggle for life" has now been transferred to the psychic plane, and those who cannot live under the intense strain on the organism, caused by this increased sensitiveness, must die off, leaving the hardier ones to keep up the stock.

Saviors.

For this reason, there is a demand from the race instinct for saviors. In supplying this demand, they come in droves, each with varying perceptions of truth. The regular M. D.'s already fear for their trade, as it is going before the incoming tide of clairvoyants, magnetic healers, "Scientists" of many kinds, and, last of all, before Suggestive Therapeutics. These are all natural results of increased sensitiveness. Nature always balances her manifestations. With the illness, due to increased sensitiveness, relief comes in methods of healing adapted to that sensitiveness. As bleeding went out with the hardy pioneer age that could stand it, in came milder systems, and finally these came that discard medicine. Through use of Nature's finer forces, Man is not only healed of disease, but is made positive to unpleasant sensations. "You do not feel the prick of the pin," says the hypnotist. So says the intelligent healer: "You do not respond now to the vibrations of pain. As you will not see that which is unpleasant, or hear that which is discordant, so you will not feel that which is painful. You have within your control the power of sensation. You can feel only what you will."

Progress.

The progress of civilization depends now not on the arts and sciences, not on schools or churches, but on attaining the knowledge and mastery of these finer vibrations. These psychic manifestations often produce some disturbance in the body, causing one to depart from ordinary customs and manners. This causes some philosophers to cry: "Degeneracy." Some peculiar mental conditions cause others to cry, "Insanity is on the increase," or some peculiarity of conduct causes the cry, "Crime is on the increase," while the cause is only an increase of psychic sensitiveness. The race is, at the close of this cycle, taking another step forward. Could one of the present croakers have seen the first eye that blinked at the sun and died from excess of sensation, but, dying, prophesied the eye of man, he would have said of that individual specimen of the species: "Degenerate." Could the medical professions that now cry "fraud" and "deterioration" in view of the many isms of to-day, have stood by the first man that made a bow, and seen how, by confinement and labor, he had changed from the rest of the tribe, they would have recommended change of climate and said: "The race is going physically and morally backward," when, in fact, it was going ahead, outgrowing the conservative's sight.

Law.

If some of the present over-anxious and meddling moral reformers who, failing to suppress vice and to regulate morals by law, are now trying to prevent the blessings of hypnotism from becoming known, could have seen primitive man lay off the skin of the animal he had worn, they would have exclaimed: "Immoral! The race is becoming too vile to live." Yet through similar changes has the race passed. The manifestations of Unity through humanity are progressive, despite prognostications of evil and decay. The race will pass safely through this change from instinctive action to intelligent and consciously predetermined action, and thus will dethrone every "absentee" god and enthrone Unity within. It will defy all law by being itself Law.

Conduct.

In all these changes, the Ego is manifesting more and more of its own infinity. The Ego power of perceiving what is, gradually reveals Truth to the intellect through sensation. "For thoughts," says Edward Carpenter, "are only dying feelings." When we feel deep enough, that is, when we suffer enough, we seek the cause and, in seeking, find and grow. Sensations that cannot be endured are avoided or cured. We learn to choose instinctively the pleasurable and to avoid the opposite. This is our only conscious way of deciding what the Ego wants. It is equivalent to Spencer's dictum, "Health-giving acts are pleasurable," and to Prof. Elmer Gates' discovery that "pleasurable emotions are healthful, and the opposite are poisonous." The Ego, which is a manifestation of Unity, finds by the sensation of pleasure the best way to unfold its individuality. It is Emerson's wise and comprehensive advice: "Trust the current that knows its way."

Ego Law.

Above By noting sensations, we discover regularity and coincidences that we call laws.

In the materialistic worship of this fetish of Law, sight is lost of the greater fact that Spirit (and therefore the Ego as a part of the undivided Spirit) is itself Law, and hence above all law.

Practical Work.

Here is a hint of the practical work of Soul Culture. It works with manifestation, with the design of controlling manifestation. It recognizes Soul not as something yet to be, or that which is beyond conception, but as something that now is. It works with Man as Soul. Soul Force, or Spirit, is as thinkable, as real, and as workable as electricity. Affirming as an individual, "I am the Spirit," the Soul Culturist Thinks Spirit, and lives Spirit, and manifests consciously the powers of Spirit. He acts that which he affirms, lives that which he professes, and knows himself as Spirit.

No Sickness.

As Spirit cannot feel pain, or be sick or die, he knows, as an individual Spirit, he cannot be sick, or have pain or die. These conditions are to him only manifestations of different mental attitudes or states of consciousness. They are real to his consciousness // he will think of them, if he will recognize them, but they are not real to him as Spirit. Whenever he changes his mental attitude and refuses to recognize them, they do not exist, for he, by recognition, becomes the creator of these conditions; they are the effects of his thinking.

Conditions.

Man His Own It is the same with all unpleasant Creator of conditions called sorrow, grief, trouble, worry, jealousy —with all that makes one unhappy. They are in man effects of his feeling or thinking. They are produced in him by Suggestion as similar ones are produced in hypnotic subjects. Man is, therefore, his own creator. He can produce within himself, at will, either pleasant or unpleasant emotions, thus making himself, at will, happy or unhappy, well or sick, wise or foolish.

Recognition.

The first thing necessary for the development of this power is simply for one to recognize himself as Spirit. Jesus, who was spiritually developed, must have meant this when he said, "He that believeth and is baptized is saved," for all the water of "the river of life" would run off the unbeliever without producing any effect, because, by refusal to recognize the power, it would not exist for him. Small discharges of electricity kill, and extremely great ones are not felt; even so does this mighty power of Spirit pass through one constantly unrecognized, until sought for; then it is found, as all else has been found, through recognition of sensation.

Scientific Faith.

This is asking of one only that same faith which the scientist has when experimenting. He would not experiment if he did not believe in the possibility of finding. Give the same ready mind to Spirit, and, in that receptivity, the Recognition will come. Once Recognition is, then all things asked for are possible.

Desire.

Next to Recognition, is Desire. It is the attitude of true prayer, "the heart's sincere desire, uttered or unexpressed." In desire, the way is open for the "current that knows its way" to flow unhampered.

Liberty.

Liberty of Spirit is thus won. Without this liberty, no spiritual growth. The last liberty to be won is "the liberty of the sons of God":—the liberty to act as Spirit, independent of all external conditions. Ignorance and fear have fettered and imprisoned the Soul with rites, ceremonies, customs, prejudices, laws, etiquette, conformity, policy, monetary considerations, social considerations, and hypocrisy, so that few dare to think their souls are their own, much less to say so, and, least of all, to live as Soul demands.

Be Thyself.

But he who would become developed in Spirit, must, above all other things, be free. "Be thyself," is the first command of Soul Culture. Hark to its Prophet (Emerson) in his incomparable essay on "Self-Reliance": "Whoso would be a man must be a non-conformist. Nothing at last is sacred but the integrity of your own mind. Absolve you to yourself, and you shall have the suffrage of the world." Liberty is the way, and the only way, to soul growth. It is the way man has ever traveled. There never is a precedent for any progressive step. Freedom never dwells in old temples. Like the nautilus, she is building herself a new dwelling each successive morn. Freedom is the ever growing stem of the tree of life. Conservatism is her grave, and the grave of all that is manly. Without liberty, man is dead; a slave lives in his place. If one would gain power to be Destiny, he must be free.

Effort.

The next demand is Effort. All effort here must be spiritual. By physical effort, we can learn in that realm of vibrations termed matter. By intellectual effort, learn in the intellectual realm. "But spiritual things must be spiritually discerned." Methods of investigation in other fields are here of no use. Spiritual phenomena (or psychic, whichever term you please) occupy a field of their own, and must be found by their own methods. Effort must therefore be made as Spirit. That is, in Recognition of himself as Spirit, one must place himself in the mental attitude of receptivity and desire, and be willing to receive whatever comes. In this negative attitude of mind, he waits for the Ego to manifest as desired.

Non- Resistance.

The next law is:— Never antagonise anything. Never antagonize anything, opinion or condition, even in feeling. All is Spirit, therefore All is Good. "Nothing but good can, or does come to me, therefore I will not antagonize any manifestation, but let it work in me the good whereunto it was sent. For all the possible evil results will be those / make by doubting the goodness of Unity in this manifestation, and, since I am m^. own Fate and since I make Fate by deciding how to receive each manifestation, I decide this is Good, for All is Good. I thus do as he did who first taught me Soul Culture. Resist not evil, but overcome it in the large affirmation, All is Good. I thus keep my mind quiet, to perceive and reveal truth. Were I to contend, I would not see clearly, neither would I reveal the truth, but would conceive much error. Therefore, I will henceforth think only Good—will never antagonize." Such must be the mental attitude of one who is anxious to lead the spiritual life.

Demonstration.

Demonstration must take the place of argument. Therefore the next law of Soul Culture is:— Never argue. "Let your light shine that men seeing your good works" shall know you are Spirit, shall know you love Truth. Affirm Spirit, and, by living as Spirit, demonstrate your are Spirit. You live Spirit by thinking Spirit and by letting that thought control your life. Soul Culture comes through doing. Here again comes in the thought of the wise Teacher: "I must be about my Father's business": "My Father worketh hitherto and I work."

"He that doeth the will of my Father, the same is my mother and sister and brother." "If ye love me, keep my commandments." He always insisted that through conduct spiritual development is demonstrated. Never once did he ask, "What do you think?" or "What do you believe?"

Self- Direction.

The next rule is: — Intend the mind in the direction in which you wish revelation. One familiar with the terms of hypnotism will understand when I say, control the mind by Auto-Suggestion. From the sub-conscious storehouse of all knowledge, the Ego itself, can thus be drawn whatever is desired in the way of wisdom. The mind can also thus be directed to the development of psychic faculties. These faculties take hold on infinity both of time and space. Nothing is hidden from Soul perception. All the Soul's powers are comprised in two, so aptly stated by Emerson thus: "The Soul is the perceiver and revealer of truth;" to perceive and to reveal truth being all that the Soul can do, yet, while the method of perception is ever one, there are many methods of revelation already recognized, and there may be many others to come in our future unfoldment. Perceptions are revealed merely as truth, or they are revealed in terms of time and space. We thus get the names respectively of intuition and inspiration, to designate the revelations of truth; of clairvoyance and telepathy, to designate those of space; of psychometry, to designate those of time. In practice, these shade into each other as, in ordinary life, shade the results of the different senses.

Life Health.

— The first manifestation of Spirit is Life. Therefore, the first function we come to is health. All conditions manifesting less than a normal state of health are those of less health, and not those of disease. They are the results of spiritual weakness; for some cause, Spirit does not properly manifest through the body. The chief, if not the only difficulty, is the impediment placed on the manifestation of Spirit by some false idea. Some affirmation of "Can't," of weakness, or some submission to conditions through belief in heredity or in the impossibility of relief, is the cause of ill health. There is no "let" to "the current that knows its way." Therefore, the first care of the Soul Culturist is "to let" his Spirit have its way in health. This is easy. Only let the body alone; keep the mind off of it, and expect it to be kept by the maker — Spirit—well. He is to think and affirm only Health.

Spiritual Gifts.

We have a number of recognized psychic powers—"spiritual gifts"— but I wish to add a few that are not generally so recognized. The first is Music, the highest and purest expression of soul. All art is purely spiritual; and the purer the art, the nearer to pure Spirit. The more any attempt in art is removed from all considerations of life, except love for the art itself—removed from monetary considerations, from precedent, morality, etc. — the purer the art and the more perfect the manifestation of Spirit. Wagner is credited with the insight of saying: "If we had real life, we should need no art." The love of the beautiful is the test of spiritual unfoldment. Beauty is Divinity. Hence all the fine arts are psychic in origin. Poetry is especially a psychic gift. It is the child of beauty and melody. Hence, from oracle to séance, we have the improvisatrice, and all men in their natural state and all children are poets.

Classification of Psychic Power.

Thus a classification of the psychic faculties which it is the province of Soul Culture to develop will include Music, Painting, Sculpture, Architecture, Landscape Gardening, Rhetoric, Poetry, Health, Inspiration, Intuition, Clairvoyance, Telepathy, Prophecy and Psychometry. We here have a field comprising all there is in life worth living 1 for, all there is to reward one for living, excepting the one thing that is above all others, and above all classification, for that one thing is the very highest manifestation of Life; it is the Everlasting Life, the pure life of the Spirit, dimly shining through the mists of error; it is—LOVE.

Love.

Love is the first and last expression of Spirit. Love is its highest and purest expression. It is the highest of which the intellect can conceive. It is ever the controlling force in life. Each individual is controlled by his loves; there is no progress for him in any line until his love is moved in that direction; he then moves without solicitation. All spiritual development is made manifest through love. It is the barometer of life recording in manifestation the progress of the soul's unfoldment. Love is all Paul declared it to be when he said: "The greatest of these is Love." It is all Jesus declared when he gave the new commandment, "Love one another," thus making it the one condition to spiritual life. It is all he meant when he said, "God is Love." To present human thought, Love is the highest known or possible manifestation of power. It represents to us the most beneficent, as well as the controlling, force of the universe within man, and, since it is such, it must be his God. It is the holiest as well as the most powerful of emotions. It is ever present, and is the force out of which all the rest come. Thought is Love reduced in potential and pitch.

Ultimate Power.

The Soul Culturist, therefore, must deal with Love as his ultimate power, just as the electrician deals with his ultimate power. He does this by methods as rational. Recognizing it as the one force, the one manifestation of Unity, he seeks in Love alone to unfold his psychic powers,

Speed of Vibration

The intensity of the vibrations of Light has been measured, but not those of magnetism, for they are too swift for any conception of time to enter into the calculation of them. Thought is swifter than magnetism by multiplied vibration, but Love is many times the multiplied vibrations of Thought. Love can be studied by its manifestations in sensation, as sound and light are studied and known.

Love's Pitch and Octaves.

Like all other forms in which Unity manifests through vibration, Love has its pitch and its octaves and, somewhere in the infinite scale, each human life is placed. The only possible development of any life is to raise or lower its pitch, to increase or diminish its potential. How to do this, and how to transform Love to Thought in obedience to the mechanical Law of Conservation of Energy, is the secret the Sphinx of Time shall yet reveal.

Love of Soul Culture—Love of Truth.

There is one ever-present starting point in Truth. This Love, it must not be forgotten, is power; as real power as is steam in the boiler. It is the power that manifests in the development of those faculties we desire. Love must be thought of as Force, must be held in our consciousness as Force, just as the electrician in the power-households, in his consciousness, Force as his thought of electricity. Love of Truth is our initial point. Love of Truth is the power with which we work. "God will not manifest himself to cowards," says Emerson; he cannot, if He would, manifest in liars, hypocrites and slaves. Only to the extent that one is truthful, brave, honest and loving, has he any independent spiritual life. All that he may seem to have is but the race accumulation for which he has no responsibility, and hence in which he has no real possession; he is but using the race and animal instinct instead of being, as he should be, an independent, self-controlled individual. To the extent that men manifest love, they are spiritual. As far as they control their love through desire for truth and goodness, they are human, are outgrowing the tiger in them and leaving the remnants of the ape behind.

Safety.

In this love of truth alone is it safe to seek psychic unfoldment. To seek in any other love, is to fall into what the occultists call "black magic," which is the development of power without knowledge or guidance; is putting power into animal, into undeveloped man. This, like all undirected or wrongly directed power, injures temporarily the individual. The ultimate result—unfoldment—is, however, the same; but this road leads through, it may be, centuries of suffering. To seek in any other than love of truth, is to repeat the scandals, the sufferings, failures, and complicated work of the Christian sects and of mediumship; or to sink into the intellectual follies of sectarian "Christian Scientists," who have abandoned love of truth for love of a certain expression of truth and for "a founder" of a sect. Love of truth, pure and simple, is liberty; and, without liberty, no independent life, no living Truth.

The Law.

To seek in love of money, power, fame, or any lesser motive than love of Goodness and Truth, is to invite suffering and development through suffering. It is "to sow corruption" that one may reap the same. The law is: "Seek ye first the kingdom of Good and its right living, then all spiritual growth shall be added unto you." There is no limit to human manifestation when once, by this means, the way is opened. One thus becomes an Enlightened man. He lives in "the light that lighteth every man that cometh into the world." The light is in himself. He lives neither by the borrowed light of his neighbors, nor of his century.

Concentration.

In this Love-of-Truth, let one concentrate all his thoughts and desires for a time each day. In that concentrated state of mind, "let" the soul be heard. After you have, by desire and expectancy, given it direction, "let" it have its way. In hypnotic terms, after you have given yourself command by Auto-Suggestion, let the sub-conscious part of your being have its expression. All knowledge and power are either latent in the soul or lie behind the soul, ready, on opportunity, to flow into expression and, whenever they are "let," they flow. This condition of "letting" is that of natural somnambulence; of the artificial somnambulence of hypnotism; that of the "Scientist" when "In the Silence"; of the Hindoo in meditation; of the crystal gazer and the card reader. It is concentration. The thing upon which the gaze is concentrated, or whether or not there be anything, is unimportant. The mental state is all.

Involuntary Concentration.

This is identical with that natural condition of involuntary concentration in which the bookkeeper calculates in midst of noise, the editor writes and the mechanic works. The one does it on compulsion of .necessity till it becomes habit, the other does it with a predetermined purpose and at will. Such concentration is the key to success in every direction; its opposite—diffusion—is the cause of all failure, be it failure in health, business or love. It is the key to all occult and ancient mysteries.

Practice.

One must, therefore, practice concentration until it becomes not merely habit, but a new instinct. One must learn to rise above the life of sense, to ignore the coarser vibrations and the sensations that arise from them, known as the five senses, and to live in the finer sensations. That the hypnotic subject does this and opens the door to the storehouse of the sub-conscious, demonstrates that every person, by the same process of Suggestion, can do the same. In Soul Culture, we are seeking to give liberty of expression to whatever latent knowledge the conscious Ego may desire and determine. The fundamental affirmation, I am Spirit, means, I am all that Spirit is. The Soul Culturist affirms:—Since Spirit is Truth, Love, Power, Wisdom, I am Truth, Love, Power, and Wisdom. I am any other possible manifestation that Spirit is. Spirit is all this in potentiality; I may be all this in manifestation. I am part of indivisible Spirit in Spirit. I am an individual manifestation of Spirit in Spirit. Even as an electric spark can say: "I am electricity in electricity, but I am also an individual manifestation of electricity," so can I say: "I am Spirit."

How to Consciously Manifest.

To manifest any of this latent wisdom and power consciously, one must believe he possesses and then try to manifest, even as he tried when a child his powers of locomotion which his parents taught him he possessed, and, believing, he tried and found. Believing he can see, expecting to see, or at least hoping to see, one looks. Even so, hoping at least to see that which the external eye cannot see, let him who would see, look; and, in due time, he shall say with the poet-artist, William Blake: "I assert that I do not behold-the outward creation, and that it is to me a hindrance and not an action. I question not my corporeal eye any more than I would question a window concerning a sight. I look through it, and not with it." And more; such an one shall see, as John saw, the spiritual city, not "coming down from heaven," but all about him, in the midst of which he lives, as he lives in this cruder city of the senses; that is, he lives in the spiritual, as he lives in the sense life, by sensation alone. He will have learned to recognize those finer sensations that come from the more beautiful and powerful, because more intensified, vibrations of Spirit.

The Coming Man.

His world will not be merely that which is seen and felt by the ordinary dull man; it will be that of the refined, sensitive "coming man" who will "feel" octaves of vibrations not sensed by one who lives in the octaves of the senses. This finer universe will be as real to him as the harmony that the uneducated, non-musical ear cannot hear is real to the ear of the leader of the orchestra; as real as the sunset, to whose vibrations the eye of the blind is not sensitive, is real to the eye of the artist. It is only a question of unfolded sensitiveness to the unseen, but ever-present vibration and the recognition of the response born within the Soul.

Scientifically Attained.

All this desired condition can be as scientifically developed and cultivated as have been the recognition of sound in music, of light in painting, of touch in blind and of tact in society. By devoting a little time intelligently each day, less than it takes to make a musician, one may become clairvoyant, psychometric, or inspirational, and thus grow to the condition desired by Rev. John White Chadwick, a desire which is almost universal; it is beautifully prayed for in these words:

I might be strong to turn my eyes away

To where the eternal stars so plainly shine—

Truth, Beauty, Good—and by that vision blest—

Lifting my heart to make its clearness mine—

Taste then, earthbound, the everlasting rest.

INTRODUCTION TO PART II.

From the Philosophy, we now turn to the Principle of Expression. From Science of Life, we turn to the "Art of Living." From "Preaching," we turn to "Practice," remembering that he who cannot "preach better than he practices" will never unfold. For the Ideal, which is the Real of the Soul, must necessarily precede all unfoldment.

That we live, is no evidence that we are now artists. That our lives are not what we desire is evidence that we are poor workmen and that we have not learned to be artisans even. We are bunglers. Disease, failure and unhappiness are evidences of the ignorant and bungling nature of our work. Since Life is power and Art, either useful or beautiful, is but the application of power under intelligent direction, we can make life an Art only by intelligently directing the one power by which Life is directed. That power is Thought. To think as we wish to be, is to BE that, which we wish to be. Such thinking comes to him who knows the origin of his thought. He chooses only those thoughts which cause health, happiness and prosperity. Our thoughts are caused by Suggestion. To know what Suggestion to accept and thus make into an Affirmation and what Suggestion to ignore, is to control life's expression— is to be Masters of Fate.

This is taught in Part II. It is recommended that this part be studied until it becomes as familiar as the alphabet. The principles will then be lived. The student will thus become an adept in the mystery of life and an Artist in living.

PART II

SUGGESTION: ITS PLACE AND POWER

Definition.

Suggestion, in ordinary speech, means anything addressed to the senses, anything that causes an idea in the mind. Thus each individual thing in one's environment is, at all times, a Suggestion. A Suggestion is whatever from without awakens a thought, whatever "sets a man to thinking." It is thus an ever present factor in life; and, in this respect, it is true that "Suggestion rules the world." But, to rule, the Suggestion must be taken by the mind as truth. It is then converted into Auto-Suggestion.

Auto- Suggestion.

This is a Suggestion given by the individual to himself; it is born of conviction of truth. Each individual is controlled by his convictions, that is, by Auto-Suggestion— by his Affirmations. In this view, it is not Suggestion but Auto-Suggestion—Affirmation—that rules the world; however, in common thought, this cause and effect, Suggestion and Affirmation, are one. Therefore, it is near enough in fact to say, "Suggestion rules the world," for, until man learns to give himself Suggestions independent of external condition, Suggestion is the primal manifestation of power. When he reaches that plane of development where he is controlled by Affirmation, he becomes, through this power of Affirmation, the creator of his own destiny.

Technical Definition.

But, while this is the meaning of Suggestion in ordinary speech, there is a technical use of the word. Suggestion, as used by mental scientists, suggestionists, and hypnotists, means an intelligent use of this ever present power with a predetermined purpose to create a certain idea in another's mind. It is intelligent use of Suggestion to cause a person to think and to act from a chosen thought. Like all other arts, it is the intelligent use of power. The Art of Suggestion is the greatest of all arts, and, as a consequence, is the one most potent for good.

Control of Evolution.

Civilization is but ideas materialized. Thoughts control life. While they are not things, they are power; thus they are the creator of things. The thought in mind of warrior, statesman, artist, becomes the victory, the state, the statute. As thoughts change, so does all external life change; all progress, all reform, began in the change of thought in some one individual. Heretofore this change has been, as in savage man, merely instinctive; but, as man, by conscious thought, has become a factor in changing the world into better conditions; as he has at will changed grass to wheat, and scrub to blooded stock, so is he now becoming a conscious factor in his own evolution. He is beginning to realize that the only power by which he has wrought has been that of Thought. He is learning that Thought is as easily controlled and made to do selected work as is steam or electricity. He has only to think rightly to have whatever he wishes, either in person or in environment.

"In His Heart"

"As a man thinketh in his heart, so is he," said the ancient prophet. The key to this Affirmation is the words, "in his heart." Interpreted, it reads: "Profound convictions control the life." In scientific terms, it is this: Man is controlled by Affirmation. Therefore, to make life's expression what we wish, we are to hold our wish as to a reality, a profound conviction; it will then materialize. Life is as easily molded into desired forms as is clay by the potter. Clay takes the shape of the thought in the mind. The child's body at birth is molded by the mother's thought; he follows the evolution of that thought until he begins to think for himself; then he begins to reshape his body; and, somewhat consciously but to a greater degree unconsciously, he is doing this every moment of time. When he shall understand his power, he will shape body and environment, at will, to his desires.

Disease Thought Created.

Thus, by Suggestion, man to-day, without intention, builds his body into disease, old age, weakness, pain and death; builds his •environment into poverty and squalor, His mental conditions of unhappiness and sorrow have materialized. When he shall never hold these ideas of bodily decay, of pain, or poverty, but, in their stead, will hold in his heart" ideals of youth, health, vigor and plenty, there will be to him no more of life's ills. He will have, instead, realization of these beautiful ideals.

Place of Suggestion.

This is the place and the power of Suggestion in the New Thought. This Art places in the control of man his fate by teaching him how to think. It demonstrates that, by right thinking, man may be now that which at times he dreams of being—ever youthful, healthful, happy and free from care. This is possible for all. The Art is as easily taught as is the use of the magnet. Many lives demonstrate it now. Would you know the law? Here it is: Never think a thing that you do not wish to materialize as a fact. I will put it in another way: Suggest to yourself that that is true which you desire to be true, "Believe and be saved," was the command of Jesus; believe that to be true which you wish to be true, and it will manifest in your life as truth, THROUGH SUGGESTION.

Illustrations.

You wish health. Affirm Health. Think Health. Hold the picture of yourself in health before your mind, just as the artist holds 'that of the statue he is carving from the marble. Hold it persistently and you will create health. Do you wish relief from poverty? Hold the idea of plenty to use, to enjoy, not to hoard, not to oppress, but to bless, and it will as surely come as rose from bud. This is the power of the Christian Scientist, the Divine Scientist, the Mental Scientist, the Soul Culturist, the Hypnotist, the Suggestionist; they all use the power of Suggestion and Affirmation, each more or less understandingly. It is the power of priest, politician, street fakir, auctioneer; of teacher, doctor, and reformer. All of these use it instinctively, for it is all the power man has—the power of Thought.

Affirmation.

The technical word in evidence here is AFFIRMATION. Affirm that which you wish and it will manifest in your life. Learn a lesson from the hypnotist. He says to the subject: "You cannot get up." He repeats it until the subject, because he accepts it as truth, cannot get up. He says: "You have a toothache," and repeats it until the painless jaw really aches. So do we say to ourselves: "I am sick, poor, old, unhappy, weak, penniless," until we make ourselves so. Now turn about; "repent" and affirm the opposite. Say, "I am rich, happy, healthy," until you find life changing its aspects. It will change when you say this from conviction. Realize that as Mind (or Spirit) you are now potentially all you desire. It lies in you, waiting expression. For what one man is, all men are. If one manifests as health, happiness and wealth, all men can. Let that power which is life in you manifest your desire. By Affirmation, direct the life-flow your way.

All is Good.

One affirmation contains all that is necessary for a perfect life. It is this: ALL is GOOD. This is faith in the Providence of the Universe, faith in the intelligence and wisdom of that Almighty Power that out of Itself said, "Let there be light," and there was light. The All-Power is good. All manifestations come from It, therefore all are good. All is Good, used as an Affirmation, becomes reality—redeems the individual from all ills.

Power of Choice.

With this understanding of Suggestion as an ever-present factor in life, goes also the understanding that, whenever one has attained power to select Suggestions and to reject those he does not wish, he has attained the power of controlling his thought. To control thought, is to be the Conscious Creator of Destiny!—to be the Master of Fate. So great is this fact that it requires desire, time and repetition before it can be realized in the daily manifestations of life. Therefore this principle of Suggestion is further unfolded.

How to Suggest.

Remember, a Suggestion is whatever is used intelligently to induce a desired mental condition in another mind. An Affirmation is a Suggestion accepted and made Truth. A statement of Truth in the indicative mood, present tense, is the controlling power in the individual life. We have here a basis from which to begin the work of assuming conscious control of life and of molding its expression to our will. Realizing that life has heretofore been controlled from without—that is, that we have Affirmed because Suggestions were accepted, that we have not heretofore thought of a choice in Suggestions we have accepted—we are ready to learn that we can suggest to ourselves; that Affirmations arising from desire can be voluntarily used. These Affirmations will control the expression of life.

The Great Law.

All the power of Suggestion is multiplied many fold when it becomes Affirmation born from desire. The Master in Life will use, as the power to control the Sub-conscious in its expression, Affirmations born in Desire. THAT WHICH HE WISHES TO BE, HE WILL AFFIRM THAT HE IS. This is the Great Law—the most important law man has yet discovered. By obeying this Law, he will control his life; will make the channel for "the current that knows its way." There is one mighty factor to use in this control: WILL. Grapple to this Affirmation— I AM—with the WILL. With this grapple, there is no failure. Every Affirmation placed in charge of the Will and let alone will find expression, will be realized. When this is understood, when the beauty and necessity of Affirmation is seen, then the place and purpose of my monthly journal— NOW—will be appreciated. No matter what the culture, position, means or external condition may be, they are valueless in the life and are enslaving conditions until, by conscious Affirmation, through Will, they are used as the means of Soul-growth—the means to self-mastery.

Morgan. J. Pierpont Morgan is not master of self, though he is almost master of all earth's transportation, for he is liable to awaken any morning ill; to find himself paralyzed; to become demented; to find fire, flood, famine or war has reduced him to beggary. He can die by disease, bullet or starvation. The poorest tramp may outlive him, may be happier and may die richer. He has not conquered Fate, and will not until he realizes that all these things, the insignia of earthly power, are of no value to the Soul, which has power to create, to call at will all it needs; until he has passed beyond the necessity of disease and sorrow and even holds death at bay; and until he has learned that he can, at will, change these manifestations of crude vibrations of flesh for the finer ones of Spirit.

The Law of Life, And yet Truth is so simple, the Mastery so easily acquired. A child may learn it.

It is laid down in this simple Law of Life:

Affirm that which you desire to be as a present reality.

Live as if it were already manifest and you shall find it manifest. I must repeat here that Truth Affirmed is the controller of life. Affirmations are the within side of Truth. No perception of Truth ever meant so much for mankind as this LAW. It means that all man ever dreamed is within his reach. He has to take it by Affirmation only. The line of evolution in man is toward Self-Control—Conscious direction of the manifestations of life. The animal is fast being outgrown, and MAN is coming into expression.

From Within Controlled in some form, life must be. Of "Without. If not from Within, then from Without. The question I now place before you is this: Which shall it be? Will you be Self-Controlled or be the tool, the play, the slave of circumstances? To control railroads, telegraphs, labor, capital, armies, is to control the Without. It is not to control SELF. The person who controls these is himself controlled by them; is the slave of circumstances. The Without-Law of Suggestion is Absolute in sway where the Within-Law of Affirmation is not invoked intelligently and consciously. No matter what or where we are, we act under Thought. As long as we obey without choice Thought born of Suggestion, we are slaves of the Without. When that Thought is self-chosen, then God has assumed the throne in His Kingdom, the Within, and His edicts are Affirmations. Absolutely he reigns. His edicts are never disobeyed. They are instantly executed. "God said, 'Let there be light,' and there WAS light." No time between command and execution—no time between cause and effect.

Man is Coming.

This development reached, MAN has come; the HUMAN is here; the animal, the instinctive, the automatic, has died out. MAN is here and all things are subject to him. This power of choice in Suggestion is the dividing line between man and brute. As soon as an individual makes a conscious choice, he has crossed the dividing line and is on the road to manhood. When that power of choice has developed so that he chooses every expression of his life and all circumstances obey his will, then, and not till then, has he arrived at MAN'S estate. MAN is coming. MAN IS HERE, whenever one realizes his power to choose, his power to BE!

Teacher's Duty.

The whole duty of the teacher in all departments is to direct, by Suggestion, the thought of his pupil. This control may be early won in life. Suggestion does not determine character, but, through Suggestion, character may be developed and molded into Selfhood. A Suggestion once accepted becomes an Affirmation. The individual then manifests, not as any person or persons may desire, but according to his inherent character. As all force acts in accordance to the instrument within which it is confined, so thought, being force, will act according to the instrumentality through which it manifests. Character is, in Suggestion, a permanent factor, changing only as the unfolding Soul—the I Am—

shall change it. To illustrate: While this essay was in progress, a friend invited me to attend the theater. I had not thought of going, was not conscious of any desire to go. But the Suggestion aroused the desire. I consented and went. The power of Suggestion ceased when I said, "Yes." I went in my thought, acted in my way and enjoyed in my way. My individuality determined how the Suggestion should affect me after I had exercised my choice and said, "Yes."

To You the Victory.

So is it in all affairs of life. To excuse one for doing anything because he or she was influenced by another, is to undermine Selfhood by destroying personal responsibility. To attain Mastery, or to assist another so to attain, insist at all times upon personal responsibility for conduct. All persons have the power to choose, and, by choice, they DO control their life. Now let each bear the effects of that choice and, by experience, learn to choose wisely. Never affirm that you are not responsible, would you achieve success in any undertaking. To you alone belongs the victory. Defeat is impossible, for all experience is victory. Wisdom is the guerdon of all struggle. Thus is the knowledge of Suggestion and Affirmation the knowledge above all other knowledge. It is the wisdom that makes all other knowledge of use. It is the only real, practical knowledge. It is the wisdom of wise choice and action.

Power of this Book.

A graduate from one of our first universities and now a teacher in a Normal Schools, after passing through my classes, said: "You have made all my other knowledge available." A physician said: "You have only made of practical value that which I knew beforehand, but I had never formulated the common experiences into Law." This little book will do all this for you if you will let it. How? Assimilate it mentally as you have yesterday's food. Make it a part of your mental constitution. AFFIRM ITS TRUTH.

Praise, Etc.

No Suggestion acts against one's desire and will. One which awakens opposition produces an effect opposite to that desired. Instinctively understanding this and acting upon the principle that each one is ready to be helped the way he desires to go, that each one is willing to accept happiness and success, the world has found praise, adulation, flattery, insignia, social distinctions, to be Power. The wise man will use all Power, and to understand Power and how to use it as Suggestion, is to win success.

Fear.

Suggestions born of duty, necessity and fear, control most lives. When one becomes unfolded, Love will give all the Suggestions. "Love is the fulfillment of the law." Fear is the "Father of Lies," of all ills and evils. "From all Fear, Good Lord, deliver us," should be in the Litany. To be free from Suggestions born of fear, is to be free from illness, failure, poverty and sorrow. These Suggestions should be ignored and the opposite ones immediately affirmed. Hold these last till they are the constant mental attitude, then no more Fear. Affirm, I AM FEARLESS!

No Power to Harm.

There is no power Without to harm. All power is lodged Within, where God's kingdom IS. Whatever is not in harmony with Truth is non-existent, hence has no power. Truth at all times is Power and is entirely GOOD. Therefore "Fear no evil." Lies and slanders have no power; for they are devoid of Truth. Pay no attention to them. To attend to them even by so much as a thought or wish, is to put power into them. The harm comes from Within, not from the lie. Soon you will come to see that no one has power to harm you but yourself. A lie harms the teller. So is it with all the evil we would do to another. In settling with a business man recently, he remarked: "Since you have kept no account, are you not afraid that I have cheated you?" "You cannot" was my reply. "You can only cheat yourself. Every dollar that you take dishonestly will reduce your power in business, destroy your happiness and injure your health. You cannot take a cent from me, for my Supply is Infinite. The Lord IS my shepherd. I DO NOT WANT." "Well, I wish everyone dealt so, it would be a better world," was his remark. "The world is all Good to me now," I replied as I walked out of the door. Take this lesson! Live it! Then ALL is GOOD to you.

Power of "Scientists," Etc.

Here again you have the secret of all the works of "Christian," "Divine," "Mental" and other "Scientists," "Metaphysicians," "Faith Healers," "Prayer Cures," etc., etc. The Power is exactly that which the hypnotist and the practitioner of "Suggestive Therapeutics" use. No matter if this be denied, he who has studied Suggestion knows that T. J. Shelton, Mrs. Helen Wilmans, Mrs. Eddy and all the rest use Suggestion. Not to use it, they must become non-existent. What other subtle forces there may be—and I think they are infinite as are the possible number of vibrations—yet the director of these forces is Suggestion. But for this power of Suggestion, they would never have a patient. Each paper, book or letter sent out by any Scientist is a Suggestion, and, as irrigating ditch carries water, so does the Suggestion carry the power these healers wield. The mistake is, that one claims All, and another All, when ALL have ALL. All work by the ALL-Power.

One Power to Heal.

As Life is ONE, there can be but ONE healing Power, and that is Life itself.

No person ever healed another. Healers have used Suggestion and will more intelligently use it. Acceptance of the Suggestion—the Affirmation — does the healing. The Suggestion may be conveyed in a thousand ways. Look, attitude, speech, anything addressed to the Ego through any of the five senses, or through any possible channel, is a Suggestion. Hence Telepathy is a most potent channel, because it arouses no opposition in the conscious life. Telepathy is the Power in absent treatments. Whoever has learned Concentration can do all Mrs. Eddy or Mrs. Wilmans does. It is the common heritage of man.

Cannon and Powder.

As chamber of cannon to powder, so is Suggestion to all Soul forces. It is the Conscious will of Man directing the expression of the Sub-Conscious life. It is Mastery ! Remember:—To thus direct, to thus realize that the Divine power in you is subject to your Thought, is to attain the pinnacle of knowledge and have the All at your command. It is to be a Special Creator under the Absolute Law of Creation. We thus create our environment— Create ourselves. We become that which we wish to be. The road is through Affirmation. To control life, understand and control Suggestion and the results are those you have desired and chosen. This is to be your Affirmation daily: "I choose my life. I affirm Truth. Truth affirmed molds my body and environment to my desire, as potter molds clay. I make my life to my choice. I am creator." By thus affirming, you have become "Conscious Law" and "King of Kings."

Millennium Here.

Knowing the power of Suggestion, its intelligent use, we who have studied and practiced it see in it the fulfillment of the prophecy and expectation of the millennium. It is here now in every heart that affirms, ALL is GOOD.

Fear.

Fear being the cause of all ills, failures and un-happiness, it is the first condition to be outgrown. To outgrow fear, learn how to Affirm Fearlessness. Let the thought used be this in any form of words you may choose to put it: "I am fearless. I dare to do anything I desire." Whenever anything comes to cause a thought of fear, make this affirmation. Then do in mind that which you fear and act it in the external when it is possible. Conquer fear by Affirmation and prove you have conquered by doing the thing feared. There is not an Affirmation that brings health and happiness sooner than this:—I AM FEARLESS !

Health.

For health, do not recognize disease in your thought. To think upon disease, to brood upon it, is to invite it—is to suggest it upon yourself. Therefore, think only of Health. Ignore disease in thought; think health. Let the Affirmation be something like this:

"I am Life. I am Spirit. I am Mind. As Life, I cannot know sickness. As Life, I am at all times well. As Spirit, I am well. Spirit cannot be sick. I am a perfect manifestation of Spirit. Perfection is health, peace and joy. As Mind, I am ever in perfect health. As Mind, I cannot be ill. I affirm myself Mind. I live as Mind above all death, pain, disease, decay, sorrow, failure and unrest. I am Soul. Soul is a perfect manifestation of God. God cannot know sickness or pain. I am ONE with God. I am well. I am not separate from Him. I live and move in this thought of Unity and manifest each day my oneness in health. I am Health ! I am Peace! I am Joy!" Make these Affirmations and forget that you have made them by living them. Be, in expression, that which you Affirm. Life flows as naturally and as harmoniously as sunlight. Affirm ! Forget! and let it flow.

Prosperity.

Affirm Success in all your undertakings. No matter what discouragements come, affirm Success. Declare yourself Prosperous. Let no thought of discouragement come into your mind. Affirm: "All is Mine. From the ALL each day comes to me that which I need."

Affirm this and forget the necessity of affirming. In the Affirmation, you have sent a message to the only Power that can bring success to the sub-conscious, the Ego—and when you LET, the Ego will bring Success. Think Success, act as if you were Success, and you are Success. Failures come because, when we are tried, we fail to cling to the Ideal of Success. Hold to your Ideal of Success the tighter when seeming failure comes. Affirm Success under all trials and discouragements and success is as surely yours as the mist is, because of the persistent drawings of the sun,

SUPPLEMENT TO THE FIFTH EDITION.

To My Readers: Greeting:

Owing to the condensation of the matter in this edition, the type being set "solid," rather than "leaded," as in previous editions, we have the same amount of reading matter in less space. I am asked by the manager of "Now" Folk to fill this space with a word to the reader concerning the book and our growth since its first appearance. This book is my first. We called it "My baby" for a year. It has sold, to our surprise, and taken my name all around the world. It has received praise and commendation wherever the English language is read. From none have I received finer appreciation than from several Hindu Swamis. An Arab teacher of occultism when reading it at the request of O Hasnu Hara, editor of "The English Magazine of Mysteries," replied when she asked his opinion of it: "That man knows!" To be tried by a jury of his peers is the desire of every author. I know by the only test possible the truth of that which I have here written. It is the test which I have recommended you in this book to use, i. e., DEMONSTRATION. "Learn to do by doing," is the only true method of education. I have demonstrated the thought of this book to be TRUTH by living it. It is not possible to estimate how much this book has done to awaken an interest in Suggestion. But I know by many letters that it has been a factor in the world's evolution along the line awakening the consciousness of the Human Soul to a realization of itself as a manifestation of Omnipotence. It has brought many to a rational understanding of an intelligent application of this most important Law of Life, which is also the only Law of human control — The Law of Suggestion.

When this book was first published there was far more confusion in the thought of Suggestion, even among teachers, than at present. The subject was shunned even by New Thought teachers generally, and was much muddled in the teaching of many and feared by others. Now it is a common word, well understood by all leading exponents of the various cults.

My magazine, then in its 2d Volume, was fearless in its annunciation of this Law, on its positive side known as Affirmation. Instructions and formulas for denials were then common. Now they are the exception. The Law of Suggestion is now so well understood that few teachers advocate negative propositions. Affirmation is Auto-Suggestion, and whatever I suggest, to myself, that I am. Students are coming to understand that this Law of Suggestion lies at the base of occultism, both ancient and modern. It underlies Spiritualism and what are termed Suggestive Therapeutics and Magnetic healing; it is the life there is in Osteopathy, "Christian," "Divine" and "Mental" Science, and in the various systems of health treatments now attracting attention. Could suggestion be removed from any system of theology or medicine, it would fail. Authors upon reform and even those writing upon business success, are realizing the value of a knowledge of Suggestion.

For these reasons this little book fills a place among the more pretentious ones, since it brings the Law home to the individual; teaching him through its conscious and intelligent use how to control his fate and make his destiny to his will. My co-laborers and myself are fast learning to direct our lives by Affirmation. We are realizing our power through Mental Pictures, through the Ideal, to direct our life. We are learning when we have made these pictures, to hold to them, and LET the Universal Life materialize them. We can build through Affirmation only. He who so consciously builds, builds to his will. This fact is one this book forces upon the consciousness of its readers. So many write me: "You have taught me that I can." I would, therefore, have this thought go with you as you lay it down: I have power to mould my life to my will. I mould it through the Law of Suggestion. I affirm and become that which I affirm. When this book was written I had but recently begun my work in San Francisco, not dreaming what its evolution has been, and I was wholly unacquainted with the work of authorship and of publishing. I had obeyed the promptings of my Soul, my intuitions in settling here; I had obeyed them in writing and later in printing the book. Unexpected assistance opened the way to is publication. I started my magazine through the same faith, in Truth as I heard it in the inner consciousness. Two young men had joined me and with the publication of this we formed the nucleus of what has grown to be "NOW" Folk. We are now an incorporated company with a fair prospect of seeing my Mental Picture materialize:—my Ideal Mountain Home founded with hotel, sanitarium, schools, printing plant and various industries where mutual lovers work for mutual good, in love of their work. This Ideal is materializing. I have held it as a reality for ten years; as a dream for twenty-five years. It comes now in accordance with the Law of Expression, which is the Law by which all Ideals materialize. Ideals find objective expression according to the fidelity with which they are held as present realities. "According to thy faith" is not limited to improving bodily conditions, but covers the whole range of human experience; war and peace, business and home, love and duty, politics and religion, marriage and divorce, birth and death, are all controlled by this Law of Ideal Suggestion— That which I think, that I am!

Realizing this power of Thought, I had written before this book, the articles now composing "Man's Greatest Discovery" which I consider my most important book thus far, as it deals with the Power and the Principle of Individual Life. Upon this fact all future science, philosophy and art will be based. From the knowledge of this fact all my works have originated and upon it all my instruction is based.

Through faith in our power, through right thinking, to create, are the plans of "NOW" Folk materializing. Thought will hereafter build that Home, Sanitarium and Schools, and whatever else we desire because we affirm I have power to build my life to my desire. Daily are we learning where that power lies; daily learning how to direct it. But it is not our thought alone that will do this; we are reinforced by every thought our readers send us, be it for or against us, it makes no difference. The windmill uses every breeze, no matter from whence it comes. All power manifests in accordance with the instrument it uses. So Thought, being Power, when it comes to us from without, is used by our Mental attitude, and since we hold to nothing but Good, all power must manifest goodness for us. Therefore, all who think of us help us in any way in our work for Truth through Love of Truth. Realizing the power of Thought to control external conditions, and the power of Suggestion to overcome conditions, I wrote my "Dollars want me," a brochure as revolutionary in its thought as in its title. "I want dollars" is the ordinary cry. "I want!" is humanity's cry, instead of being, as it should be, "I POSSESS!" Affirming possession, we enter into the realization of possession. Without ,this realization we may be poor with millions in our hands. "He is poor who thinks himself poor!" says Emerson. I can imagine no greater good I can do my fellows than to enable them to replace poverty thoughts and pictures with those of opulence. I wrote for this I say in my "Introduction" "To help you to rise above the drudgery of enforced labor!" I believe in freedom and in free men. Necessity is as much a Master as the slave-driver with a whip. I have the consciousness of knowing that the mere Suggestion "Dollars want me!" has changed the conditions of hundreds of its readers. I would like this little book to be scattered as a tract, for there could be no more effective arbitrator between capital and labor; no more humanizer for the selfish and idle; no more stimulating thought to the weary rich, than is the thought it bears: Wealth is for enjoyment through use.

"How to Control Fate" soon after its publication called forth my "Not Hypnotism but Suggestion," than which no book is more needed today by the masses. It is becoming common for the idle, the foolish, the weak and the vicious to use "Hypnotism" as a scapegoat, and to excuse themselves by saying: "I was hypnotised!" when every expert in Suggestion knows that character determines the reception or rejection of a Suggestion; that where it is used as an excuse it is a case of lack of self-reliance, a case always of self-hypnotism. No greater evil is possible than that teaching which lessens personal responsibility for conduct. The weak and vicious are ever seeking an excuse for that which they alone are responsible. Because of this, theories of predestination, heredity, karma, circumstance, influence, spirits, devil, or hypnotism are created and used as an excuse. Excuse is one of the most poisonous of thoughts, for it undermines character, weakens the powers of resistance, lessens faith in self and inculcates a belief in what is worse than ancient demonism by locating power in things outside the Soul. There is but one sure foundation for individual and for national integrity, but one sure foundation for character, and that is SELF RELIANCE. Self-reliance must find its rise in Self Knowledge and Self Respect. For this reason I feel that I am in my work practicalizing America's greatest essay. . .Emerson's "Self-Reliance." All my writings are pitched to the one keynote. BE THYSELF!

The object of this book, and all my books, magazines and lessons is to assist others in finding themselves, for each is Power to overcome all conditions and circumstances, and the Power with each is directed in the Will. This Will is trained and directed only through faith in self. "I Can is the Affirmation of Character, Health and Happiness. Self-assertion its one name.

Through the success of these books I became aware of the world-wide interest now manifested in New Thought, and felt that this stream needed guiding and clarifying. Therefore I wrote my "New Thought Primer; Origin, History and Principles of the Movement." This book is also a child of "How to Control Fate," for my purpose was, as much as anything, to bring to the intelligent the thought this movement was also Evolution, and that human unfoldment had ever been controlled by the Law of Suggestion.

There is no creation. Progress is but the coming into expression of that which eternally has been. New movements arise in a conception which is but an extension of a previous conception, and that of a previous conception, and so on back to primitive man, of a divine, infinite and eternal idea, which finds expression through human ideals. These ideals become incorporated into institutions, and a civilization which later ideals modify. Thus external conditions are but the materialization of Thoughts born in Suggestions. So arose New Thought. From previous glimpses of Truth we have now grown to a larger vision.

In like manner came the philosophy and the art of Suggestion. It began in Mesmerism, came up through "Animal Magnetism" and other forms of using Thought consciously, to control conduct, until the discovery was made that Thought was the only power used, and that it was one's own thought within himself that did the work in him. Suggestion lies solely in the individual's power to think and power to choose what to think. From its conscious use in controlling conduct and curing bodily infirmities we have learned that it is equally powerful in changing material conditions and in creating environment to desire.

Thus my six books have arisen. They are the evolution of the one idea: Thought is Power and can be intelligently directed to the creation of one's own self and environment.

Had this first book, "My Baby", .not been received, the rest would not have been. This opened the way for these others and those which are yet to follow. In its effect upon author and publishers it demonstrated the truth of the principle it taught. It has been also a material help in carrying on our work, for it used to come to us that they might assist in the work.

The theme is not exhausted. In dealing with Thought we are dealing with the mightiest Power subject to Human control. In dealing with the Soul we are dealing with Infinity and Eternity. The growing consciousness of Power will be an eternal unfoldment. The evolution of an idea is endless. Every day a new book is needed to record the increased perception of this idea of Thought as Power. I have many new ones as ideals in my mind and I will print them as soon as they can materialize. I propose to write twenty-five pamphlets like this.

Thus there are twenty more to come. These written I then propose to write several large volumes, unfolding a system of "NOW" Philosophy. It is for this reason that I desire the Home I mentioned above to materialize. This will give the leisure, the opportunity and the means that I need. What I will call the system I am as much at a loss now to know as was Herbert Spencer for years concerning his own. But the name will come, the means will come and at the right time the books will materialize. We control Fate through Suggestion made as these are in faith in Principle, faith in Self. I know all who read this book wish me to see them materialize. Your thought will be an added power to help. Means are to come for the preparatory work of pamphlet printing, which is but an introduction to the greater work.

I am just entering the productive period of my life. I write this on my sixty-fifth birthday. Was never so well in body, so clear in mind or so in love with, or so enthusiastic in, my work as now. I never listen to a Suggestion of Age, weariness or relief. I am in embryo all now that I wish to be. As bud unfolds into bloom, so will you and I unfold only that which we now are. Suggestion to this effect creates a mental condition which makes it easy for the germs within to come into expression. Therefore now affirm with me:— I am ALL now, I desire to be and I have power to bring that which I am into manifestation. For this reason that Philosophy which I am will write itself at the right time. This little book is the first chapter.

It seems proper for me thus to take you, my reader, into my confidence since this little book that introduced me to the world starts out on its new edition. I desired to tell you how successfully the Law has worked in my case since November, 1901, when it started on its mission. Ten thousand copies have been disposed of, and each one has carried its message—BE THYSELF! They have won for me the love of thousands whose words of cheer I can only in this way reciprocate.

Soon I will come to you with a little book upon "Concentration." I am so often asked "How to Concentrate?" and what it means, that in answer to these questions, I write this as the next number in this series. I have also ready for publication a work on "The Practical Application of

Suggestion in Daily Life" If you are seeking unfoldment we shall long keep company. We will be companions on the way.

A most encouraging feature of modern progress is. a realization of the interest in things material giving way before interest in Soul. Psychic Research Societies and investigations in laboratories for the beginnings of life are but evidences of a demand for that for which there is as yet no adequate supply. From personal experience and from the testimony of thousands, I affirm that rest is found only in the Principles upon which all New Thought cults are based. Hunger drives birds to grain fields and deer to the winter corral; so soul-hunger drives men and women from the starvation of fashion, social dissipation, from business mart and sanitarium to the Mental Scientist, where they learn that their only Power, their only Possession, is themselves. Where they come into the realization that happiness does not consist in material things, friends or conditions, but does consist in a purely mental attitude toward one's self and the universe. Happiness, like all else, is a mental habit. He is happy who decides to be happy. The Suggestion of happiness creates happiness. A Suggestion of misery will create it in a palace. A Suggestion of peace will create peace in the midst of tumult. When one says, "I am unhappy," he or she creates that condition within the mind. When one says, "I am happy," they create happiness within the mind, its only habitation. "The kingdom of heaven" is the kingdom of happiness. It lies only within the consciousness, and depends only upon the Affirmation one uses. Thus does one become the Master of Fate through decision and self-determination? "What shall be the Affirmation under which I live?" is the question. It is as easy to say, "I am Happy" as it is the reverse; as easy to create a habit of using these words as it is the habit of using their opposite. Optimism and pessimism are mental habits. Which shall it be? is a question each must decide for himself. A gentleman said to me last night: "I cannot tell you what I owe to your instruction. I was a pessimist and unhappy when I entered your class. I now see everything from an opposite point of view, and am an optimist." Through a course in Suggestion he had learned that not only was he that which he thought, but that each thing had the effect upon him that he thought it would. Through expectancy he created the conditions for the effect affirmed.

This change will come to every one of my readers when this Thought, I AM THAT WHICH I THINK I AM shall become to them the mental incentive of action. As I think I am. I will think only that which I wish to be. I will think ideal things, and thus create happiness. Dear reader, as my last admonition, I affirm that Happiness is the subjective side, the Cause of health. Unhappiness is the subjective side and the Cause of disease. Choose! Which shall it be? The old prophet said, "As for me and my house, we will serve the Lord." "The kingdom of God is within." Him I serve. Truly your friend,

HENRY HARRISON BROWN.

San Francisco, June 26, 1905.   THE END.

BOOK TWO

CONCENTRATION, THE ROAD TO SUCCESS

INTRODUCTION

WHAT IS SUCCESS?

The force of that mysterious, but irresistible power—Humanity's common and concentrated Thought.— Senator Beveridge.

In what does success consist? Many persons desire to know how to be successful. How to win success. Before this question can be answered there must be an understanding as to what they mean by success, and what success stands for in this Book. I asked a correspondent what he meant by success, and his answer was, "I am in business, and I wish to make money from it," Another wishes to win an office. Another to outstrip a rival. Another to succeed in her book. And here are two young ladies writing me, one wants to pass an examination in school and the other to learn to ride a bike. This is called success. But it is success without Principle. Success that leaves Life out of count. It is the success of some undertaking. This is not success. One may succeed in any and all these and similar undertakings and yet be a failure.

Success must be measured by a larger standard. Can we call these U. S. Senators under indictment for breaking the laws; these men of whom

Graham Phillips is telling in his "Treason in the Senate". Can we call these millionaires who are under the indictment of public opinion, and these society women who are passing through operations from their doctors, Successes? Can we call the student broken in health, though he wins the valedictory, a success? Success in things may mean failure in Life.

How may I succeed in Life?" is the only question that any conscientious metaphysician can answer. He will not answer the questions as to success in any enterprise. Those who attempt this are not metaphysicians but charlatans. The Greatest of Metaphysicians gave us the rule for SUCCESS, any other is a mere temporary advice or makeshift. Here is the only possible way to SUCCESS, that is written with capitals —"Seek ye first the kingdom of God and His righteousness and all these things shall be added unto you." A simple and scientific Law. It simply means.— Live by Principle and not by detail! It is as if the professor of electricity when asked, "How shall I make a battery?" should answer, "First study up on electricity till you learn its principle of action, then you will know how to make any apparatus."

Let us analyze this law as laid down by Jesus. First where am I to seek for the Kingdom? Answer, "The kingdom of God is within you!" What does kingdom mean. Kingdom stands for Power. Here then is the Law, Seek the Power that is within your SELF, then you will add to yourself things you desire. Success thus lies in the consciousness of Power to do whatever I wish to do. Success lies in the consciousness that one can meet any situation with satisfaction to himself. The manifestations of success are Health, Happiness and Supply.

He is a failure who finds that his body will not allow him to do what he wishes to do. He is a failure who must depend upon another to do that which is necessary to be done for the accomplishment of his plans. A successful man though he may employ a thousand men, will feel that were it necessary he could carry out his purpose alone. The leaner is a failure. The successful man is filled with joy. The "kingdom of G-od" is "the kingdom of heaven" and heaven is happiness. Therefore any condition in life which does not bring happiness is failure, and happiness is the subjective cause of health. There can be neither health nor happiness till wants are supplied; therefore poverty is failure. I care not how honest, generous or noble a person is, if he wants any of the necessities of life, he is a failure. For the Power of God in the Soul when once found will see that Supply ever is at hand. He who has found this Power will find the ability to draw to himself Supply. But Supply does not mean anything to hoard or to lay by for a rainy day.

Therefore in Soul Culture the definition of Success is:— The consciousness of ability to meet every occasion in life and convert it into Health, Happiness and Supply. The way to this consciousness is first:— Believe it; then affirm it till you become it. This is the Affirmation of Success: I AM POWER TO BE AND TO DO THAT WHICH I WILL TO BE AND TO DO

SECTION I.
THE "WHY" OF THE BOOK.

Present power requires concentration on the moment and the thing to be done. — Emerson.

I swear I see what is better than to tell the best, It is always to leave the best untold. — Walt Whitman.

"Another book upon this subject?" the reader may exclaim. Yes; because concentration is the secret of human power in action. Waste is prevalent everywhere and the consequences are poverty, illness, unhappiness, and failure. It is a libel on nature to think that any person should be in any kind of want because there is not supply and ability in him to appropriate it. The unconscious perception of this fact has pushed man onward to present civilization. A more or less clear perception of the Law and the Way has given rise to many schools of Human Culture. Each generation has had its seers who have studied the operation of the Power within man and discovered the Law, so simple, that all may intellectually grasp it. But because the ordinary person goes no further than to have a mere general perception of Truth, this book is added to the great metaphysical stock and others will necessarily come after mine. I am but one among the million. This book is but one stone cast on the cairn that authors are building to the worship of the God of Success.

Concentration is not something to be learned as one learns mathematics. It is a mental habit which is to be acquired just as the habit of solving problems in geometry is to be acquired by practice. Concentration is that mental attitude attained by practice, that characterizes the book-keeper and the mechanic, who know not that others are about, and who do their work almost automatically and unconsciously.

Concentration is that mental state, acquired only by practice, which enables the actor to forget self in the part he is playing, or the author to forget self in the thought he is writing. Only practice and more practice, can produce it. For this reason text-book after textbook will be needed, and the thought must be reiterated, "line upon line, and enforced example by example, till the habit of concentration is formed. Because of this I feel it a duty to give my testimony and to help those still struggling as once was I. But I have another reason. My magazine and books have caused a large clientele to look to me for assistance along the lines of soul unfoldment; they turn to me with questions, and I must answer. From this feeling and this need, this book is born. It has not been of predetermined growth. It arises from my articles in magazine, from my lessons in class, from letters and conversations. Because I feel these persons have made inquiries that others are asking; these others will find what so many have already found in my thought; so I let the matter stand just as first given, knowing that the sometime repetition of the same thought in a little different way, will through suggestion strengthen the idea. I simply talk to you, my reader, just as I should in "writing you a letter, or in answering your questions, were you in my room. In fact much of the thought of the book comes from my class conversation. I trust you will feel the inspiration from which the instruction sprung.

I wish most in these first pages to emphasize the fact that it is a mental habit you are to cultivate. I am not giving you a treatise for merely intellectual comprehension. It is a book of conduct, rather. Any book can help you only in so far as you put what you are told into practice. As soon as you grasp an idea, lay down the book and think upon it and begin, then and there, to practice what you have learned. Repeat it over and over as an Affirmation. Tell yourself that you live that. Practice this till you unconsciously, through habit, think in that line. It will ultimately become a habit for you thus to think and you will live from that Affirmation. This alone is Concentration.

When I was a boy I was an omnivorous reader; read every book no matter of what kind I could obtain, from Sunday School, library, or neighbor. I thus created a habit of reading anywhere and of paying no attention to whatever was about me. Often has mother shaken me with the words, "Henry, where is that armful of wood you promised to get me T Or, "Henry, when will you get that pail of water?" "Why mother," I would reply, "I never heard you call me!" "My son," she would say, "I have spoken several times, and you have answered me, 'yes. Mother, right away!' and now I can wait no longer." But I had not heard her. So at least I thought then. Now I know that my hearing was then perfect, but that I paid no attention to what I heard. I did not let the sound then cause me to think. I was deaf because I did not use my power to convert sound to thought. The old saying is true; "Deaf people hear when they wish to!"

How many of my readers have this habit of abstraction or of absent mindedness? And yet they are the very ones who tell me they "cannot concentrate.' Please change this expression to this form, and it is true: "I do not concentrate upon that which I desire! I let myself drift through habit!" Study this last sentence till you get the meaning. It will help to develop the power of conscious concentration.

All I am trying to do in these conversations is, to bring you to consciously do that which you are doing unconsciously and automatically every day. I wish you to rise from habit formed through neglect or necessity, to a habit formed because you desire and choose it. In the first place you are a slave of, and in the last place you are the Master of, habit.

Note—Since Concentration is only paying attention to right thoughts, I have prefaced each section with extracts from best literature, and recommend that the reader memorize them, as they are Power-thoughts and will, when meditated upon, lead to Success.

SECTION II.

CONCENTRATION IS NATURAL.

If the first rule is to obey your native bias, to accept the work for which you were inwardly formed,—the second rule is concentration, which doubles its force. — Emerson in "Greatness."

The power of concentration is one of the most valuable of intellectual attainments. — Horace Mann.

Judging from letters and questions of pupils, no part of the Mental Science causes so much difficulty as the demand that there be Concentration. I propose to take from this demand all that is difficult, and remove all obstructions from the mind so that there will be a clear understanding of what is meant by "Concentration" and what by the phrase so much in use,—"In the Silence"

There is no break in the methods of nature. Truth is identical whether uttered by ancient or modern teacher, by eastern priest or modern Mental Scientist. He who finds Truth, finds it by Nature's one method. There are no patent rights upon any of her secrets, and no corners upon any method of arriving at the perception of Truth.

The cave man found it just as Moses did, and Moses just as Socrates, and Socrates as Jesus, and A. J. Davis as Jesus, and Mrs. Eddy as Davis, and Henry Harrison Brown as they did. Therefore, unless we are to admit the claim of special revelation and arbitrary selection on the part of a Creator, we are to analyse our own mental action, and from the way we have come to Truth, realize that all in like manner come. From the study of our own unfoldment, we are to deduce ways for still more extended progress, just as we have by study of nature's methods in other lines of manifestation, learned to assist her in her unfoldment.

As man, by interrogating nature has learned to become a factor in the evolution of the material world, as he has, by the same process learned to be a factor in his own evolution, mentally, artistically, esthetically; so by the study of our mental conditions we are to learn to be a conscious factor in the evolution of a control over ourselves.

The child and the savant learn by the same means. The slave and the king develop by the same process. The workman and the poet win success by obedience to the same law. The victor and the vanquished are results of the one instrument. Nature is no respecter of persons. All the old conception of any special revelation; of any peculiar method; of any newly invented process; of any specially prepared series of directions; of any collections of teachings, or of any prepared formulas, being of value, must pass away. You are to realize that in you abides the same power; in you lies latent, the same intelligence; in you awaits the same germ, that all other men possess, to be brought into unfoldment by the same methods. You are to declare,—"What man has done I can do! When I know how others achieve I also can achieve. When I have learned the Law, I can use it! When I find the Way I can walk in it. When I see the Light I can follow it. When I know the Truth I can demonstrate it."

So long have the old ideals held sway that it is important that you see that all of the old growths of error, of self-depreciation, of beliefs in the supernatural and in the special are rooted out of your mind. Too many are trying to come into the New Thought and hold on to the old thought at the same time. For such, Jesus spoke, when he admonished us not to put new wine in old bottles. New perceptions of truth will not fit old statements, and new perceptions must not be limited to old methods. Truth is never old and her methods of revelation, the processes of awakening to the perception of Truth, are ever the same. Do not confound human perception of Truth with Truth itself, nor fix it at the ancient limitation. Lowell tells us that:—

God sends his teachers unto every age, To every clime, and every race of men, With revelations fitted to their growth And shape of mind, nor gives realm of Truth Into the selfish rule of one sole race.

Do not make one and the same, the thing and the maker, the seer and the perception. The methods of seership are always the same; the methods of applying the truth perceived to the objective life are as various as are organizations and the lives of the seers. No one can either perceive Truth or live it for you; therefore while you perceive Truth by the absolute law of Mind, you will apply Truth by the special law of your own individuality. Thus Truth common to all ages and all men is so differently stated, and so differently applied that there are thousands of sects and schools. But under all these, lies the one Substance named God, Brahm, Allah, Joss, Force, Mind, Energy, Christ, Spirit, &c., &c. And no matter what the rite, form, ceremony, formula, method, law, rule, or regulation proposed or imposed, all these have their base in the same natural phenomena. Therefore no matter what claim is made for any system you are to understand that no system ever was, or ever can be, made that will embody all possible methods of attaining any desired unfoldment. No system can be made that will exhaust the possibilities of infinite Principle. Systems, forms, and rules arise in the observance of details. When you rise to Principles you will make your own rules or have none. Reliance upon Principle and reliance upon rule, make the difference between a master and a slave; between a leaner and one self-controlled. To rest upon forms, formulas, rites and rules is the custom of church, state and public opinion. To rest upon Principle is the demonstration of—Individuality.

A clear conception of this point is necessary because so many teachers, leaders and founders, are springing up, claiming to speak with authority, or to have devised, or found, some plan by which one may attain unfoldment, success, health, or happiness by some new and original road. Know this: all such claims are based upon some merely individual perceptions of the one and the same law which every person has obeyed who ever attained success. There is but one way, because Life, Truth, Principle, and Law are unchangeable. The Spirit of Truth through Jesus said—"1 am the way!" So It says through every Human Soul. "I am the way V says Life. "I am the way!" said Nature to the scientist, and seeking out her way, it is now his way. In New Thought we only interrogate Nature; seek her way! When we find her way we shall have the only way. And since all Truth is simple; since every discovery man has made of Nature's way is simple; we are to infer that when we find the way to health, success and happiness it will be so simple that we shall be surprised that we did not always know it.

I admonish you at the beginning of any study, to put aside all systems that have anything strange, difficult, mysterious, occult, or supernatural; anything hard to understand, or peculiar to do. They are not Nature's way and will never be yours. Mistrust everything you find difficult to understand. Only so far as any system conforms to your own simple life, does it have any value to you. When you are inclined to take up any method of self-culture, ask, "Is this Nature's simple way? Have all men in all ages found success through obedience to this Principle? If so, I will adopt it."

Again, I advise you to refuse to deal with any teacher, or system, that proposes to do all for you; to make it easy for you. There are no easy, no royal roads. Though the New Jerusalem "lieth four square with gates on each side;" there are no chariots on either side to carry you in. You must get in by your own unaided efforts.

"Where did you come from, Topsy?" "I growed!" Each person must grow into any condition he desires. Teachers may do what the gardener does—make conditions for growth. This book and any good book or teacher, can make conditions for you to grow, by teaching you how mankind has ever grown.

I would that you bring very closely to yourself this thought—"All men are created equal V' In this consciousness concentrate your forces in the thought.— "What man has done, I can do! What men know, I can know. When I know what they know, I can do as they do!' This is the only possible rational, self-respecting mental attitude. It is the only one under which I wish to claim you as a pupil or as friend. In this mental attitude we shall win. In any other we shall fail.

In other words I have been during all this lesson, advising- you to concentrate upon FAITH IN YOURSELF. This is the keynote to the Arch of Character and its presence or absence constitutes success or failure.

The key to success in the line of all mental and spiritual achievement, is CONTROL OF THE ATTENTION. The ability to concentrate and hold the attention upon any given point at will, and resist all diverting tendencies and desires, is an absolute necessity to high attainment and rapid progress. Happily this is an art that all may acquire by resolution and persevering effort. The very practice itself is a wholesome and efficient mental discipline. — Dr. J. H. Dewey in "The Way, the Truth and the Life."'

SECTION III.

PAYING ATTENTION.

Careful attention to one thing often proves superior to genius and art. — Cicero.

Let us labor for an inward stillness, An inward stillness and an inward healing. — Longfellow.

Not in the clamor of the crowded street. Not in the shouts and plaudits of the throng, But in ourselves, are triumphs and defeat. — Longfellow.

In the Study of metaphysics, the awful bugbear of 'The Silence" has been let loose upon yon. As you have been thinking of what I have written and paid no attention to anything else, you have been "In the Silence!" As you have "paid attention" to the thought of these pages, you have been "concentrating," and the difficult task you have feared is accomplished; the condition you thought so hard to reach, is gained.. How? By not thinking of it! By forgetting you have done ihat which you wished to do. Never yet did a person concentrate while thinking, "I am going to concentrate T or, "I wish I could concentrate!" or, "o, how hard it is to concentrate!" As long as you think of what you wish to do, you will never do it. As soon as you forget your wish to do, in the doing, the thing is done. It is this continual thought of concentration, that troubles so many of my students, readers, and correspondents. "I have been a New Thought student for years and cannot concentrate," is a frequent expression. But there is, nevertheless, in the expression, the concentration sought. It shows that the person has concentrated, not upon the thought desired, but upon the wish to concentrate. This is concentration. I have said that we must win by that method by which mankind has ever won: That there is but one method. Study the life of any successful person in any age and along any chosen line; seek one among your friends or acquaintances; what is the dominant mental quality that gave him success? Be he gambler or poet, find the trait which gave him power. Find among your friends those who have failed and see what thought caused their failure.

Lady Macbeth said to her husband:

But screw your courage to the sticking place and we shall not fail!

We have the proverb—"Too many irons in the fire!'

This is diffusion.

"One thing at a time, and that done well Is as good a rule as I can tell!" is an admonition I learned as a lad. Success is his who concentrates; failure lies in diffusion. "Concentration is power; diffusion is weakness, says Emerson. Study persons of strong character among your friends. They are not the fickle ones, not those who jump from topic to topic in conversation. They are those who can tell a coherent story, and who are not easily thrown off their poise.

Men who succeed are those who attend to their business, that is:— pay attention to business. The rule for success in every department of life, be it desire for health, happiness, success, or prosperity is—MIND YOUR OWN BUSINESS. First, have a business. Then, mind it. That is, put your mind into your business. Think of your business. Keep your thoughts upon your business. MIND—PAY ATTENTION TO, which is merely saying, "Concentrate upon what you are doing." Men whose minds are off wool gathering when they should be attending to business, are men who fail. Men whose minds are full of fears, anxieties and doubts, fail. Minds, uncontrolled, are like horses uncontrolled; neither arrive at any desired end. They fly the track, they put no eye on the goal. Winners see the goal; keep that end in view all the time. Concentration is an ever-present element in all human success and if you wish to succeed in applying the Affirmations of "Soul Culture," you must do as all successful persons have done, i. e., concentrate upon them. In the simplest and strongest terms, make these Affirmations your business, and mind your business. M. Y. O. B., (mind your own business) must be your watchword of success. These letters are of value equal to those to which men attach so much value, those granted by college or king. Following the name of every successful person, I see the invisible M. Y. O. B., which is God's insignia of nobility—"A successful man!"

New Thought is but bringing prominently and simply into view, the good old admonition, "Have something to do and do it." Jesus gave the same when he said, "Not every one who saith to me Lord! Lord!' But he that doeth the will of my Father!" No doing without thought, and that thought is concentrated thought. Powder flashed in the pan never sends a ball to any mark. Powder concentrated by the chamber of the cannon does the work; tons can only destroy recklessly without the chamber.

The lesson—Powder in pan has the same power as that in cannon. So with men—All have equal power, "All men are created equal/ in life, power and possibilities of Spirit. Some concentrate and win; others scatter and lose. Some make a lot of noise, and go off with a whiz, like a Chinese pin-wheel; others work silently like the fuse of the sappers and miners, till the moment of action, then you hear them. Do you take this all in? You do not as long as you hold any person or condition or circumstance to blame for your success or failure. As long as you thus hold circumstances responsible, you will never cure life's ills. You have as much life, as much power, and as good conditions as any other person. We are not all alike in desires, tendencies, or loves; but for us, as we are, the whole universe is ours. We have only to use the power we are. Circumstances are opportunities through which we are to express the power we are. Emerson says: "The great heart will no more complain of the obstructions that make success hard, than of the iron walls of the gun which hinder the shot from scattering.'

From this, understand that Concentration is the universal Law governing the manifestations of Power in any line. In what is known as physics, concentration is the secret of power. Mechanics lies in power to concentrate the stream, wind, lightning and thus make it possible to bring it under direction and control. Diffused power cannot be directed or controlled and is therefore subject only to the laws of the Absolute and the uses that it has in the Universal Mind. Winds that blow without any human direction, streams that flow without being controlled in some channel, have use in the economy of Nature, but are not directly of use to man.

As soon as man begins to concentrate, not only these invisible forces, but also to concentrate the visible like fusing or forging the minerals, he increases their power.

Concentration is the secret of directed power, wherever man has made it available. Emerson tells us that Napoleons success lay in concentration, his only rule.

He says:—"On any point of resistance he concentrated squadron after squadron in overwhelming numbers until it was swept out of existence."

When man shall learn to still more concentrate power he will master aerial navigation. Storage batteries and small dynamos and small engines are opening the way.

Therefore, when you are learning concentration, you are learning to use Power, in the same manner as man has learned to use those powers he has harnessed to his machinery.

Mental concentration is the application of the one method through which all nature applies her forces to any particular end.

You are ever to remember that you are living in a universe; that all force is one and is subject to the one law; that methods of the laws operation in the visible universe are parallel with methods in the unseen universe. Says Emerson: "The laws below are sisters of the laws above!" Mrs. Browning tells us: "There is not a flower on earth, but has its counterpart on the Spiritual side." They are reflections in the slower vibrations of what is actual and permanent in the higher. As the picture in a mirror is a reflection of the object so every so-called material circumstance is, but the reflection of a mental reality, or if you prefer, a spiritual reality. All laws are spiritual laws. Or it may please you better if we say, all Laws are Laws of Mind. Mind is all, and All means ALL. It does not leave out Man or rock, angel or energy. ALL means God, and God means ALL. You are thus first of all in your demonstration to concentrate the thoughts you have had of Existence into the OKE Substance that fills the Universe. You are to affirm ITnity until it becomes a mental habit to think from Unity. Think of God as not far away, but as being ever-present and IN you. To think of your life as God's life; your thought as God's thought; your strength as God's strength; your action as God's action. You must create this habit of concentrating God, yourself, and your friends into the All. You are to accustom yourself never to think of anything, or any manifestation as separate from the All. It is the All that manifests; it is the All that thinks, loves, acts, works, hates, grows, blossoms, ripens, and decays. You will soon grow to FEEL God, as you think of IT (or HIM) as present in yourself; and to think of yourself as present in Him, and of your thought and deed as being His thought and deed. You will soon realize that the idea of separateness between yourself and the All is the beginning of all your ills.

Paul held and taught this conception of Unity. He said: I am persuaded that neither death, nor life, nor angels, nor principalities, nor things present, nor things to come, nor powers, nor height, nor depth, nor any other creature shall be able to separate us from the love of God!

SECTION IV.
SOME CHANNELS OF WASTE.

Work while you work and play while you play;

That is the way to be happy and gay. — My Old School Reader.

Too many irons in the fire.

Jack of all trades and master of none. — Old Proverbs.

Laurel crowns cleave to deserts

And power to him who power exerts.

Hast not thy share? On winged feet

Lo, it flyeth thee to meet! — Emerson.

While happiness is to be desired and is the source of health and power, being the subjective side, the cause side of these, it is often confused with mere excitement, —especially the excitement of change,— or of stimulant, and also with mere pleasure. Pleasure arises in the sensations of the physical body and while it is to be encouraged as a means and as such becomes a source of power, whenever sought as an end it is diffusive of power, destructive of happiness, through the reactions that follow, and thus productive of failure in line of health and a successful life. Rational pleasures are to be sought temperately. With Self-Control they are healthful. Intemperate use is diffusion, weakness. All emotions not controlled—all intemperance in any form, —is the opposite of that concentration, which is the "Road to Success. It is the concentration of mere physical enjoyment, and since all power is Mind, (or Spirit) and not body, to concentrate upon the physical in any form, is to close, to a greater or less degree, the channels of inspiration of Spirit, which is life. The physical is the animal side of Man. And until he attains mastery over the flesh, it is as natural to concentrate upon physical enjoyment as do the lambs and colts. This is the exuberance of animal life. Man can keep this exuberance down to what is termed old age will he be temperate, and the word means—Self Controlled. Under right thought, all this animal spirit is curbed, and reined, and guided by the Master—Soul. Through this mastery it is possible to avoid disease, unhappiness, poverty and even physical death by ripening out of physical conditions through some form of de-materialization.

It is not because there is anything inherently wrong in this, that I refer to the fads, follies, fashions and social excitements. Only so far as they are indulged in to kill time; are taken up because they are in the air; indulged in to emulate or to vie with others; enjoyed with no serious purpose; and allowed to absorb time, attention and labor that, would we win Success, — would lead to Success. I am writing only for those who are willing to purchase success. "Laurel crowns cleave to deserts" and no one ever won the crowning success who did not buy it with a price. And no one wins social distinction, or place in the fashionable, political, or athletic world, who did not pay for it by losing success in other fields.

"In the devil's booth all things are sold, Each ounce of dross costs its ounce of gold."

"It is natural to concentrate upon pleasure," it is said, and also:—"It is natural to concentrate under excitement l" Yes: but is it well? Has not man a higher motive? Anger, jealousy, envy, hatred, avarice and kindred passions are concentrative and belong naturally to man; but unfolding man leaves these behind and finds happiness, power, prosperity in concentrating upon their opposites.

It is because, all forms of concentration that have not behind them noble ideals, are diffusive of power and weakening to character; because they are a form of intemperance; because they are manifestations of a lack of self-control, of self-sufficiency, that, for those who have a desire to nobly win, I mention them here. Society has much "busy idleness/ The ladies crochet, make crazy quilts, take up china painting and kindred fads to "kill time." Not with any serious purpose, but because they don't know what else to do, or seek them to show their productions for the approval or envy of neighbors. There is much dissipation in what is termed "Art." "Art is man added to Nature," but there seems to be no purpose "to add" in much that today passes by that name. The test? Only a few years and all these productions are relegated to the lumber room. The productions of real Art, live. True, some unfoldment comes to those who really enjoy; who really love the work; who truly have a real desire; but when it is done only because others are painting; because "I must do something" it is a diffusion of power and an element of weakness.

To follow this course is to take the road to failure. Concentration upon any occupation means success in it. Have a purpose in what you do and work with a will.

Whatever is done to kill time; to help one forget one's self, because it is the fad or because society demands it, is weakness. "Conformity is weakness" says Emerson.

Companionship, social intercourse, exchange of affectionate and love expressions are sources of power. Man is a social being and needs to mingle with his kind, but what are known as "social functions" are diffusive and interfere with Success, as determined in "Introduction." What is termed "society" is dissipation; a loss of opportunity and power and leads to ill health and failure. Many who feel compelled to live lives in conformity to social demands have said to me, both men and women, "Society is hell!" Physicians tell me so and the records of sanitariums and homes echo,—"Hell!" Why? Because it is the opposite of Peace—Rest—Happiness— Health.

Concentration upon pleasure for its own sake, kills. Games are right and necessary in their place. They are means of relaxing; a means of rest from our over strenuous life. But the tendency is to carry the same strenuousness into the game, and instead of enjoying the game, enjoy the winning. And there is no more nerve wearing and diffusive means than gambling in any form, be it at stock board, roulette table or at any thing where there is striving to win. Let me tell you something:—when you become so interested in winning as to lose the enjoyment of each step of the game— stop! I will not play a second game with any one who "crows" over his winnings, or who feels bad over his failures. And I would prefer he would, like myself, forget to name who won the evening before. To play in any other thought than that of enjoyment of expression at the time, is not to make the game restful, but only to change the kind of excitement. To change from concentration of business to concentration in winnings is not to change the principle, is not rest. The same is true of athletic contests. The motive determines the benefit. Herbert Spencer loved to relax at billiards. A young man once played with him who showed great skill and declared that he was champion at the game.—"I am sorry to hear it/ said the philosopher. Time, skill, effort and life wasted for that which represented no power, no real success.

President Livermore said to us at Meadville: "Young men, you cannot devote yourselves to society and at the same time attend to your studies!"

"Choose this day whom you will serve," says nature. You cannot have success on a high ideal plane and at the same time in a lower one. Cannot win in business, art, politics, literature, or any chosen field, and dissipate your time, thought and power in other fields. Concentrate upon some chosen ones and use all others as a means of relaxation and rest.

"Too many irons in the fire!" is the old proverb. Have one purpose. Concentrate and stick, is the soul of success.

I recently heard a young man in conversation with a young lady say—"No, I had to give up night school; I had too much to do!" and a few moments later I overheard him say: "I was at the theatre a few evenings ago, and with skating rink and theatre I shall be out every night this week." The probabilities are that in a few years he will complain of his "luck," because others get promoted over him. He had concentrated upon pleasure, the sensations of the physical man. Gossip, the daily papers, latest novel, the new dance, and other trifles occupy too much time for health and success. I have listened to conversations between men on some political trifle and between women on some society gossip for over fifteen minutes that was not worth a passing thought. This loss of life means loss of health and success.

Yet these people will tell me they cannot concentrate. True they have not learned the law of mastery—concentration at will,—but they naturally concentrate upon the thought that comes under present desire, or habit. What shall these do? Follow the advice given in Matthew:—"Repent,"—for the kingdom of God is at hand I" Repent;—turn about;—do the opposite. Think the opposite. "At hand." Yes, reach forth and take it. It is waiting for you—is the realization of your Ideal of happiness and success.

SECTION V.
"I AM LIFE"

I am the Way, the Truth and the Life. — Jesus.

The infinite always is silent, 'tis only the finite that speaks. — John Boyle O'Reiley.

The granite rocks disorganize
To feed the hungry Life they bear!
The very moss drinks daily Life,
From out the viewless air. — J. L. McCreary.

I am the Way, the Truth and Light;
In me all Being flows.
I'm one with rock and star so bright.
God's spark within me glows. — Sam Exton Foulds.

There is but one Life and I am that Life. This thought you are to hold and thus concentrate Life into One and not as in the past diffuse and limit it in amount. ALL the one life is mine. With this thought you cannot either lose or waste. All life is yours and you may use it as you choose. You have no less life at any moment than you had at first. You have as much at 80 years as you had at birth. Under the old thought habit of scattering and diffusing Life, you were at times weak, weary, or ill. Under the New Thought you are never thus, but are at all times One with the All-Life. Learn to think from this thought of life. Concentrate upon it. Do not lot your mind wander off into old channels, but keep your attention fixed always upon some aspect of the ONE.

It is an excellent practice to image yourself as an inlet of an infinite ocean of Life. Imagine a current setting into you as a bay, just as it comes through our beautiful Golden Gate; and as it fills this magnificent bay, so see Life fill you. Say to yourself,—"I am a bay filled through the Golden

Gate of Love from the Infinite ocean of Life. The tide never ebbs. I am at all times full. I have but to let Life flow through me into expression, and as fast as I let it flow out, I am filled again. Thus I have life only as I give it expression. O Life; Healthful Life; Beautiful Life. Mine now and forever!' Be this your constant song.

Constantly keeping a chosen thought uppermost is Concentration. As you practice it will grow easier, till you will have formed the habit of thinking of God, of Life as One, and then think of yourself as God and as Life in manifestation. You will grow to think of the fullness of life, just as you have been accustomed to think of your want of life.

Mental habits are the only habits you should cultivate or allow. There are good mental habits but there are no good habits in the objective life. To think rightly is to allow fullest liberty in the objective life, because Thought cannot take the same objective form through you to-day, as it did when you were five years old, or as it did when you were ten, or twenty or thirty years of age. As you change, your environment changes; you will find your thought of Unity taking a new physical manifestation. For instance—You may to-day, under the thought of the Infinity-of-Life, find it to your happiness to attend theatre or attend the sick, and be up all night, but your ordinary habit is to retire early. But when you make it a habit to retire early you fetter yourself, and will feel the loss when you do not.

Create the mental habit of doing what you think is best at the time and for the occasion and you will either retire or remain up with equal physical comfort. Mental habits are formed from Principle, from love of right; ph5sical habits are formed from attention to details. Principles have millions of applications. Create a habit of temperance and you will need no pledge, and any pledge will fetter you when you wish a larger liberty. A mental habit of thinking no evil will keep you from fault-finding and criticism, while a habit of overlooking the faults of others will shut you out from seeing them and open the better to your vision. Mental habits are results of demonstration along certain thought lines. "I don't demonstrate" Why? Because you have created a mental habit of letting the mind run at random. Create a new habit. How? By doing as you always have done save to choose your thought. There is no change in law or method. It is a simple thing to choose other thoughts where you have been thinking unpleasant ones. This requires will and effort till you create the habit and then the right thought will think itself. Automatism is to be made of conscious use; habit is automatism,. By a course of right thinking we change nerve tissue; build cells which like storage batteries hold the thought and, when cells enough have been created, they do the work without our conscious volition. We materialize our thoughts and our will into muscle and nerve. Gray matter is secreted in the ends of the fingers of the blind and in the fingers of the pianist and the deft artisan. The fingers do not think, but the thought out of which they have been made, does the work. So is it in any line of labor; the body becomes materialized so that the less of conscious thought is put upon it the better work it does. This is done under the universal Law of Concentration. You are consciously to obey the Law to a chosen end, as you have in the past involuntarily and unconsciously obeyed it, to an end chosen for you by necessity. In the old thought and labor you were slave; in the New Thought you are Master through Self-direction.

You do not suffer from lack in concentration, for without concentration nothing is done. Every step you take and every word you speak is the result of concentration. What you complain of arises from a lack of proper thought choice. People differ in the power to concentrate at will upon a chosen thought and their power to hold by will to a chosen thought for any definite time. Some people have persistence and consecutiveness while others are fickle, veering, and easily discouraged. But discouragement, fear, grief, pain, sorrow, worry,, anxiety, jealousy, anger, and weariness are all like their opposites, the results of concentration. What is the difference? Is it because some persons possess less will? Can one person have more Life than another? Each one has All Life and can draw at will. Can a person then have less will than another? The All-Will belongs to each, and each has all of the All-Will that he or she wills to use. There is no such thing as a weak or a strong will, any more than there is a strong or a weak life. There may be a strong or weak manifestation of life and will through the same individual. No person exercises the will in the same way at all times. The very fact that we notice the difference between the exercise of will on occasion, is evidence that will is limitless and we can use all we desire. Therefore it is not a valid excuse for a person to say of another, "He has a stronger will than mine! because each person has a will of equal strength. It is merely a question of how you will to use the Ego as Will.

SECTION VI.
HOW SHALL I CONCENTRATE.

Let your yea be yea and your nay be nay. — Jesus.

Whatsoever things are lovely and of good repute, think on these things. — Paul.

No man can choose what coming hours may bring

To him of need, of joy, or suffering;

But what his soul shall bring unto each hour

To meet its challenge—this is his power. — Priscilla Leonard.

It is profanation for you to ask how Life will do its work tomorrow. It is sacrilegious after telling Life, the Omnipotent and the Omniscient what you desire, for you to put your finger into the work. You are to let the One in the sub-conscious materialize your ideal. Every time you interfere with Life, you get burnt fingers. Your entire business is to build in the Ideal. When you have created the mental image you are to concentrate upon that image and LET the MASTER BUILDEE—LIFE (GOD), do the work while you enjoy the conditions that come to you. I think this advice is plain; Concentrate upon the mental image and let that image, through the operation of mental laws, direct the 8oul in the manifestation. Simply do your work in imagination; do your work by thinking. God will through necessity do the rest. Thinking is all you can do. Therefore watch your thoughts and when they are inclined to stray away from the chosen image, bring them back. Soon the Will by that faculty must body itself forth in the physical becomes so trained to the fact that it must hold to the chosen picture, that it will keep your thoughts from straying. This is the ultimate of Concentration; it brings REALIZATION; then you and the mental image become one.

I give you in this connection a fine mental picture to hold of your power, from Edwin Arnold's "Light of Asia V Concentrate upon it till it becomes your thought of yourself, as body, as Will, and as Infinite Life. Look upon Spirit as the rider! take The body for the chariot and the Will As charioteer! Regard the Mind as reins; The senses steeds, and things of sense The ways they trample on. So is the Soul The Lord that owneth spirit, body, will. Mind, senses, all. Itself unowned.

Thus think the wise! He who is unwise, drives with reins Slack on the neck o' the senses, then they romp Like restless horses of a charioteer. He that is wise, with watchful mind and firm. Calms these wild fires, so they go fair and straight Like well-trained horses of a charioteer. The imagination is the real creator. The pictures it creates become objective realities. Henry Wood deserves a much greater recognition than he has yet received for the Principle he lays down in his "Ideal Suggestion." This form of Suggestion controls the life. The ideal is the real in Spirit and that which is spiritually created must take objective form. As every picture was first a mental image in the mind of painter, and painted itself; as each statue was first a mental picture in the mind of sculptor; as palace, hut, or stable in the mind of architect was once a mental picture; so every form of human expression is in the inception a mental image, created upon, or by, or through, the Imagination. What is once impressed upon the mind universe. Pictures created by Affirmations become, according to the fidelity with which they are held imaged forth in the body. "According to the fidelity with which they >are held." Note this well. Rest here and give the thought time to affect the body. Rest an hour and it will have an hours effect. Make a mental habit of holding this thought constantly as a picture, to the exclusion of all pictures that mar, and it becomes reflected in the body as does the mental image in mind of artist or workman. "Let your yea he yea." This is why you are at all times to keep before yourself the picture of health, happiness, and success. "Think on these things." These pictures are to be held as realities in Principle; not to be wrought out in detail, save as day by day, the need of detail comes. As soon as mentally created, they are Powers and Realities in the Soul Realm. There alone you have creative power. Details are the objective conditions with which you are to deal with reason when the time for reasoning comes. "NOW is the accepted time" for you to deal with Principle. Principle will take care of the detail that now is, and with other details, when the evolution of the mental image brings them into the present. Make not the mistake of planning the how, and the way, in which this mental image will objectify. That is not your business. Do not think on these things. Give to Life the outline of what you desire and trust Life. Let Life carry out your desire. Life is omnipotent and is the only builder. Life will decide when to give the picture objective form. Hold the picture in your mind and trust. Be yourself the architect; Life is the workman. Keep your hands off. The only work for you is:—Think, Concentrate, and Trust.

SECTION VII.
THE WILL.

The education of the Will is the object of our existence. — Emerson.

O living Will that shalt endure

When all that seems shall suffer shock. — Tennyson.

The mind of a human organism can, by effort of will, properly directed, produce measurable changes in the chemistry of the secretions and excretions; in the vasor motor blood supply to areas and organs, and in the temperature selected areas, and so on. All of this goes to prove that the mind has a direct effect upon the functioning of the cells that compose an organ, and that if we can properly train the mind, we can produce definite effects upon any physiological function.

— Professor Elmer Gates.

An educated Will then is the first necessity to happiness, health and prosperity. The Will should be as subject to desire in us as are the muscles of the gymnast to his will. This can be done by creating right mental habits through voluntary concentration. The mechanic educates his hand to hold the saw; the engineer his to hold the throttle; the pianist, his fingers to play; till it is now 'second nature for them to obey. In like manner can the Will be cultivated in other directions. Its function is to obey; to carry out the orders of the judgment. When it has been trained to stick to a thought, it is easy, and we say, "A person of trained will I" But if the thought wanders then we say, "Weak will!" But the Will is equally strong in both cases.

It takes as strong a Will not to do as it does to do; as much Will to sit in the chair as it does to get up; as much to stop walking as to start; as much to refrain, as it does to perform. "I can!" "I can't!" and "I won't!" require an equal expression of Will. But when we have trained the Will to our decision, "I can't!" then it is easy, natural," for us to say "I can't." When we have trained it to our decision, "I don't," that is also easy; but when we have trained it to say, "I can," it is equally easy to say "I can," and to do. The trouble with the majority of persons is that they never have been trained into habits of self-reliance and self-assertion. Lacking these it is natural, because it is habit to say, "I can't." In fact, it says itself, so accustomed are they to say and to think, "I can't." "I can't" is really "I won't try!" "Can't" means, I will not will to do. Therefore when you tell me that you do not concentrate because you "lack Will," this is not the fact. You really tell me that you have created a habit of letting yourself as Will drift without conscious direction. All you have to do to win your desires is to train yourself as Will through Affirmation, till it is as natural and easy for you to say "I can!" as it is now for you to fear, doubt and say, "I can't." This Affirmation, "I CAN!" is born of the consciousness of ability to do because you possess All-Life and All-Will, and may use as much as you desire. You do use at all times as much as you have trained yourself by thought to use. Would you possess the power of self-direction, you must have power to choose your thought, and to hold it as long as you choose; have power to shut out all thoughts that weaken or interfere; that make sick or timid; must have the power as trained Will to hold, because you choose, pleasant thoughts of health, success and happiness. VOLUNTARY CONCENTRATION" is the secret of personal power; is the secret of all who have won in lifers battles. These victors decided to think success, and nothing but success, and to never give up, thus from the very jaws of defeat, to win the mead of victory.

Concentration is but sticking as Will to the thought you have chosen. It is thinking "I will." I am asked, "Shall I affirm all the time?" I answer,— Should you spend all your time thinking or saying "I can!" and "I will," you would do nothing else. Think "I can," and "I will" whenever opposite thoughts would enter the mind. Sit quietly a few minutes each day, by yourself with the chosen thought and hold it because you choose to hold it. While you thus concentrate voluntarily, keep all other thoughts out of your mind by willing them out. I will to think thus. This is not easy. You little realize how you have encouraged tramp thoughts, unwelcome thoughts, uncalled thoughts, "calling" thoughts, superficial thoughts, until you begin to direct your mind. You then find how unstable you are as Will. You find as one of my pupils said when she first tried to enter the Silence, "Every other thought, I ever had, came calling!" We have not been trained to choose our thoughts, and are too much of the time subject to wandering, vagabond, tramp thoughts that finding us undirected, pick us up and abide with us. It is important that you fully comprehend what is meant by "Going into the Silence !" It is voluntary concentration. It is wilful concentration. It is concentration upon a chosen thought. It is doing voluntarily and with a determined purpose that which you have been letting yourself do involuntarily all your life. You have learned that when you decide to do a thing and get up your grit,—will to do it,—you can do it. Now what you do, in case of necessity, or under the stress of must," or when you develop a positive determination, you are to create into habit of doing consciously all the time. By this time you will have perceived that what you are learning is not something for occasions, but something for all time. You are changing your manner of life, through this change of mental habit and learning, through thinking in the New Thought method, to live New Thought.

Success goes thus invariably with a certain plus or positive power; an ounce of power must balance an ounce of weight. And though a man cannot return to his mother's womb and be born with new amounts of vivacity, yet there are two economies which are the best succedanea which the case admits. The first is the stopping off decisively our miscellaneous activity and concentrating our force on one or a few points: as the gardener, by severe pruning, forces the sap into one or two vigorous limbs, instead of suffering it to spindle into a sheaf of twigs.

— Emerson in "Power."

SECTION VIII.

HABITS.

You cannot dream yourself into a character; you must hammer and forge yourself into one. — Anon.

We must build the ladder by which we rise And climb to its summit, round by round. — G. Holland.

If my mind is not engaged in the worship, it is as if I worshiped not.— Confucius.

We are creatures of habits most of which we have formed involuntarily, or at best in ignorance of the Law. Now we are beginning to learn and to live in conscious and intelligent use of the Law. Under necessity the bookkeeper concentrates upon his column of figures and hears not the noises about him. Under necessity the workman learns to concentrate upon his machine, his tools, his material, and to hear and to think of nothing else. Under necessity the musician and the artist concentrate upon their task. Under the same necessity the mother attends to her duties unheeding what is going on about her. So with all successful business men. They learn to mind their business; to concentrate their thought upon it. So with us, when we are interested in music, in a play, or conversation, or in the communion of love's expression. Concentrated upon the thing in hand, we think of nothing else. This condition you are to cultivate. It is the rapt condition of the saint; the condition of prayer; the condition of hysteria; the condition of meditation; the condition of absent-mindedness. All these we enter into instinctively. you are to learn to enter them at will, and to understand the method and the purpose. Drifting is not navigation. Neither are these instinctive conditions, —even though they are productive of good,—self-control. All instructions under the New Thought name lead to self-control, which is the culmination of all true education.

Paul enumerated the 'fruits of the Spirit' thus,— "Love, joy, peace, long suffering, kindness, faithfulness, meekness, temperance.' Temperance is also given in the margin of the revised edition as "self-control,' which is the pure meaning of the word. Therefore temperance is the realization of spiritual consciousness. Temperance is self-control; is man's coming into his inheritance of power; is man taking possession of that kingdom which is his. He can never take it until he shall realize that he is one with Infinity. This is accomplished only by hammering and forging the Self into the expression desired. "Man is a bundle of habits," says Emerson. Whence come they? Many by inheritance. Are they mine or do I belong to them? Only that which I appropriate from heredity by choice, belongs to me. All the rest if I continue to manifest it, I belong to. Heredity owns me till I convert it to my desire. That which I do not thus choose and which yet remains in me, is uncontrolled tendencies which bear me on as wind bears the leaf and as hunger bears the wolf. I yield to them and when the habit of yielding: is formed, I excuse myself by saying:—"Heredity. I can't master." When the fact is, I have not tried.

Without attempting to stem the current, or to direct the bark of my life, I have been content to drift. This habit of submission to tendencies is non-human. It belongs to the brute. Man has not yet left heredity behind. My humanity consists in my power to choose. My power to move, to think. He who does not exercise his power of choice is losing his opportunity of selfhood.

Habits are unconsciously formed. They grow while we are sleeping. They are born of our thoughts, and thoughts we take into our sleeping hours are most potent in controlling our lives.

For this reason mental habits have power over us. Mental habits are the only ones to cultivate, are the only habits that are good. Any habit of physical expression is bad, because it becomes a fetter. But a correct mental habit is based upon Principle, and leaves the individual free to act as he feels is right under all conditions.

Cultivate the habit of thinking pleasant thoughts and you will wear, as a habit, a smile. Take a pleasant thought to bed with you and you will smile all the next day.

The rain falls upon the newly plowed hill and makes a little streamlet down the field. The next shower fills the little channel and cuts it deeper. So does the next and the next, until the traveler of a later generation than the plowman, finds a deep gutty or ravine. The water was trained to a habit of flowing in one place. So with thought. Thought is Power. The same thought repeated creates brain and nerve conditions, thus like the rain-fall, preparing for itself a physical memory. Application of this principle gives the fingers of the pianist and the typist, such automatic power. In like manner every thought creates the nerve cells through which to express itself. Fear, worry, anger or any passion becomes a mental habit and creates for its expression the right machine. Grey matter is already secreted for that purpose through previous thoughts of fear, and worry. Each time an Affirmation is made there are nerve cells created that make it easier for the Affirmation to control the body the next time. And the next time the Affirmation is made, a thrill passes through the whole system, as the prepared cells respond to the thought. Thus through Affirmation, after a little while, we have a new mental habit, with a new physical memory written in our nervous system, through which that habit finds easy expression. The sympathetic nerve is like my father's old horse. Father rode around the country buying produce, and the old horse would stop at every farm-house where he had been accustomed to stop, no matter whether we were on a purchasing tour or a picnic. It is necessary that we guard our thoughts, and especially our words, for the vibrations of our voice create nerve conditions through which the thought will work automatically, like the old horse. Have you never had a tune ring in your head all night, or some song, or word of friend? The listening had made a nerve-condition that keeps up automatic action. Much of fear and worry continues in this way. Stop it by will.

Understanding that nerve cells vibrate from habit without our conscious thought, it behoves us to be careful of the thought habits we form; to be careful of what thoughts we express; careful of what thoughts we hold but do not express, for the silent holding, creates also nerve-conditions that later compel expression. From unpleasant thoughts, people so create their bodies, that they find it impossible to live in them, and move out through disease.

Out of the chasm of a bad mental habit, we can build the ladder on which to climb, only of pleasant thoughts. Each time the Affirmation is made, a lung is placed in the ladder. Repetition will create the habit of concentration, so that soon nerves will readily respond, and the habit of health and happiness be formed. Whoever says to me, "I can't concentrate!" is simply repeating the cry of an old habit. I reply, "You can, but you don't! When you will to, you will concentrate.' The habit of willing soon becomes a pleasure; becomes chronic. You learn that you can, when you think you can. Concentration depends upon the habit you create. Therefore, to tell me you cannot, is to make conditions so that you do not.

If you really wish to concentrate; wish to enjoy the Silence, you must make it a habit to do so, by giving thought, will, effort and love to it, till it becomes as natural to concentrate then, as now to fear. You know how habits of any kind are formed. Do with a chosen Affirmation as you have been doing with Affirmations of fear, worry, and illness, and soon you will find yourself living in the Silence; for the habit of concentration, of paying attention, to a chosen thought, will have been formed. This habit will grow upon you until you realize that you can think whatever you choose to think. And be whatever you choose to be.

SECTION IX.
"IN THE SILENCE"

The Soul contains in itself the event that shall befall it. — Goethe.

You are in "the silence" now. The only way to realize it is to get still, physically and mentally. It takes time and practice to do it, and there are no short cuts except as aspiration, faith and suggestion help to quiet your mental chattering. But the spiritual and mental and material rewards of such practice are enormous. Eye hath not seen nor ear heard the glories that are free in the silence. — Elizabeth Towne in "Nautilus."

In the silence of the Spirit,

In the higher realms above, In the deeper life within me,

In the world of perfect love; I have found my Father's kingdom

And His righteousness divine; I have sought and found my heaven.

And all else is ever mine. — C. J. Larsen.

I will be silent in my Soul,

Since God has girt me round With His own Silence in which

There is no space for sound. Only His voice perchance may drop

Like dew upon the ground. — Anna Hempstead Branch.

Thus far I have dealt directly with the Philosophy of Concentration; now I shall give what has been called out by pupils and patients. If some thoughts are repeated, it is because I feel it is necessary to repeat for power, and that conclusions be reached from as many points of view as possible. My notes cover answers to many questions and each reader will find here, I trust, answers to those he is asking.

This phrase, "In the Silence/ so much in use does not mean any peculiar condition. Often it is expressed thus, "Going into the Silence!" There is no "going." The Soul lives in Silence. We are there constantly. Silence is that mental attitude which shuts out the external world through lack of attention. We come en-rapport with the external world through the five senses. Closing these, we listen to that which we hear in the silence of the soul. I like best to use the phrase, "Listening to the Silence."

The noise and turmoil of the objective, which is the physical life, never reaches the Soul. The Real Man— the Soul—is never disturbed. It is the conscious part of our Being that is disturbed; made unquiet; taken out of ease and placed in that condition we term disease. The Soul is like God, always at rest; always at peace; always silent. The Self-Consciousness of Man alone knows worry, fret, pain, trouble, disease, and death. The Soul never dies; no more can it suffer any inharmony. These conditions of un-rest are merely disturbances in the manifestation, and not in that Reality which manifests. The man who runs a machine may be quiet and peaceful, yet the machine may run with racket and in disorder. So with the Soul; all the disorder is in the mental part of our Being and is but the necessary education for our unfoldment. We shall ultimately reach that serene condition, "Where we neither wish nor will;" where we shall, in the words of Emerson, "Trust the current that knows its way." These disturbed conditions are but the preparation the 1 ignorant man makes for that later condition of spiritual maturity, where in Faith and Trust he "Lets the light shine the "Light that lighteth every man that cometh into the world." The Intelligence that is latent in the Soul; the Power of the God-in-man is awakening into Conscious expression. When there is sufficient unfoldment conditions of inharmony pass away and there is At-one-ment; our will is one with the Absolute, the Universal Will. In this condition, one is led as the Quaker and all saintly persons are, by the Inner Voice. Whittier says of that time when mankind shall recognize this Inner Voice, that above the harsh and discordant noises of the present,

A sweeter song shall then be heard, The music of the world's accord, Confessing Christ, the Inward word! That song shall swell from shore to shore, One Hope, one Faith, one Love, restore The seamless robe that Jesus wore.

This same poet also makes this excellent prayer for us all:— Cease not Voice of holy speaking, Teacher sent of God, be near, Whispering through the day's cool silence, Let my spirit hear.

The Hindoo, the priest, the seer, the poet, the inventor, all have learned to listen in the Silence and what is there spoken they proclaim.

In this knowledge of the Silence we are only making common property of the ancient secret of Concentration, meditation and prayer, which has ever been the methods of psychic unfoldment. An ancient occult saying is "Silence is Power!" Silence is the condition in which all power exists, and in which all power operates. Power is silent. The Hebrews spoke of God as dwelling in Silence. No one hears the rustle of the robes of Gravity as it draws earth and sun into equilibrium. There is no noise as the sun each day lifts billions of tons of water. Electricity makes no sound as it ceaselessly works amid the spheres. "When the morning stars sang together and all the sons of God shouted for joy," the objective world was silent; only the ear that hears in the silence heard the song of joy. The Trappist monks have this saying—"It is silence that shuts out new ideas, worldly topics and controversy. It is silence that enables the soul to contemplate with singleness and mortification the infinite perfections of the Eternal!"

During my youth I learned this extract which has been an inspiration to me. I know not the author.

"In silence mighty tilings are wrought—

Silently builded, thought on thought.

Truth's temple greets the sky;

And like a citadel with towers

The Soul with her subservient powers

Is strengthened silently."

The Bible contains many passages upon the power of silence and none more valuable than the admonition of Jesus to "Enter the closet," which I interpret, from my experience, to mean, "Close the external senses and listen to the Silence and what you hear there you shall manifest in your life." All the possibility of Demonstration in all lines of mental science must lie in the unfoldment that comes through meditation—Silence. The Hindoo mystic does this when he sits under the Bo-tree and hears nothing. Concentration in Silence is the only road to inspiration, in any of its forms of Life, Love, Truth and Power.

The Power of Silence and the Power in silence are the most important lessons the present century has to learn. Prof. William Crooks estimates that "a cubic foot of ether which fills all space has locked up within it

10000 cubic-foot tons of energy which have as yet escaped notice. To unlock this boundless store and subdue it to the service of man is the task that awaits the scientist of the future. The later researches give well founded hopes that this store house of power is not hopelessly inaccessible!" Thus reasons the physicist; but the power he sees is both in, and of, the Silence. All these foot-tons, and all the varieties of power the scientist knows, do not exhaust the possibilities of God as Power. Science is but bringing the old conception of God into more intelligible terms. The physical scientist is not the one who reveals God as power. The metaphysician does this, and harnesses this power to human Ego as Will. Prentice Mulford, an early New Thought teacher, said:—

The source of all strength of muscle is in your mind. Your amount of physical strength depends upon your capacity to call force to act upon whatever part of the body you choose. Forever, Spirit, Thought, means for us the same!

But all action of Mind is in silence. Not till thought finds objective expression is there any sound. Through Mind we are in touch with the Omnipotence working in silence. Through this union man possesses all, because he is but a manifestation of All, and the All is indivisible. In Silence man can learn how to use, through his intellect, the All of which he is but the conscious manifestation, directing this sub-conscious manifestation in his life. Considering that we have all of God for a reservoir, we can well ask the question with John White Chadwick:—

"Where such a wealth of perfect things

How dare we ask for more."

Carlyle understood the value of Silence when he wrote to Emerson:— "Silence is the greatest thing I worship at present; almost sole tenant of my Pantheon! Let a man know rightly to hold his peace. I love to repeat to myself 'Silence is of Eternity V " To attain the power to listen at any time, and at all times, to the Silence, is to have unraveled the secret of the Sphynx. In her. Silence is deified and made vocal. All who have learned the secret of living through Concentration, have lifted the "Veil of Isis V I recommend you to memorize this little poem of mine that it may lead you to Life, through Meditation. UNITY.

I stood by Sphynx in desert lone.

Impassive and cold her face of stone;

Stolid and dull those ancient eyes;

Her lips refused me any tone;

Her ears were deaf as stone on shore;

Heart still as in eons before.

In awe I bowed to material guise,

Nor deemed for me the great surprise,

To greet me from those stony eyes.

Musing, I said, "All are divine!

Kin art thou to this Life of mine!

We're children both of the Infinite One!"

Then vocal became those lips of stone;

Her ear had caught my gentlest tone;

From eyes a flame of Love-light shone;

Heart beat as once to priest of yore!

I was lone ho more on desert sand—

A companion held my hand.

I'd solved the riddle of all time—

The SOUL of Sphynx was one with mine.

SECTION X.

COMPENSATION OF CONCENTRATION'.

Though no human eye behold thee Odin sees and hears each word.—Fridthjorfs Saga.

Hush! the sevenfold heavens to the voice of the Spirit Echo:—He that o'er cometh all things shall inherit.— Owen Merideth.

You laugh at monotones, at men of one idea, but if we look at nearly all heroes we may find the same poverty; and perhaps it is not poverty but power. The secret of power, intellectual or physical, is concentration, and all concentration involves of necessity a certain narrowness.— If you ask what compensation is made for the inevitable narrowness, why, this, that in learning one thing well you learn all things. — Emerson.

"How shall I concentrate?" "I can't concentrate. Will you help me?" "Please tell me how to concentrate!" "I have been a student of the New Thought for years but have not mastered concentration. Will you give me directions?" These and many more questions are among the letters on my desk. Yes. I will help you all by as simple illustrations as possible. But I have already said that you all do concentrate, though upon wrong thoughts.

Every art is the common property of mankind. No faculty can be created. No new power is ever manufactured. If what you desire really exists, then you possess it in common with all persons. The chances are that you have held in connection with your desire, some thought of the mysterious, or the supernatural. If Concentration is "the secret of power/ then wherever you find power it must be the result of concentration. Man uses power. You in your Life are Power. Did you not concentrate you were powerless and to the extent that you have voluntarily exercised power, you have to that degree concentrated. So much power in manifestation, so much concentration.

The motto for Concentration is, "One thing at a time!" Concentration is only paying attention. How many times did we as children hear parent or teacher say when our mind was wandering—"Pay attention" The cat watching at the hole for the mouse and the pointer dog on scent, are types of concentration. Follow evolution from cat and dog to Newton and Darwin and you find that Success is but materialized attention. Newton expressed it as—"Intending the mind"

A person naturally concentrates. The mind develops through concentration. The child concentrates but he can hold himself to one thought but a few moments. Upon this fact the kindergarten teacher instructs. Changes are frequent in the school day of her pupils. Parents forget this inability of immature minds and set too hard tasks for children; demand too much of them and then complain that they are not quiet, are restless, fretful, fickle; that they are inattentive and forgetful. All this is true. The wise parent would not have it otherwise lest the child have no childhood, and be old before his time. Wisdom recognizes this native condition and takes advantage of it by not over-taxing the child. As the powers of mind unfold, this power of concentration should increase, but the chances are one hundred to one that it is lessened by false training. The child concentrates at play. Every boy concentrates at his games. Watch how every muscle is tense and every faculty alert in the game of ball; when he is on his skates; or when sliding; or when riding on his bicycle. How still—concentrated—is even the baby when he is "in mischief," which to him is as much business as is the bank, or shop to his father. Concentration is the one method of accomplishment, and the power to concentrate at will, is the sign of mature mind. The masses of people still have child minds. They have little power to hold to a thought and thus wander in conversation; change constantly the premise in argument and lack logical acumen. The scientist has power over his mind; the pseudo-scientist reaches conclusions that are false because he lacks this power of concentration and cannot hold to all the facts till the result is truth.

The need of present humanity is revealed in this lack of power to concentrate upon chosen and desired thoughts. Few have the power to concentrate at will. The great majority are led through involuntary concentration to illness, failure and misery. They let thoughts pick them up, instead of picking up the thought they wish. They are children in man's guise and estate. Therefore when you tell me you can't, or don't, concentrate you are merely telling me that you are in mental babyhood; are not self-directed; but are the creature of any thought that circumstance happens to throw in your path. For this reason it is expected that beginners in Soul Culture will find difficulty in voluntary concentration. Every New Thought cult is but a method of bringing the individual into more perfect expression of his power of self-control. And the manifestation of this control lies in the power to choose, and to hold, the chosen thought. Present conditions of mental chaos, weakness, fickleness, sensationalism, wandering and unsettled physical conditions are the result of a false home, school and social education. Too much is attempted; too many things merely skimmed; too much superficial attention given to too many studies. *Beware of the man of one book is a wise proverb. Too much compulsion is put upon children. They are driven by force, or through competition, as in prizes, at school and Christmas trees, by hopes of promotion, and in college by degrees. The motive is ignoble, selfish, diffusive. The child is not drawn by the love of a noble ideal. What is done by compulsion weakens character. What is done through love strengthens it. The child to become educated should LOVE his school, his teachers. He will then go, drawn by his ideal. He should love to read, to study. The whole duty of parents and teachers is to create this love, to inspire this love of growth, in the child. There is no lack of attention where there is love, no diffusion then over many things. It is the one loved thing. Notice the child at play; the man at congenial task; the man in love with his mistress. Where this love is not, then through effort, under necessity, a habit of concentration is formed for some particular thing; and the man becomes a machine. There is an equally weak condition of character as balance.

One of the best bookkeepers I ever knew was so perfectly concentrated while at his work that nothing ever disturbed him; but he was one of the most fretful and nervous of men at home and in society. A merchant of my acquaintance, most genial and concentrated upon business in his store, was cross and fickle at home. A professor among my friends, is completely self-posessed and absorbed in his study and class, but is a most timid and nervous man elsewhere. I have a friend so concentrated in his base-ball game that he knows no pain when injured, but possesses so little indurance at other times that a cut on his finger while at his work unnerves him. I knew a surgeon most cool and impassive when at the operating table, that would walk the floor all night before an important operation. I know of actors so concentrated upon their part that they do not remember anything that has transpired during the play, but who are so nervous at other times that they break down in insomnia. I had a friend, a most successful orator, so concentrated when talking that he would not sense his body, who was in his home and office the most restless and sensitive of men. I know a woman who is so fretful and fickle with her children that she spoils them, but who will play croquet with perfect abandon, forgetting everything.

This is the case with many gamesters at cards, and habitues of race-courses. These are all examples of concentration under necessity or habit. This condition is a dangerous one for health and happiness, because uncontrolled. All excitement is concentration, where the person has completely lost self-control. For this reason Emerson says, "When you become interested in a book put it away." Proper development gives one at all times, the power to concentrate in any chosen line and at the same time keep self-control. Understand me, it is not that condition where we call a person cold and unsocial. That is not concentration, but constraint, repression, and is equally dangerous to health. Self-possession is very different from self-repression. This latter is common to find and is the result of a fashionable education and of social etiquette. Because of repression doctors and undertakers are reaping a rich harvest. "Except ye become as little children V is the true thought of concentration. The only natural concentration is under desire; is in the line we love.

The only proper way to concentrate is at will, and not because we have to. Let there be no "Have to!" in your life, would you be self-centered and self-directed. A friend often replies when asked why he does not do a certain thing,—"I don't have to!" An industrial and social condition that compels a man to do that which he does not love, and which civilization has not taught him to love, which has not inspired him with an ideal that lifts him above the thought of necessity or starvation; is not entitled to the name of civilization. It needs Edward Carpenter's book used upon it as a surgeon. He entitled his book—"Civilization, its Cause and Cure!" Present civilization needs to be cured. The prophet's cry is applicable to the present condition. "These people honor me with their lips, but their hearts are far from me!"

Heartlessness must be the case where necessity rules. Never a child loved its parent because it was driven to. No husband ever loved his wife because she demanded, "I am yours and you shall love me!" This demand kills what love there was in the marriage. As water flows down hill, so, naturally, do we concentrate upon that which we love.

The first thing to do as one comes into this New-Thought-life, is to do what he loves—or love what he does. He must abolish the thought of must, of necessity. Any method of concentration is lost upon one who will not cultivate a love for present conditions and let that love lead him out of unpleasant ones. Because every thought of antagonism is a concentration born of weakness and of unhappiness, learn to love present conditions and you will naturally concentrate upon the right thought. Learn to love the Affirmations that lead you out to health and happiness and you will naturally concentrate upon them. Learn to love your neighbor as you love yourself and you will concentrate upon thoughts of helpfulness. Love that which you are trying to do and your love will lead you through concentration to BE that which you desire.

SECTION XI
WITH EYES, SEE NOT.

Let us aspire to that heaven where all is eternal and where corruption never comes. — Ancient Aztec King.

*I speak to them in parables because having eyes they see not and having ears they hear not, * * * * Their ears are dull of hearing and their eyes they have closed, lest at any time they shall hear with their ears and shall see I with their eyes and should understand with their hearts! — Jesus.*

These words reported of Jesus have been shortened into the proverb, "None so blind as those who will not see; and none so deaf as those who will not hear!" This fact is a common one. A person does not see or hear that to which he gives no attention. But within this fact lies the deeper fact, that one does not see and hear, because one wills not to see and hear. That is, each person has the power of choice and may see and may hear that which he chooses, and may not hear and may not see that which he does not choose to hear and to see. To exercise this choice is to be the master of fate. This choice is the prerogative of humanity alone. It is the patent-right of manhood; the entail of God's heritage to Man. To the degree in which we exercise this choice we have outgrown the animal in us; have made it sub-servient to the Human.

To see is to pay attention to. To hear is to listen to. To understand with the heart, is to so concentrate upon what is about you, to so think upon what is heard, seen and felt, that you shall know the meaning it has in your life.

Concentration is the simplest thing to understand when you realize that it is thinking upon that which you do; paying attention to what is about you. It is a habit that can be acquired, but one so often neglected in childhood. It is the fault of teachers and parents that children do not grow up conscious of their power to choose and hold to the thought chosen. Wandering minds are formed from uncongenial tasks. Study the children at any school and see how uncongenial are the tasks to many of them. It is a common thing to see children pretending or trying to study, but often glancing from the book, watching what is going on. This cultivates insincerity, pretence, hypocrisy, affectation, fickleness; all of which arises from a lack of attention.

Concentration means that we shall be absorbed in the task of the hour. The biographer of Agassiz tells us i that he would bring his work into the parlor of an evening when it was filled with young company and devote a portion of the time to social converse and enjoyment and at the next moment turn with complete abandon to his study, oblivious of those about him. In this he showed complete control of his mind,—of himself. Tennyson tells a friend in a letter, that he practiced concentration before his literary labors by centering his mind upon his own name; then allowed no interruption.

To affirm that you can't concentrate is to affirm lark of faith in yourself, for the first necessity of success and happiness is faith in your possibilities. Where this faith is not, there is very little accomplished in the way of character-building. Therefore the first step you need to take is to cultivate this faith in yourself. Practice affirming the infinite possibilities of the Human Soul. Think of yourself as an incarnation of God with all the possibilities of the God-head in you. Meditate upon the words of Jesus, The kingdom of God is within I you!" till you feel able to accomplish anything you desire. This meditation is concentration. As you I meditate upon this thought you will grow into the ! power of expression. Affirm—"I, as spirit (or mind) ' possess all power I need to accomplish my desires." I The thought of "Cant" is born in recognition of the power of circumstances. As long as you think they have power you give them power. Circumstances in themselves have no power for either good or evil. The thought you have of them determines their effect upon yourself. If you fear them, you give them power to harm, that is, you are harmed by the thought you put into them. You may think whatever you choose of any circumstance or condition, and it becomes to you that which you think it is. Let me take a simple illustration. When I was a boy we planned a picnic one summer. The morning arose rainy. I felt so badly over it as an evil, that I cried, but others of the family rejoiced, for a drought was broken. They were happy, but I went to bed with a sick headache. The fact was, but a rainy day, and it became to each one that which his thought made it. Fire, defeat, loss of property are mere circumstances; one, by them, is stimulated to I greater effort, another is crushed into lethargy. Concentration in the fear of things and of conditions, creates anxiety, worry and defeat. Concentration in Faith in the All Good, upon things and conditions, causes cheer, clearness of vision and success. How you shall consider any circumstance, is for you to decide and as you decide, that circumstance is to you.

But having made your decision, stick to it. Concentrate upon the thought which you have decided as the right one to hold in relation to that circumstance. Through this concentration you will make your decision a fact in the objective life, because by your decision you have already made it a fact in the Cause-Life.

I wish to emphasize this fact because it is most important. You need not see or hear, need not feel or recognize, anything you do not desire to sense. You can make any circumstance bear to your objective life, whatever relation you desire, by deciding in your mind what that relation shall be, and by then concentrating upon that decision. Why do I affirm this? Because I am doing it every day, and because I know others who are doing it. What one person does, all can and may do. This fact was impressed upon me years ago by the experiments in Suggestion.

As soon as you become convinced that the position I take in my little book, "Not Hypnotism but Suggestion," is correct, and it is the position of all expert practitioners of the Art, you will understand, that by thinking a coin is hot, when held in the hand, the thought will produce a blister. By thinking a drop of water is a drop of Croton oil, a blister is formed; by thinking a door knob is the pole of an electric battery, a shock is received; by thinking a handkerchief is perfumed, an odor is perceived, and by thinking a bread-pill is medicine, one is cured. From these facts you can draw only one conclusion:—All have like effect upon the body and environment. To hold a candle before a mirror is to cause a reflection in the mirror; in like manner to hold a mental picture is to cause its reflection in the body. To change that picture every moment is to cause a change in the bodily reflection. To hold a picture continually in the mind is to keep its reflection constantly in the body. This Concentration does:— it holds the candle of desire before the mirror of flesh until the flesh reflects permanently that picture. Concentration carves in the marble of the material, the model held by Imagination, the creator, who builds through thought. From this fact is reached the conclusion which I state in these Affirmations— I am blind and deaf to all that is unpleasant, ill, painful, weak, or that carries failure. I recognize only that which I wish to recognize. I pay attention only to chosen ideas. I see only that which I wish to see. I hear only that which I wish to hear.

You can gain this power by deciding and training yourself as Will by practice. Practice lies in the use of Affirmation. Concentration is the incubating process which brings the seed thoughts into physical expression. See that you place in the incubator only those thoughts which you wish to run about in the garden of your life. "None so blind as those who will not to see.'* Be thus blind through will and you will open your eyes to see only the Good, the Beautiful and the True.

SECTION XII.
THE IDEAL.

Among thy sons O God! let me be one. —Edward Egleston.

To live divinely is man's work. — Theodore Parker.

The thing we long for that we are
For one transcendent moment,
E'er yet the present poor and bare
Can make its sneering comment.
Still through our paltry stir and strife,
Glows the wished Ideal,
And Longing moulds in clay, what Life
Carves in the marble Real. — Lowell.

I have suggested in previous sections that it is the picture in the mind that is of importance; that the Imagination is the creative power. I wish now to intensify this thought. All things are but material reflections of mental images. You realize this in the statue and the painting, the temple and the machine. On my wall hangs a most beautiful painting, "The Coming Light." The light is breaking through brilliant clouds, "In hues that envious make the pearl-shell, gem and flower." This picture is but a faint representation of the picture that was in the Soul of the painter. He did his best to catch it with canvas and brush. Had it not existed for him before the brush was in his hand, it would not have become my joy. There stands a statue in yonder museum that I love to gaze upon. Story saw that "Greek Slave" long before he took marble and chisel; but when the Idea possessed him It carved itself. A mental picture then; now it stands a marble dream, for the delight of man for ages.

Which is the real and which ideal? Which is transitory and which is permanent? Which is Truth and which illusion? Which is the thing, and which is the reflection? Fire, flood, age, neglect, may destroy the picture and the statue, but the idea cannot be destroyed. The eternal thing is the Idea; the transitory is its reflection in the sense-material. That which eternally exists is the unseen and the permanent; is the Ideal, created by the Human Mind from Divine Ideas. I wish you to memorize that most beautiful extract at beginning of this section from Lowell. It is scientific and better yet, it is Truth. And Oliver Wendell Holmes has something only a little less perfect which is also worth remembering:

Deal gently with us, ye who read!

Our largest hope is unfulfilled—

The promise still outruns the deed—

The tower but not the spire we build.

Our whitest pearls we never find;

Our ripest fruit we never reach;

The flowering moments of the mind

Drop half their petals in our speech.

These are my blossoms; if they wear

One streak of morn or evening's glow.

Accept them; but to me more fair,

The buds of song that never blow.

This is but repeating in Holmes' beautiful way, the adage, "Men preach better than they practice!" And this is the most important fact I have for you in this lesson in Concentration. No progress without this Idealism. No practice without preaching proceeds it.

To see the buds mentally is to create them, and they will bloom not only in the eternal realm but also in the objective life. They lose beauty only when compared with their reflection in the realm of decay and death. Dr. Holmes and James Russell Lowell will find the greatest joy in creating, now they are freed from this sense-limitation of expression. The creator—Mind—is superior to the created—things—and the creation is, that the creator may still more perfectly create. We are now devotees to appearances, to creations, to things, Emerson tells us:—

Things are in the saddle

And ride mankind.

He tells us also that this "Law for Things," "Doth man unking," and adds:—

And what if Trade sow cities

Like shells along the shore,

And thatch with towns the prairie broad,

With railway ironed o'er?

They are but sailing foam-bells

Along Thought's causing stream,

And take their shape and color,

From him that sends the dream.

And again he says of England's abbeys and the pyramids:—

Out of Thought's interior sphere

These wonders rose to upper air.

I add to these words of Emerson these other words from him, prefacing them with that great line of Richard Realfs:—

Vast the create and beheld, but vaster the inward creator I Emerson looking to the "Over-soul," says of human creations:

These wonders grew as grows the grass,

Art might obey but not surpass.

The passive Master lent his hand

To the vast Soul that O'er him planned!

Mazzini, the Italian patriot and statesman, said to his countrymen:—

Love and reverence the Ideal; it is the country of the Spirit; the city of the Soul!

In no other country can the Human Mind live. The Imagination is the "home of the Soul." No happiness save the Ideal. Hope dwells there and Peace makes the Ideal her habitation. From that realm come all the manifestations of Thought. Man, through thought, is creator. His workshop is the unseen. His material, divine ideas. His tool, the Imagination. The product. Ideals. Amid Ideals, we live. They are our only companions. No man buys, wears, marries, or buries aught but his Ideals. He lives among them always and enjoys or suffers only through the creations of his mind. Life, world, men, conditions, the hereafter are to me what I think them; are to me what my Ideals of them are. It is important that you realize this, for your health, happiness, and success depend upon your realization of your creative power.

To realize that you possess, and that you do, either consciously or unconsciously, create every condition, is for you to become a conscious creator at all times, so that by creating Ideals to your desire and concentrating upon them, they become material actualities. Concentration is the only mental attitude under which Ideals shape themselves into the physical life. As long as you hold an Ideal before you, that long is it shaping itself in your body, your business and your social life. When you change your Ideal, then the new begins to shape itself. What has been your practice? Have you, like the sculptor, held to one Ideal till it "Carves itself in the marble real?" Or have you taken the Life-block and placed it in the hands of an Ideal to-day, changing to another to-morrow, and then to another, till you have had as many Ideals as there are days? Have you not changed the details of the work every hour? You decided in the morning you would have a statue of Health, but before noon you changed it to Pain, at midday to Grief, at mid-afternoon to Success, and at sunset to a Satyr laughing at Failure, and at bedtime to Remorse, and awaken at morn with a statue of Hope? Is not your life a composite of all these and a thousand more? And this because you have not held one picture before it long enough for the picture to become fixed as a mental habit. Concentration means holding the chosen mental picture to the exclusion of all others till your objective life becomes the picture. "1 AM THAT WHICH I THINK MYSELF TO BE!" The Ideal Life is the Real Life and this unseen Ideal Life is the one that alone concerns us. The laws of matter, are the Laws of spirit. They are but reflections of the unseen Laws, because Nature is one. No line can be drawn between the Here and the There; between the present and the past, or the future;

between Cause and Effect. The Universe is a Unit, and as such we are to live It. Not to live in it, but to live It, for we are It. This Life of the body that has so troubled us, is the life of appearance, and with appearances hereafter we are not to deal; will deal with eternal verities, i. e. with Ideals which cause these appearances. The goal of every endeavor is Ideal, and that Ideal is REALITY OF SPIRIT. Let this Ideal manifest in perfect faith, by letting it alone, save to hold to it as Will. The Ideal will carry you to the goal of its own manifestation.

"A thread of Law runs through thy prayer

Stronger than iron cables are;

And Love and Longing towards its goal

Are pilots sweet to guide the soul.

So Life must live, and Soul must sail

And Unseen over Seen prevail

And all God's argosies come to shore

Though ocean smile or rage and roar." And you are to remember that this voyage of unfold-ment is eternal and you are to be happy every rod of the way. The joy of life is in creating, in unfolding, in going on.

I must turn to the poets at this stage of the discussion, for they are the truest philosophers, sages and seers, because they live in and report the Ideal, which is Truth.

I close this section with a little poem by an unknown author, prefacing it with extracts from Sam Walter Foss and from Kipling. Foss says:— There is no bourn, no ultimate. The very farthest star, But rims a sea of other stars extending just as far. There's no beginning and no end. As in the ages gone The greatest joy of joys shall be—the joy of going on.

Kipling says of the Ideal:—

Our face is far from this our war,

Our call and counter-cry,

I shall not find Thee quick and kind

Nor know thee till I die.

Enough for me in dreams to see

And touch Thy garment's hem;

Thy feet have trod so near to God

1 may not follow them.

But all these poets fail to give us the practical lesson which I wish you to draw from their lines and that is— by worshiping the Ideal, ie become that Ideal. Therefore there is no better practice for you than to concentrate upon beautiful extracts of Great Thinkers and saintly persons. You can easily find them. The

Twenty-third Psalm and other poetic, and therefore wise passages of scripture are familiar, so I do not quote them. But I will give you these 'foiled down" expressions from the poets for memorizing, that the mental pictures they create may become in you physical manifestations. This little poem tells you that the realm in which you really live is never perfectly reflected in the objective life. So regard it a lesson how to live the Ideal here and now.

"I think that the song that's sweetest. Is one that is never sung— But lies at the heart of the singer, Too grand for mortal tongue, And sometimes in the silence Between the day and the night, He fancies that its measures Bid farewell to the light.

A picture that is fairer. Than all that have a part. Among the master-pieces, In the marble halls of art. Is one that haunts the painter. In all his golden dreams, And to the painter only A real picture seems. The noblest grandest poem. Lies not in blue and gold, Among the treasured volumes The rosewood bookshelves hold; But in bright and glowing vision It comes to the poet's brain, But when he tries to grasp it. He finds his efforts vain.

A fairy hand from dream-land

Beckons us here and there,

And when we strive to grasp it

It vanishes into air.

And thus our fair Ideal

Floats always just before,

And we in love and longing.

Reach for it ever more."

— Anonymous

I wonder if ever a song was sung
But the singer's heart sang sweeter!
I wonder if ever a rhyme was sung,
But the thoughts surpassed the meter!
I wonder if ever a sculptor wrought,
Till the stone echoed his ardent thought!
Or if ever a painter in light and shade
The dream of his inmost heart conveyed.

— J. G. Harney.

That haunting dream of better, forever at our side,
It tints the far horizon, it sparkles on the tide.
The cradle of the present too narrow is for rest.
The feet of the Immortal leap forth to seek the Best.

— Lucy Larcom.

In my first little book I gave the Law thus, and I have never been able to improve upon it. Let it close this section:

Affirm that which you desire as a present reality.

Live as if it were already manifest.

And you shall find it manifest.

I will here, in view of what has been said, translate it thus:—

Create an Ideal.

Live that Ideal; and

You will become that Ideal.

Concentration upon, and consecration to, the Ideal, brings it into manifestation.

SECTION XIII.
PEAYER.

Prayer is the Soul's sincere desire. — Hymn.

Men pray cream and live skim-milk. — Beecher.

Prayer is a form of concentration. Men pray to their ideals. — Theodore Parker.

Uttered not but comprehended Is the Spirit's voiceless prayer. — Longfellow.

More things are wrought by prayer Than this world dreams of. — Tennyson.

And so I sometimes think our prayers

Might well be merged in one,

And nest and perch, and hearth and church,

Repeat "Thy will be done!" — Whittier.

O Indra! have mercy upon me and give me daily bread! Sharpen my mind like edge of iron! Whatever I now utter longing for thee, do thou accept it! Make me possessed of Thee. — Rig Veda. (Quoted by Max Muller.)

The influence of a calm trust and faith expressing itself in prayer, uttered or unexpressed, over the functions of organic life, cannot be over-estimated. It is a spiritual and potential influence and force brought to bear upon the hidden spring of disease. It is one of the most potent prophylactic agencies against the inception and cause of all morbid conditions, —F. W. Evans.

Among the many forms and methods of concentration, prayer is the most common and the most potent. The secret of the religious world has been that by prayer at altar, with prayer-book, through hymn, ritual, rite, and environment, it has led the soul to contemplation of holy thoughts, and through concentrating upon them, the thought thus sown in the mind has influenced the life for good. You can learn valuable lessons from any church service. Any form, any rite, any book, any ritual, written prayer, or hymn has a value to the one who concentrates upon it as Truth, oi as a way to Truth It is not through form or book, but through the thought —through the attitude of the Mind that benefits come. There Power lies. We would partake of the charity and humility of Whittier when he says:—

A bending staff I would not break,

A feeble faith I would not shake,

Nor even rashly pluck away

The error that some truth may stay,

Whose loss might leave the soul without

A shield against the shafts of doubt.

All these religious institutions grew out of human needs and minister to human needs, because they are but methods of concentration under holy thoughts; to the extent they are accepted in faith, they produce results in holy living. For this reason noble characters are found in every clime and under every creed. They concentrated upon their Ideals in religious services. The Ideal element in each draws, inspires and holds. Paul gave the Philippians a most excellent rule, when he said:—"That ye may approve things that are excellent; that ye may be sincere and void of offence." Sincerity is the only condition of receptivity and that Ideal which we sincerely accept, we cling to till it manifests. But prayer is the "Soul's sincere desire!" we pray from the Ideal and to the extent that we are persistent in our prayer, it becomes realized in the objective life. "Pray without ceasing!' can only mean, "Concentrate upon the desire expressed in your prayer" Again we are told, "Whatever things ye desire, when ye pray believe that ye have received them and ye shall have them!" This is the statement in another form of the principle of Affirmation. Affirm that you are the Ideal and through that Affirmation you create conditions through which the Ideal shall manifest.

Thus there is but one Principle, uniform in all its operations in all religions and in no religion. Without understanding men have unconsciously obeyed the Law. That Law is found in the Principle of Concentration in sincerity upon the ideal. This is but another way of saying "I AM THAT WHICH I THINK I AM!" I pray, thinking I have received, and lo! I have received. Thus prayer is a common and instinctive method of arriving at health, happiness and success through Concentration. Tennyson tells us "More things are wrought by prayer than this world dreams of," because through prayer the Principle of Concentration is applied to daily living. When the Law is understood and practiced by you, you will have found the only way in which conscious man has directed his development. He has wrought through the concentration as Will, upon that thought which is born of desire. Any form of prayer which one sincerely uses, will work the end which is desired in the Thought expressed. Thoughts are materialized into life through prayer. Therefore the selfish and the generous, the proud and the humble, the ill and the well, the failures and the successes, may all use the same formulas, utter the same prayers, but

the results in each life will be as different as are the feelings awakened by the petition; for the objective results are decided by the real desires of the heart and not by the words. Since most of the prayers are selfish and personal, looking to some outside power for help, asking for something which the petitioner really possesses, but is not conscious of possessing, the answers, like the petitions, are selfish and limited to temporary and personal likes. Should a person of quick temper pray sincerely to be cured of the habit, he will be cured as he says:—"Lead me not into temptation." But should he pray through fear of the pain which an outburst of anger brings, he will find relief from present pain, but not from the cause, which will remain to bring pain again through another outburst of anger. So with sickness; a prayer for health will be answered according to the faith in which the prayer is uttered. "Lord! Save or I perish!" will bring salvation according to the thought embodied in the words expressed, and not according to the Power really dwelling within any person, potentate, or God, outside the Soul of the one who prays. God-In-You answers His own prayer. He cannot answer till you give him opportunity by making conditions by faith.

Prayer is the best method of cultivating faith, for through it one learns to "Cast his burdens" off his conscious mind and allow the thought born of the Ideal to fall into the sub-conscious, there to become the director of the conscious expression. Prayer is the state of forgetfulness of the present and of the objective self; a state of concentration and is entered into with some dominant thought which has the power of an Auto-Suggestion. This Auto-Suggestion is received by the Sub-conscious and creates the spiritual condition desired, and that condition produces the desired objective results. Therefore when one says, 'I cannot concentrate," I reply—Each time you sincerely desire you are concentrated. Each time a wish becomes desire you are praying; you are concentrating. The thought of this section is beautifully expressed by a poem translated from the Arabian, by James Freeman Clarke:

"Allah! Allah!" cried the sick man, racked with pain the long night through,

Till with prayer his heart grew tender,' and his lips like honey grew.

But at morning came the tempter, said,—"Call louder, child of pain!

See if Allah ever answers, 'Here am I, again'."

Like a stab the cruel cavil through his brain and pulses went.

To his heart an icy coldness, to his brain a darkness sent.

Then before him stands Elias, says, "My child why thus dismayed?

Dost repent thy former fervor? Is thy soul of prayer, afraid?"

"Ah!" he cried, "I've called so often; never heard the 'Here am I!

' And I thought, 'God will not pity! Will not turn on me his eye!'"

Then the grave Elias answered, "God said, 'Rise Elias, Go;

Speak to him the sorely tempted; lift him from his gulf of woe.

Tell him that his very longing, is itself my answering cry.

That his prayer, 'Come gracious Allah!' is my answer,

'Here am I' Every inmost aspiration is God's answer undelBled;

And in every 'O, My Father!' slumbers deep a 'Here my child.'"

SECTION XIV.
DESIRE VERSUS WISH.

Want fewer things but want those few things more. — Elizabeth Towne.

Hunger goes selfishly thinking of food; Evil lies painfully yearning for Good. — John Boyle O'Reily.

I only ask a will resigned, O Father, to thine own! — Whittier.

The one prudence of life is concentration; the one evil, dissipation. Everything is good which takes away one plaything and delusion more, and drives us home to add one more stroke of faithful work. — Emerson.

"Will concentration bring me what I desire? I want something so much" thus writes a friend of many years.

What is desire? I must consider it, as the consciousness of the pressure of the unfolding soul. Could consciousness be given the rose-bud in spring-time, I think it would be filled with desire; outward pressure is ex-pressure. So desire in the Human consciousness is but the demand of the soul for expansion through expression. Every desire must be gratified. Hunger is the prophecy of food. The hunger would not be were there not that which can satisfy it. Hunger and food are the two sides of one fact. Hunger the subjective side and food the objective. So is it with every desire; it not only can be but it is gratified.

But here is one important thought, one which will help you to an understanding of my assertion. There is here all the difference between principle and detail; between the universal and the individual; between desire and the thing desired; all the difference there is between hunger in the abstract and hunger for a particular food. Desire is soul-hunger—for what? For expression only. The soul, like the starling in Sterne's essay, cries, "I want to get out V But it does not cry for any particular way or place in which to get out. Desire is of the subjective, of the spiritual life. That which gratifies desire is of the reason, of experience, of the objective life. When you ask me, "Will my desire be gratified?" I answer yes. "Will my desire for that particular thing be gratified?" That depends upon your choice, your persistency, your will. Desire causes us to want. Then we ask ourselves, what we want. Often in this condition we wish. Wishing is weakness; is dissipation of our forces. In wishing the Ideal is held momentarily and is changed so often that life becomes a composite of many pictures, none of which have taken shape and given satisfaction to the conscious mind; but because there has been expression in wishing and the soul has partial satisfaction. No habit is more weakening than that of wishing—day-dreaming. It is idling away hours, vitiating the stream of life with mental poison, "vain imaginings," that simply flit through the mind leaving it weak, because as Will, the Ego is not trained to hold any one of them till it makes an impression upon the objective life. Desire, taking form in a mental picture held by the Will until it materializes, gives satisfaction to the conscious mind. Lowell says:—

But, would we learn that heart's full scope

Which we are hourly wronging,

Our lives must climb from hope to hope

And realize our longing.

Then aside with wishing, day-dreaming, absent-minded hours, where we drift without helm or rudder; and in their stead, select that thing, or that condition, which will satisfy desire; lop off all others; give away one more delusion and go home through this concentration of desire to more faithful, because more earnest, work. Be sincere in your desire for things; be persistent in your desire for any one thing; then you must win. Desire things less, and desire growth, unfoldment, and expression more. It is not the thing that is of benefit, but the power to thus express:—

"I've found some wisdom in my quest

That's richly worth retailing;

I've learned when one has done his best,

There is no harm in failing.

I may not reach what I pursue

Still will I keep pursuing;

Nothing is vain that I can do.

Since soul-growth comes of doing."

Desire less things in number but desire those less things tremendously, but not anxiously nor nervously. Keep at it with as steady a pull as do the crack crew of the college. Jesus gave the law which is never failing: "Seek first the kingdom of Go(o)d and its righteousness and all things will be added." I think if I state the law thus you will understand it:— Seek first the consciousness of Power within your soul where All-power centers; live in accordance with soul laws, then things become subject to you. Before you can make effort to the attainment of anything, you must feel it is possible for you to attain it. There must be the Affirmation first of all—I desire this. Then there must arise the sense of power to have, to do, and to be, which finds expression in, I can! Then there must come the important decision I Will! Now comes the tug of war, the point where so many fail. They will to do, and do not. Having willed, you must put that decision into the keeping of the Will, and know, that at that moment you possess the thing desired. The affirmation for this, be it a thing desired, is I have! Be it an action, the Affirmation is I do! Do you desire health? Follow the evolution of the thought thus:— I have power to heal myself because Infinite Life finds expression through me. Being infinite I can heal myself. Because I can and desire it, I will! Because I have the power, desire and will, and have so decreed I am healed"

From the moment you make this decision let not that mental picture of health pass from your mind. The healing must begin at Cause, which is your mind, and the effect will show as health in your body. This desire for expression is seen in children. They want to do something. Wise parents and teachers give them something to do. Soul demands expression. When it is denied to children in a channel we desire for them, they take the one that offers, and we call it mischief, if we do not brand it, evil. But remember the law of all force. It moves in the line of least resistance. Human desire is a manifestation of force. It will move in the easiest line if not directed. The same tendency to do, and to let, blind desire lead them is seen in grown people. "What to do?" is their cry. And when there is not purpose, direction and self-control, they move in ways we deem unwise. Ills, evils and crimes are but the results of undirected desire. All desire will find expression. It says:—"I'll find a way or make one!"

And it must make one, for the individual must express or die, because what we call Life is the expression of Soul through the body.

Therefore where you have desire, give it expression, for if the way is not chosen and direction is not given, it will find some way. Repressed desires, and repressed emotions arising from them are the cause of every ill of body, mind or estate. You are even to remember, that you as Will must take charge of your judgment, must direct desire, or it will run riot. Directed desire is the source of all success. Undirected desire is the cause of all that we term evil. Desire is soul-force. Never forget this, then you will never ask: "Will my desire be gratified?" Force will find expression. Desire is your Life demanding expression. Will you diffuse it like heat lightning on a summer's night, or will you confine and direct it till it is the light upon your path and the motor power to your success? A story is told of a student who upon entering college placed over the door of his room a large red V. "What is it for?" he was often asked, but he never told. There it remained during the four years of his college life. He came out the valedictorian. On his last evening in his room, he invited his friends and pointing to the V, said:—"You know what V stands for? I have won. I determined when I entered here to be valedictorian. That was placed there to keep in mind my decision."

Is this not what is meant by "keeping thine eye single, then shall thy whole body be full of light." This young man, ignorant of the law, acted under it. He may, in his concentration upon this one thing, have lost his health, but it illustrates this principle, that you cannot scatter your mental powers over too many mere wishes. You must "climb from hope to hope and realize your longings," by holding them as mental images and letting them materialize. Can you realize your desire? Yes. This lesson tells you how. Will you pay the price? Is it worth your endeavor? Will it give you satisfaction? How many of the illusions and playthings in your life will you give up for it? You cannot have every little whim gratified, and then have some great desire satisfied also. Put your powder into Fourth of July explosions and your energy into social dissipation and you will have no power for defense, and no energy for the battle. "Why do I fail?" so many ask me. Here is your answer:—Dissipation of your energies by the satisfying of mere whims, in the dream born of temporary wants; by mental pyrotechnics; by living under ignoble motives, sacrificing to superficial social pleasures or directed by low aims. Concentrate upon something worth while and then stick. You will then win and the result in the treasury of Eternity is Character. It is the sticking that counts. Hence this is your Affirmation— I am persevering. I never fail.

Memorize these glorious lines of Emerson and never doubt your ability again:

Laurel crowns cleave to deserts,

And power to him who power exerts.

Hast not thy share? On winged feet

Lo! it flyeth thee to meet.

All that nature made thine own,

Floating in air or pent in stone.

Will rive the hills, and swim the sea,

And like thy shadow follow thee.

SECTION XV.
MENTAL POISE.

My peace I leave with you. — Jesus.

But when the heart is full of din,

And doubt beside the portal waits,

They can but listen at the gates

And hear the household jar within. — Tennyson.

Right is Right, since God is God, And Right the day must win!

To doubt would be disloyalty! To falter would be sin. — Old Hymn.

Where concentration is, there is a mental peace. Unrest denotes a mind wandering and unstable. Therefore would you have reflected from the sub-conscious storehouse of wisdom into the consciousness, the wisdom for the moment, there must be mental quiet. In this quietness the mind becomes like a still lake and the light within is so reflected that you know what to do. Concentration means peace of mind. Seek this condition for success in any undertaking. A good way to seek this is to concentrate upon some passage of literature that has quieting power. The story of Jesus stilling the tempest illustrates the power of the soul to still the storms of the mental life. Think, "Peace be still," and hold the mind upon some passage of quieting verse or text. I find myself repeating verses long ago memorized, and as it has been my habit from youth to memorize poems, there is always in my mind one ready for the occasion. If you will memorize the following stanzas, or passages at beginning of sections in this book, they will bring that mental poise which will prepare you for any particular thought you may wish to hold. Many have found in this stanza of Whit-tier's power to help them and out of the maddening mazes of life to bring peace of mind. You will find John Burrough's, "Waiting' helpful and from the volumes of NOW, you will be able to cull Affirmations and stanzas that will give this mental quietude.

Amid the maddening maze of things

And tossed by storm and flood,

To one fixed trust my spirit clings—

I know that God is good.

This stanza from one of my poems may suit those who have any objection to the word "God.'

Trust is now brooding in my heart

As thus I float o'er Passions's grave,

I'm Spirit and of All-Life part.

As such unmoved by wind or wave.

Affirmations of peace and of restfulness are always to precede any special Affirmation, for until Peace of mind is reached, there can be no concentration. Therefore the Affirmation— I am peace —is recommended. The words of one of Mrs. Scott's "Truth Songs" will help you as you repeat, hum or sing them:

God is peace; (or—I am Peace.)

That Peace surrounds me. In that Peace I safely dwell.

'Tis above, beneath, within me. Peace is mine and all is well;

God is Peace, sweet Peace! God is Peace, pure Peace!

That Peace is mine—mine— And all is well.

Keep repeating the thought of peace, till peace is yours. When once you have attained self-mastery in this direction, you can follow it up successfully in all others. Can affirm; Health, Happiness, Success, or any desire as a present reality.

SECTION XVI.
METHODS OF CONCENTRATION.

Resolve to be thyself; and know that lie
Who finds himself loses his misery. — Matthew Arnold.

No longer forward nor behind
I look in hope or fear;
But grateful take the good I find,
The best of now and here. — Whittier.

Our efficiency consists so much in our concentration, that nature usually in the instances where a marked man is sent into the world, overloads him with bias, sacrificing symmetry to working power.

— Emerson.

People have interpreted Concentration to mean a kind of worrying over some "ideal"—a mental treatment has been understood as a strained holding of a certain thought— will-power has been looked upon as bulldog tenacity. Instead of all this mental wear and tear, let us now ascend to the throne of Faith and Love, and with cheerfulness and self-reliance build better conditions.

Instead of holding on so tightly, why not let go—give a chance for the expression of the infinite potencies. The control of one's thoughts should be undertaken easily— no impatience—no hurry—no strain. What is there to strive for? We are now heirs to celestial conditions; happiness is immediately ours if we will let go, if we will keep quiet, keep quiet.— Fred Bury.

Understand that peace of mind will not allow you to be anxious, or fearful, or timid or rigid; will not allow any thought of doubt of the righteousness of your conduct. You can hold no *must" over yourself. "I do this because I like to do it!-* is the true spirit. In this spirit you can relax; throw off all care and simply let the thought, which for the time you have chosen, have its way through and over you.

In applying these, or any directions do not think any serious loss will be yours if you do not obey them. Never rigidly hold to them. If you do not use them, you only place yourself where the boy is who prefers play to dinner and goes without. You are to give yourself perfect liberty, cast aside all fears and then—trust. In this mental state, select that portion of time you can readily give to Silence, be it ten minutes, or an hour. When you have selected it, make it as much your business to attend to it, as you would to attend the lesson of the professor you have engaged for music or painting lessons. Be as prompt to an appointment with yourself, as to one with a friend.

Sincerity demands this. Reasonable excuses will be accepted here as elsewhere, but neglect will tell upon your unfoldment. It is your business at this hour. "Attend to business in business hours." Failure to feel the importance of punctuality, and failure to realize the importance of time and effort here, are the great cause of the many not attaining the power of the Silence.

Having chosen the time, select the place. It should be away from all other persons if possible, in a room by yourself, where you can have external quiet. But when you have mastered, you will enter Silence anywhere, at any time. Alone or in midst of a crowd. To be able anywhere and at any time to concentrate upon a chosen thing is to be your purpose.

If you cannot have a room by yourself, then give yourself the Affirmations silently wherever you are. The hymn says:—

"Should holy thoughts come o'er thee

When friends are round thy way,

E'en then the silent breathings

Thy spirit sends above,

Will reach his throne of glory,

Who is mercy, truth and love."

Having selected time and room, take a restful position, one of perfect bodily ease. Not a lazy or careless one, but one of perfect relaxation; relaxation for a purpose. Let go of all thoughts of material things, including body, home, business, and friends. Draw a few long breaths with the thought:—*I am resting. I am peaceful.*

Fix your mind upon yourself as a Divine Being; as a manifestation of the One Universal Principle that fills all space and time. Think of yourself thus as a child of the One, possessing infinite possibilities. Affirm:— I have power to do and to he whatever I wish to do and be. See yourself perfect, because you are this child of the Infinite. Make yourself in thought one with All-that-is. Affirm:—I AM ONE WITH INFINITE LIFE AND WISDOM.

When you become perfectly peaceful, take the special thought you desire to have manifest. If you are there to rid yourself of illness take this thought:— In the One I possess all life. I now let Life manifest in perfect health. I am Life and in the life of the One, I am healed.

N". B.—You are not to be particular about the form of words. Take the thought in any form of words you choose. It is not the words but the Thought, that I wish you to receive. It is not the words but Thought that direct the Sub-Conscious Power. Also remember it is not the thought that heals or does any work. Your body was built before you were capable of thinking. The Power that heals, or gives success, is the Power that built your body, and that Power, is the Universal Life. But since you are a self-conscious individual, your thought directs the Life into the mental mould you make for it, in your Imagination. Therefore all you have to care for is your Thought. You "press the mental button" and Life does the rest.

If your desire is success in any particular line, create a mental image of success. Do not try to see how, or when, it will manifest, but in faith create it and as you wish it to be know that since you have created it in thought, it will manifest. Use the thought in this Affirmation:— I am a manifestation of Infinite Wisdom and I possess the power and the knowledge to bring success. I now decree for myself success. It is now mine and will manifest. I am success.

Whatever be the desire of the hour, in like manner think upon it, and know that through mental concentration it does manifest. Forget time and way, and expect it to come at the right time, in the right way. It will be there at that time.

This is in a great degree but a repetition of a previous section, I know, but you need it. I am writing a textbook.

Do not try to think. After you have decided what the thought is, you are to make no effort, but are to give yourself up to it, and let it think for you. When the boy whistled in school, over the discovery of the mistake in his problem and was chided, he replied, truthfully:—"It whistled itself!" Let your thought do the whistling while you simply enjoy the session. Soon Life will pulse through you; will fill your Being. You will have a sense of interior power. Gradually a sweet peace will steal over you, and you will sense the Infinite Mind thinking in you; the Infinite Life vibrating in you; the Infinite Love, loving in you and Infinite Wisdom guiding in you. Life, Love, and Strength will fill your entire being. If you sink into unconsciousness, do not fear. Let any condition come and go at will. If you have set any time for your seance, you will come back to the objective life at that time. Passivity, you must have. When the thought entirely possesses you, you are entirely oblivious of the objective life; you have no attention for anything else but the "letting" process,—letting Life, Love, and Truth fill you.

Every day no matter where you are, whenever any thought in antagonism to the selected one would come into your mind, affirm the thoughts you have chosen. They will bring the desired condition. Overcome any ill thought with the use of a good one and you will soon grow into the power of controlling your thoughts. This is health; this is success. Mind,—You must grow. "Consider the lilies," when hereafter you ask "How" — "They grow!"

SECTION XVII.

DIRECTIONS FOR PRACTICE.

Like a beautiful flower full of color but without fragrance are all the fine but fruitless words of him who does not act accordingly. — Dhammapada.

Time was, I sat out Truth to find. Heart-sick, foot-sore, aweary grew my mind; When haply—oh my pride! what bitter cost! — Truth found me wandering. I, not Truth, was lost. — Alfred Young.

The only way to change conditions effectually is to change "the heart," the habit, or instinct-mind. This can be done with more or less ease, according to the degree of setness of character and the degree of will and enthusiasm brought to bear.

The key to all change of character lies within that little five per cent conscious mind, which with all its littleness is a sure lever by which to move the ninety-five per cent ponderosity below it. For conscious thought is positive thought, dynamic; while subconscious thought is negative, receptive. That little five per cent mind has stronger compelling power than several times its bulk of sub-conscious mind, and there is not an atom of all that ninety-five per cent sub-conscious mind which cannot be moved by that little five per cent mind which lies at the top. The conscious self is the directing power. Just as it directed your fingers to change their fixed habits, so it can direct any change in other lines of mental or bodily habit— by directing persistently, quietly insistent practice on the desired lines. Insist upon right conscious thinking, and in due time you cannot fail to have right sub-conscious thinking. — Elizabeth Towne in "The Life Power."

Many teachers give formulas; there is a belief extant that certain positions; directions in relation to points of the compass; certain minerals, crystals, amulets, talismans, medicines, herbs, token, are necessary to the attainment of power.

This is an error. Any form, formula, position of body or potion; any point of compass; any condition of environment; believed to be, or found at any time to be of assistance, is of present assistance; and may be used as long as it is regarded merely as a means to a development that will enable one to dispense with it. Used that it may be outgrown.

But, the moment any particular thing, or condition, is considered necessary, it becomes a fetter and a limitation; here lies the danger of all such aids. The only necessary condition is your mental attitude. Horace Greely said; "The only way to resume specie payments is to resume;" the kindergarten motto is— "Learn to do by doing." In like manner I say to my reader:—"The only way to concentrate is to concentrate." No outside aid is necessary and the use of aids, unless guided by the thought of mere temporary assistances, is attended with the serious danger of limitation. Any place, any time, is the proper place and time. Any chosen thought is the right thought. The ideal of Concentration is—Ability at any time to so concentrate at will upon a chosen thought as to become oblivious of objective environment. This ability extends to business transactions, social intercourse, literary and oratorical exercises, and all forms of psychic manifestations, and all forms of healing.

Not long ago while waiting in hall for lecture and chatting with friends I was called upon to give an absent treatment. It was successful. A friend met me on the street, handed me a letter with request that I psychometrize it. Immediately, as we continued our walk, I became oblivious of my surroundings and described the writer and those persons consulted before the writing; told the business; the motive; gave advice as to meeting the results; and the way to answer.

Too many sensitives, psychics, and healers, demand conditions. The only condition is the mental one of Attention. Notice how concentrated and still is a regiment of soldiers at the command—"Attention!' Learn like obedience to your own Auto-Suggestion.

The use of crystals, sacred words, cards, names, and like instrumentalities is a staff better dispensed with than used.

But as children need text-books, slates, pencils, blackboards, apparatus, the quiet of school-room and presence of teacher, that they may develop the power to do without all these, so one may use temporarily some external means for concentration.

Once I used to develop my hypnotic subjects and somnambules by having them concentrate their gaze upon something bright; I would help my patients into quiescent mental attitude, by gazing at some bright thing; but I found it harder to break up this habit when once formed, than it is to form one of concentration without any external aid. "Think sleep; and you will sleep!" This is my method;—through Affirmation.

But for those who, without assistance, must develop voluntary concentration, I give a few simple methods. You can, until you develop power to do otherwise, subdue the light in your room to a twilight. May choose a convenient room and time, when and where you can have external quiet; but at same time remember, that your lesson is not learned, until you can concentrate in bright sun- or gas-light, anywhere. Even in midst of noise, or a crowd.

Having selected time and place, put yourself in easy position; one in which you forget body. I do not recommend a recumbent one as the position suggests sleep, and you do not seek involuntary sleep.

Take an easy position, read, or repeat some quieting extract. Bring some pleasant picture before the mind. Relax the body. Close the eyes and concentrate upon that picture. The first lesson is to gain the ability to look upon this picture you have created with the same steadiness you would look upon landscape from the window.

The next lesson, is to connect some thought with the picture and concentrate upon the thought. Do not make the séance so long as to tire you. Do not strain. Do not become conscious that you are making an effort. Intend the mind, and then let it float with the current. Concentration is the condition of perfect ease. No task, no strain, no effort, no conscious thinking. You have directed the thought; now let it go without bit or rein. If you do not succeed in this, you may choose something upon which to concentrate the gaze. Something with bright color, or something with metallic luster. A bit of sunlight on the wall, a flower, a gem, anything. Gaze upon it till you see nothing else, then close the eyes and see it still.

But with any of these conditions, or one you may gather from any other author, remember it is the thought that is of importance. Know that you can before you begin, and know that you do while you are at the lesson. The ideal condition is that which while in it, you do not notice the external; you pay no attention to it, but when you take up the objective life again with positive-ness, you will recall that certain sounds, persons and events occurred; and that all sounds seemed subdued and far away. Somnolence, sleepiness, passivity, is the ideal condition when entered into voluntarily. Do not let these séances degenerate into mere reverie or absent-mindedness, nor allow yourself to go into these conditions when about your work. If, during your séance, you feel like sleeping let sleep come, with the Suggestion that you will waken when the time set has expired and will gain what you seek while in this condition. Fear not and let what will come. You will so waken. Be prompt to begin and to close! Bring yourself to time, system and order; this is mastery. It is probable that you will fall to sleep for quite a period while you are learning. It is well. Do not resist. It is nature's way of producing an equilibrium. Most people live at such tension in this complex, strenuous life of ours, that nature by reaction rights our nervous system in these rests. Produces an equilibrium. Thou shalt not come out thence till thou has paid the utmost farthing," we are told by Jesus. Enjoy these séances. Soul-growth comes in them. They are not the sleeps of the night, for you have given direction to the sub-conscious and while you are thus relaxing your will from the body. Life is building the nervous system into condition for the expression of your desires. Take with you the right Ideal into the Silence, and then give Liberty to Soul, to have its way.

SECTION XVIII.

HOW TO DO IT.

It is the same Force in the human breast,

That makes us gods or demons. If we gird

Those strong emotions by which we are stirred

With might of will and purpose, heights unguessed

Shall dawn for us. Or if we give them sway

We can sink down and consort with the lost. — Ella Wheeler Wilcox.

The truth is that really all have untold treasures of power locked in their inner being. In fact all are millionaires, but their priceless treasures will remain useless to them, till some one informs them of their own possessions and hands them the key with which to unlock them. —E. D. Bablitt.

Though at the expense again of repetition I add here and in the following sections, some extracts from my "Mail Course in The Art of Living." This art of controlling one's self which we call "Voluntary Concentration," is not merely learning, it is living; and to live this Principle means that there must be repetition, "line upon line" till the thought becomes a part of the whole mental man, as the food of the morning has become in results, part of the physical man. In as many ways as possible, I am repeating the simple principle of Human-control, of Self-control through Concentration, which is only control through Auto-Suggestion.

I wish to clear from your mind the confusion that exists in the minds of many students along New Thought lines as to the meaning and the use of this term Concentration. This thought take with you:— you do concentrate. But it is the concentration of habit, a habit created by necessity. All successful men win through concentration, but it is a concentration that costs them the pleasure of living. Business attention is concentration. Business care follows them home, absorbs the domestic virtues. It follows them to church and deadens the sound of sermon and hymn. It follows to theater, and obstructs the view of stage. It follows to bed and prevents sleep. This is concentration. Through habit, it has become involuntary. When any concentration becomes wearisome, when we wish it would leave us, it has then become unwholesome. Thoughts connected with limitations will so become. Any thought limited to the external, when held long, will cause weariness of the flesh. Business men, professional men, are prone to let their thought born of necessity rule them. Success in any sense cannot be his who does not rule himself, that is, does not choose his thoughts. Involuntary concentration is slavery, is disease and death.

Voluntary concentration is mastery, is health. Concentration upon a thought you chose and then laying it aside and taking up another, is Self-Control, is POWER. Concentration is only Paying Attention to a Chosen Thought, paying Attention to the thought you have chosen for the time. To illustrate:—A procession passes the window. I see it, but pay no particular attention to any one person. Something attracts my attention and, to that particular thing or person, I direct my attention and I see only that. My attention is concentrated upon that and it absorbs my whole thought. I know, however, that the procession is passing. I may later recall much that passed. That is a secondary attention. All that passes before the eye is photographed upon the psychic sense, so that, while the conscious mind is paying attention to one person, the sub-conscious is paying attention to all that is present. To concentrate, is to let the conscious will hold to the one thought out of the procession of thoughts that are all the time passing in the mind. Other thoughts will be there. It is impossible to make the mind a blank, but it is possible to notice only that which you choose of what passes through it. It is possible to choose a thought and to so hold it before consciousness that no other is present with us. This is the case in all excitement. Fear is concentration upon the thought of fear; pain upon the thought of pain; grief, upon grief; worry, upon something that causes intense anxiety. What the man does thus instinctively, he can do under intelligent direction. In learning concentration, you are learning to supplant instinct by self-control. Instinct is control by the Absolute, by race-thought. Concentration, as we now use it. is control of the manifestation of life by the Individual will. To attain this control, it is first necessary to believe it possible. Where this belief is, next is the declaration that you will learn it. Having so determined, you can develop it. "Where there is a will, there is a way.

When you determine to so develop, you will make effort, you will do. Effort requires time. These steps and intermediary ones you will follow. Failures come from wishes, temporary likes, but never from real desires. Do you desire it? Then you will make effort and will win. If you only wish, the desire for something else will overshadow your wish. Convert a mere wish into a desire and LET the Desire take possession of you and lead you to its own expression. Put no conscious effort upon any desire. Hold to it in faith and it will manifest. The danger is that you will try too hard. The chief thing that causes failure in all psychic attempts is that the person tries too hard. You are ever to remember that you are to LET the Current have its way through you. You can guide it by your Affirmation, but you are to know that it will run in the channel of Suggestion without effort on your part. Negative to the Soul, positive to all externals, is the law. "Trust the current that knows its way," is Emerson's direction. "Thy will be done," is Jesus'. "Float with hand on helm," is my direction. "TRUST;' is the word.

SECTION XIX.
SOME PRACTICAL SUGGESTIONS.

We may question with wand of science
Explain, decide, discuss,
But only in Meditation,
The Mystery speaks to us.— John Boyle O'Reiley.

He always wins who sides with God.
To him no chance is lost.
God's will is sweetest to him when
It triumphs at his cost.— Old Hymn.

Into that realm of reverie where the soul feeds on immortal fruits and communes with unseen associates, the body meanwhile being left to the semblance of idleness—of all which, the man have given this valid justification: — "I loaf and Invite my soul. I lean and loaf at my ease observing a spear of summer grass." — Moses Colt Tyler. (Life of Patrick Henry.)

Affirmations are power and used in any manner are to be recommended. Used till one forgets to use them, by no longer needing them. The Affirmation serving to create the mental habit of looking at affairs, conditions and experiences of life, from the point of view of the Affirmation.

But Oral Affirmations have great power and in beginning to obtain the self-control that comes from Concentration it is often wise to suggest aloud to yourself until you shall have grown the power of Silent-Suggestion. And even after you have attained considerable attainment in this silent power you will find great help, when new conditions demanding new Affirmations arise, by speaking the words to yourself. The spoken word has a power in affecting the nervous system that the silent word has not. The gray matter of the brain and nerves vibrates with the spoken word, as the violin string does to the stroke of the bow, and each vibration helps to make the cells responsive to the thought the words convey. It is wise to take possession of every factor that will help us in the development of Mastery. In the beginning of my study thirty years ago, I would repeat the chosen words till I became unconscious. Tennyson says he went into a trance through repeating and concentrating upon his own name. You choose an Affirmation in line with some desire. Talk to yourself in line of that desire. Place yourself, in imagination, in a chair opposite yourself and talk to yourself. In imagination, see yourself there. If you are in the habit of doubting your ability in any line, tell your SELF that you have power, that you are a son of God, that you can do anything. Keep at it till you begin to fill up with power, till you feel as if you had taken stimulant, till the brain Joegins to reel. Let it reel till you fall to chair, lounge or floor unconscious and lie there till you awaken, saying, "I have won! I have won!

Take a case of absent treatment! You wish to heal. Go into a room by yourself. Sit down by lounge, couch or bed. Imagine the patient there. See him, or her, lying there before you. Imagination is the CREATIVE faculty. Develop this power till you can FEEL that he is there. Then talk to him as IF he was there. He IS there when you SEE him there, for there is no space to thought. In this way, you can heal or help in any desired way. Learn to so concentrate upon this patient that you are oblivious of everything else. Imagine him well. He is well. Spirit knows no sickness. You are to see the spirit well and full of life. Tell him so. You will, in this way, learn to concentrate when you desire. A lady once came to me for treatment of her daughter. I agreed and, when the mother left, I sat down by my treating lounge. I brought the daughter there in imagination and made passes with my hands from head to foot, just as if she was there in body. Then I said: "Go to sleep and sleep till 3 p. m., when you will awaken with all these conditions passed entirely away." She did so awaken.

Suppose it is a case of business dealing with a man. Place him in like position. Talk to him as if he were really there. You will grow to think it without talking. This is concentration. It need not take you an instant to concentrate to give the thought power over yourself or to send it telepathically to others.

Absent-mindedness is involuntary concentration. Cultivate that condition so that you can enter it at will. Let it be voluntary concentration. Choose some theme and speak upon it when alone. Grow into the habit of losing yourself in thought and recalling yourself at will.

When you wish to know anything, tell yourself that you know and let it come to you as you let go of the conscious thought. An illustration:—I had an article to write to-day. Before I was fairly awake, it thought itself through my mind. After I dressed, I tried to recall it. The title included three subjects. I could not recall the last. The more I tried, the more it eluded me. At last, I gave up and said: "Well, if it is necessary, it will come." Later in the day, while I was dictating a letter, my thought ran in the same channel and took up the theme I had forgotten and followed it to the end. I let it run itself. This is concentration. Suppose you have a patient and you are puzzled as to what to do. You have studied the case and are undecided. By this study, you have given yourself an auto-suggestion born of desire. Now say, "Well, when the right time comes, I shall know," and forget all about it. It will suddenly dawn you from the sub-conscious. This suggestion and this forgetfulness IS concentration

Suppose it is a thought of business. You have considered the question and are unable to decide. Tell yourself that, at the right time, it will be clear to you. It will come when you let go of it. "My word shall not return unto me void V How shall it return if you do not let it go? It goes from you when you forget it once uttered in faith. Thus are you learning concentration.

You wish to go voluntarily into the sub-conscious. Do the same. Tell yourself what you wish. Sit down and let that wish be the controller of the hour. Give up! Forget that you have made the wish. Forget that you have the desire or that you have given the direction. Let your thoughts take, without your conscious direction, the line you have previously desired. Practice alone will bring the power to do this. By a systematic application of the above, you will grow into a conscious control of your thought, as you have heretofore, through necessity, grown into an involuntary control. You can readily concentrate, when compelled, in your business. Affirm that it is easy to concentrate at will and DO it. LET the thought have full sway over you. I know of no other way to accomplish this but this: Pay Attention to a chosen thought. It is a good plan to practice self-suggestion in going to sleep. Tell yourself you are sleepy and go to sleep on Suggestion. Tell yourself you feel like yawning and let it yawn. Tell yourself that you are hungry and let the hunger come. Tell yourself that you wish some food and suggest the kind and let hunger for it come. Tell yourself that you wish to go, or to do something, and let the desire grow and obey. In this way, you get into the habit of living from the sub-conscious by self-direction and are "in the Silence" all the time. Concentration is not a thing for special occasions; it is for all times. When you have learned to "let the current have its way," you have learned the greatest lesson of life. You will live above sense, will live subject at all times

to the Spirit; will be led by intuition; will use your reason to apply Truth which flows into the consciousness by intuition to the objective life. Concentration, "in the Silence," is not a thing for special occasions; it is the condition of the devotee made constant. "Pray without ceasing," is the law. Desire, suggest and let. That is all. It is the lesson Jesus learned when he said: "Thy will be done." "May thy kingdom come," really means, "Let thy kingdom come." The kingdom of self-control ! The kingdom of self-mastery! Concentration is the shutting out of the objective life. It is closing the five senses and letting the Soul he felt and heard in the silence.

Follow these directions. Practice as suggested and the Silence will become vocal.

The exercise of the Will, or the lesson of power, is taught in every event. From the child's successive possession ol his several senses, up to the hour when he says "Thy will be done!" he is learning the secret that he can reduce under his will, not only particular events, but great classes, nay, whole series of events, and so conform all facts to his character. Nature is thoroughly mediative. It is made to serve. It receives the dominion of man as meekly as the ass on which the Savior rode. It offers all its kingdoms to man in the raw material which he may mould into what is useful. Man is never weary of working it up. He forges the subtle and delicate air into wise and melodious words and gives them wings as angels of persuasion and command. One after another his victorious thought comes up with and reduces all things, until the world becomes at last only a realized will,—the double of man.

— Emerson in "Nature."

SECTION XX.
SELF-STUDY AND THE LAW OF LIFE.

Buddha appealed himself only to what we should call the Inner Light. — Max Muller.

Do your work, respecting the excellence of the work, and not its acceptableness. This is so much economy as that, rightly read, it is the sum of economy. Profligacy consists not so much in spending years of your time or chests of money,—but in spending them off the line of your career. The crime which bankrupts men and states is job-work; declining from your main design, to serve a turn here and there. Nothing is beneath you, if it is in the direction of your life; nothing is great or desirable if it is off from that. — Emerson in "Conduct of Life."

It is' well to have some definite methods for practice in the beginning but there is a danger that I warn you of, and that is that you will grow to consider them a necessity. Beware of this.

Use them for self-development. Remember that you will soon outgrow them. I give them to be outgrown. But use them until you can concentrate without these preliminary steps.

First—Study yourself. Understand your own mental conditions. See where you are positive and where negative in your thought. All thoughts of any lack in yourself; all thoughts of want; all tendencies to complain, wish, or find fault with yourself; all criticisms, regrets and self condemnation; all thoughts of inability to cope with any condition; all thoughts of shrinking, avoiding, fearing any person, thing or condition; all thoughts of reliance upon friends, money, position, reputation or culture; all thoughts of any assistance from without yourself; all these are thoughts of weakness.

They have no drawing power. They are non-attractive; produce mental conditions that are a lack of what is called "personal magnetism," but which is only a lack of those character-radiations that create success.

Study yourself and see how much you concentrate upon such thoughts. Realize how much they influence your life; how much time you waste in thinking them over and over; how much you diffuse power in this worry, fear, fret and complaint. This is riding the hobby horse of childhood, ride all day and you are not an inch further on your way. This method of using thought is but mental gum-chewing; disgusting to the observer and destructive of all healthful mental digestion. Where you learn that you have been holding a thought of these kinds, immediately change to its opposite. Study the tables on pages 36 and 37 in "Self-Healing" and concentrate upon the opposite thought. If you have held thoughts of failure, of want, change them at once to thoughts of possession. Never think want! Never wish for anything, for you, as Spirit, possess all in potentiality, as the egg possesses all the songs the bird shall sing. Turn your attention to this germ within, and claim possession, and in concentration give it an opportunity for expression. Concentration is mental incubation. Brood over the desire as a present reality, as the mother bird broods over the egg. She knows by instinct that the chick is there and by brooding she brings it into expression. In the faith of reason and instinct which you possess, brood over that which you know is, and which you, by Affirmation, have called forth, until you see it with eye and touch it with hand. Take what Lowell says of this bird-condition as your own, and sing:

His mate feels the eggs beneath her wings And the heart in her dumb breast flutters and sings. He sings to the wide world, and she to her nest,— In the nice ear of Nature, which song is the best?

For this reason whenever you are inclined to say "I want!' think—"I possess ! and seek, and you shall find it within. Then let it out.

Feel that you thus have; others then will feel the same, for you will radiate those vibrations of power that cause them to feel, to believe in you, and to act under those feelings. This is "Personal magnetism," and it is but the concentrated rays of the whole man turned to one purpose through concentrating upon one thought. And thought is the directing power of all Life's vibrations. As I think, so my radiations are. When I think diffusively my radiations are diffusive, and people do not feel, do not recognize me. I make them feel by shooting my vibrations from the chamber of Concentration. Then the projectile is felt. Otherwise the powder flashes in the universal, and the projectile lies in the magazine of the soul.

Feel, and you make others feel. This is the law. Be a dynamo and the currents will flow. Feeling is the power which thought directs. Therefore cultivate the power to feel. Enthusiasm is its name in conduct. Be enthusiastic. This can all be done in silence. But FEEL enthusiastic when you are in silence, and then Power, concentrated Power, will go on the line, over the wires of your thought, to create success. "Mean business!" and feel business when you think. This power to feel, this feeling of power, this sense of possession, characterizes all great characters of history. We credit it to personal magnetism. But it is character. Emerson says of certain great men in his essay upon "Character," "The larger part of their power was latent. This is character—a reserved force which acts directly by presence and without means!" This reserve force creates success, wherever success is found. Therefore will you succeed, create this reserve power. It is done by concentration, by patience, by entering the Silence with the consciousness of possession and there letting your whole personality be filled. "Blessed are they who hunger and thirst after righteousness for they shall he filled" is the promise. Enter the silence of meditation with sincere desire with "an earnest and contrite heart/ and you shall be filled with power to bring into manifestation that which you have in silence affirmed.

Here is the Law as laid down in my first book "How to Control Fate through Suggestion" and time has enabled me only to enter into a deeper realization that it is the one and only Law of Success. Build for yourself a 'perfect Ideal! Think from that Ideal as a present reality! Affirm that Ideal a present reality! Suggest from that Ideal as a present reality! Act from that Ideal as a present reality! And it he-comes to you a present reality.

It may be briefly stated thus:— Think, speak and act just as you wish to be, and you will be that which you wish to be.

Those who thus think become that which they think, because the Law of Life is: I am that which I think. To think is to be! Destroy my thinking power and I am destroyed. Therefore the only thing I have to do to control my life is to control my thoughts and think— Control! Concentrate upon the thought of Self-Mastery. Self-control is the keystone of character. Faith in Self the source of personal magnetism; the source of power; the source of success. Therefore the first thing to cultivate is faith in Self. Affirmation to use:— I believe in myself as the source of Truth Love, Wisdom and Power. Concentrate upon this thought and then "look within."

Read Emerson's "Self-Reliance" and commit to memory the passage commencing, "Trust thyself! Every heart beats in unison with that iron string!" Also memorize and use this quatrain of Mrs. Helen Wilman's:—

He who dares assert the I,

May calmly wait,

While hurrying Fate

Meets his demands with sure supply!

SECTION XXI.

SPECIAL DESIRES VS. PRINCIPLE.

God alone can make the work complete, Give to Cause its perfect ending. — The Kalevalla.

An honest heart, O Helga, of pure endeavor With Odin's runes is written, misleading never! — Fridthjofs Saga.

The power of man increases by continuing steady in one direction.— Emerson.

One question that frequently comes to me in various forms concerns the act of concentrating upon special desires for some certain condition or thing. These questions will illustrate, and are each from either recent letter or interviews:

1. "I wish supply; shall I concentrate upon a specified sum?"

2. "I wish a companion; shall I center my thought upon any particular person?"

3. "I wish to win a prize in a lottery. How shall I concentrate?"

4. "I am a school girl; I wish to stand well in my class. How shall I think that I may win?"

5. "I wish our foot-ball team to win. How shall I use Mental Science?"

6. "I wish a certain present. Is it right for me to concentrate upon it?"

7. "I wish relief from rheumatism. How shall I affirm?"

8. "I am unhappy with my wife. Shall I demand that she become harmonious?"

9. "My son smokes cigarettes. How shall I suggest that I may break him of the habit?

First let us understand what has already been said— Build your Ideal from Principle and not from details. The ideal, after we have built it, becomes the objective actual.

The Ideal should be permanent; if built of details it must continually change. Principles alone are eternal. Then for us there is this choice:— Either to assume that we know just what conditions and things are best for us and then concentrate upon these; or to assume that we are expressions of Intelligence that knows better than we, in our partial unfoldment, can know, and trust that Intelligence to bring that which best satisfies our desire.

Assuming the first position we shall decide just what we want and concentrate upon that and draw it. Be it money, we shall fix upon a certain sum; be it friend, upon a certain person; be it environment, we shall fix upon a certain locality; be it fame, upon a certain prize, and by constant expectation, affirmation and concentration win that we have chosen.

But every person has learned that he, or she, has not correctly measured the value of things thus coveted and won. There is still a lack. Things do not satisfy. "Things shall be added," said Jesus, when in Principle you gain the Power.

For this reason I advise you to assume the position, that the sub-conscious Wisdom knows better than you know in the conscious mind, what is needed for your unfoldment, and consequent happiness, and to trust that sub-conscious Wisdom to direct you to, or to draw to you, what is best, to satisfy your Ideal. By desire, give the Auto-Suggestion to Soul as to what you wish in Principle, will it only, and then let that Suggestion in the Soul bring about conditions and things to the objective man.

You know but few of the million factors that are shaping your destiny and cannot possibly judge what conditions will arise tomorrow or next year. Therefore you cannot wisely ask for things, lest they be not those which fits to-morrow's needs. Besides, from every point of the great circle of Infinity, and from the Infinite Supply, your needs can be met. To concentrate upon any one point is to close all others to you. To concentrate upon any one thing, is to keep all other things that might come, away; to concentrate upon any particular time is to close other and perhaps more fitting occasions.

With the when, where and how, I advise you not to deal. Deal with the fact that in the All-Embracing Good;—in Infinite Supply,—everything necessary for your Health, Happiness, and Prosperity already is, and all you need to do is to suggest to this All-Power through your sub-conscious life, and then to let that which you ask for come at the right time. This is the truth in the words of Jesus:—"When ye pray believe that ye have received them, and ye shall have them.'

This leaves you free to receive, and leaves the Power that supplies you limitless. Any concentration upon a particular thing limits the Power you ask to bring it, to that one thing. Be limitless in your faith and know that Supply is limitless.

In light of this Principle I will briefly answer the above questions, referring to them by number:

1. Concentrate upon all you need, upon sufficiency. Use no specified amount and know that what you need will come as you need.

2. Know that in Infinite Supply the companion you need already is, and that your call will reach him (or her) and that he will come to you at the right time. Any particular person among your acquaintances is more likely not to be, than to be, the one fitted for you. With Miss Philura in the story, feel assured that he is in the All-Embracing Good, and will come at the right time.

Make ready for him in mind and environment. He will come.

3. I would affirm— If it is for my good, I shall draw a prize, —and think no more about it. I know" two cases where such prizes have broken up homes and ruined characters.

4. Make your desire into the Suggestion— I have won the test place for me, —and then work conscientiously and sincerely, without anxiety or worry. Care for health; and above all seek the place with the noble motive of self-unfoldment is wisdom and power, and banish all thought of competition and of envy.

5. Make in your mind the picture of success of your team without any feeling of rejoicing over the vanquished, and willing to accept the gage of battle, let the Omnipotent that works through both teams, settle the matter, and rejoice whatever may be the result. Your thought can control your life, but not the life and the expression of others; your attitude can

be that of success, no matter which wins; when one has done his best, that is Success.

6. It is your privilege to do as you choose and if conscience says to you it is right—it is right. The question is—Is it best for me so to concentrate? No! for it is pure selfishness, and selfishness never- brings happiness. The best Affirmation is—If it is best for me a present will come.

7. In faith in the Divine Life within you, concentrate upon the mental picture of Health. Affirm:— Life is abundant I I have my share. The Omnipotent Life is within me and I am healed! Banish all thought of symptoms from your mind. Recognize only Life and its healthful manifestations.

8. No! give her liberty; the same liberty you demand for yourself. Make yourself harmonious. Radiate joy and gladness. Fill the home with your healthful love-vibrations and then, if she is not herself happy, you will be. Your happiness does not depend upon her, or upon any person. It depends entirely upon your own mental state, and you can make that what you will. You have power of choice. Affirm— I depend on no person or condition. I am happy because I choose to he happy! and home atmosphere will change.

9. In your mind free him from the habit and give him liberty. If you depend upon the Power of Thought to cure him, never chide nor call attention to the habit. Suggest to him from the Ideal you hold for him. Concentrate upon this mental picture of freedom and all your conduct and speech will be from that. "I am glad to notice that you are outgrowing the habit," is a wise Suggestion.

From the Principle from which these answers arise each person can for himself get a solution to his problems. The Principle never fails. Trust it! Think from it! Affirm from it! Suggest from it! You thus become that which you think.

The principal factor in Self-Mastery through Concentration, is the formation of a mental picture of that which is desired. Mental imagery is the one creative power of man. Make this picture and then, despite all seeming evil, amid all discouragement, cling to it as to an objective reality and you make conditions for it to become that reality.

I am that which I think I am. Because I made the picture and the subconscious is obliged to manifest in the form I made.

SECTION XXII
MY ONE RULE—AGREEMENT.

Resist not evil but overcome evil with good. — Jesus.

The foolish have one master, that is fear.— Old Proverb.

If you wish to become acquainted with Nature you must deal with her sincerely.— Prof. Tyndall.

How can we secure concentration? To this question, the first and last answer must be: By interest and strong motive. The stronger the motive, the greater the concentration. — Eustace Miller, M. D.

The one only rule I give my pupils is this—NEVER ANTAGONIZE. Elaborate this and it becomes, Never argue! Never contend! Never contradict! Never oppose! Never resist!

Resistance is pain. Antagonism creates those conditions against which you contend. Opposition but increases the evil. Contradiction breeds ill feeling. Jesus has the law thus:—"Agree with thine adversary quickly while thou art in the way with him; lest at any time he deliver thee to the judge and the judge deliver thee to officer, and thou be cast into prison" Agree! dont resist, lest it become worse with thee. Resistance will bring an increased penalty.

Resistance is concentration upon that which you do not want. But since concentration brings into expression that upon which thought is concentrated any resistance brings to you that which you resist. This is a negative and weak condition. Antagonism is weakness. Resistance is negative. You are influenced by outside suggestions. Denials, "Don'ts," are negative.

They leave you nothing upon which to rest. Affirmations are solid foundations. For this reason say "I like! Tell not what you do not like. Think upon what you wish, not upon what you do not wish, for your thought is creative.

I wish you to think upon this until you can live in non-resistance, by ignoring all conditions of antagonism; by so concentrating upon the thoughts of things and conditions desired, that you will recognize no excuse for contention. No one thing in all Mental Science is harder to accomplish than this. It is the fulfillment of the law. "Mind your own business. Remember the reply of Jesus to Peter when asked by him what John should do: "What is that to thee? Follow thou me V' Any argument or antagonism, is minding another's business. All persons have an equal right with yourself to think and act as prompted within. In giving them this right in your thought, you cannot resist anything they do. You will think and act your thought freely. And since Goodness, Truth and Love, are realities and are all; when you affirm these you will be powerful. To lack faith in them and to antagonize renders you negative and weak. You have separated yourself from Principle which is power.

Peter resisted and lost his ear. Jesus did not resist and was crucified! "Who is victor?—Pilate or Christ?" Remember the motto which is constantly on the cover of NOW:—"Nerve us with incessant Affirmatives. Don't bark against the bad; but chant the beauties of the good." When you are concentrated in "chanting" you cannot bark. Which shall it be? Will you be a growler, or a chanter, in the arena of life? So important is this attitude and yet so liable to be misunderstood that I give some illustrations. From them you may learn to apply the law. While I roomed in Topeka, Kansas, there was placed in the next room, and against the partition wall, a house organ; some one would practice on it much of the time. At first it

distracted my attention and annoyed me;, till suddenly it dawned upon my comprehension, that they paid rent for that room, and had the same right to play organ there, as I had to play on my typewriter; that if I minded my business and became concentrated upon it, I would not be listening to anything, and be disturbed. Now, whenever I am asked if such or such a thing does not disturb me I reply, "I do not allow myself to be." A friend who boarded where I did, was annoyed by cats under his window at night. Complaining of it to me, I asked, "What are you going to do about it?" He answered, "I have done everything I know!" I then asked, "Do you think the cats think of you? Why not treat them as they do you? They probably are about their business; you attend to yours. The room is yours; you pay rent for it and can decide what shall be done in it. They are in their room, why not let them do as they wish in it? In other words, why not let them attend to their business while you mind yours? That is, why put your mind upon the cats and allow them to trouble you? 'None so deaf as those who will not hear.' By antagonising you magnify the trouble till you are loosing sleep and will soon be ill! Concentrate upon your sleep and pay no attention to them." After a few moments silence he said: "I see! I will!" He did not hear them thereafter.

Complaining of the weather, a friend said: "I don't see why it rains so much!" "My dear," I said, "will you fight a battle with Omnipotence? Are you setting yourself up as the superior of God? Why not leave his business to Him, and you attend to your own, which is to use the weather He makes?" "True! Forgive me! I will never complain again!" "O, this headache! I don't see why it comes. I have been fighting it all day, denying it, and it does no good!" pitifully cried a patient. "Well, suppose you now in love agree with it. Stop fighting and begin to love the Law that caused it. The Universe is wise.

Cause and effect are divine. Love the Law. Agree with it. Denials are antagonism. Agree with thine adversary! Be passive and let Love, which is the fulfilling of the law, have sway. Affirm: In love I am healed. Soon peace of mind and relief came to her. I gave this law of non-resistance one evening in my class. The next week a very intelligent and positive lady said: "I tried the law of non-resistance in my case and it works. A week ago Sunday morning a news-boy got under my window at five o'clock, and began to call out his papers. He annoyed me till I thought how I would shake him were I out there. It so affected me that I got no more sleep. Yesterday morning he began again at the same time. For a moment the old feeling came up. Then I thought of what I had been taught and I said: God bless the little fellow, he is attending to his business. How smart he is to be out so early. I hope he will sell every paper!' and thinking thus I fell asleep. I felt good all day."

"I lost some money from my pocket," said a student of my books. "At first I was inclined to feel badly when the thought came, What is your business now? It was your business to put a guard over your money; you did not. Now is it your business to feel badly and lose the lesson, or is it your business to so learn that you may lose no more? I decided I would not fight the inevitable, but rejoice that I had learned all that the lesson cost me."

Learn from these how easy it is to apply the Principle of Agreement. It means "Stop fighting!" Non-resistance ! Expression of faith in the All Good! Reconciliation with Divine Will, acceptance of present conditions as the best for the present. They are to be outgrown in love. "I grateful take the good I find. The best of now and here."

SECTION XXIII.

LOVE.

A new commandment give I unto you: That ye love one another.— Jesus.

Now abideth these three, Faith, Hope and Love, but the greatest of these is Love—Love is the fulfilling of the Law. — Paul.

I swear I begin to see Love with sweeter spasms than that which responds to love. It is that which contains itself, which never invites and never refuses. — Walt Whitman.

A man has two needs: that of knowing and that of loving. — S. Barring Gould.

The lover needs no law. He'd love God quite as well Were there no heaven's rewards; no punishment of hell.— Angelus Silesius.

The verdict of this world is short, Long and vigorous its report: — To love and to be loved. — Emerson.

Now a section the most important of all, for without Love I am "as sounding brass and tinkling symbol." So much Love so much Power.

Life is universal, but in Man Life is transmuted into human form and is Love. The only Power Thought can direct is Love. Thought is the individual expression of Life; and Love, the race or the Human expression. Love is the Absolute in the Soul. Love is in reality God, for it is the Omnipotent in Human form. Therefore so much Love so much am I a man. The subconscious Power that I direct by concentration is that form of Life, that Mode of Motion, we name. Love.

Therefore Success depends upon your having a warm heart and your radiating at all times, Love. This radiation is called improperly, "Personal magnetism." It, like magnetism, is a Mode of Motion, and it is like magnetism, one of the forms of Universal Attraction, and in its attractive power, it acts as magnetism does. But it is Love under control of the individual Ego as Will. Will directing the Life-force, which is Love, is the secret of Success. Therefore only as you love and throw yourself into your Thought will you succeed. Love as force can be diffused, expended upon a variety of things; under a variety of wishes, passions and endeavours; failure in high endeavor is the result. Sexual passion is but one way and not, by far, the most destructive. For with it does go some human feeling. But concentration upon mere business success, upon mere money getting, upon a life of mere superficial excitement; a life of mere pleasure; these in time completely absorb the Human element; are most vitiating in the making a success in Character.

For Health let your love manifest to all about you. A smile, a word of cheer, a helping hand, a generous deed, are stepping stones to success in business, in health and in happiness, because they are openings for the stream of love; are developing those radiations of personal influence that cause others to feel us, to respect us, to confide in us, and to do as we wish them to do. Cold heartless men may succeed in their special line, but they succeed at the expense of health and of the love of their fellows.

Remember, Love is Power. As such it will either use us in its blind animal way, or we will use it intelligently, as we do other forms of Power. I can give you no greater thought, were I to exhaust all language, than this. The Sub-conscious is God manifesting as Love and this Power of God is subject to Thought, the Human expression. Love can be, is to be, directed by Thought. "By my Thought, by my Auto-Suggestion, I direct the expression of the Infinite Power which I am!' This is to be your Thought as you enter the Silence. Then the Silence becomes to you the Holy of Holies; becomes the Altar of the Most High; the inner Sanctuary where is the Ark of the Covenant which God, the Absolute, has made in the Soul.

Therefore to the extent you are in Love with Beauty will you succeed as an artist. As much as you are in love with Goodness will you be happy. As much as you are in love with Truth will you be wise.

To love what you do, is to succeed in it. To love your life is to make it a success. To love your home is to make it a happy one. To love your business is to succeed. Providing, in all these cases you have first built a noble Ideal of all these, and Love that Ideal (which is your highest conception of God) "'with all your heart and soul." "Son, give me thy heart!" success says to every man. From concentration where heart and intellect both join, comes the only success worth striving for—Happiness, Health and Supply. Love begets Faith, and Faith begets enthusiasm; enthusiasm begets effort and effort begets success. Love is the beginning and the end of Life, and it continues a companion all the way.

Therefore the Genius of Success says to each:—"Lovest thou me?" and well for him who can truthfully say, "Lord! thou knowest that I love thee!" Then shall come the condition of proof,—"Feed my sheep."

A noble Ideal is the only possible salvation, for that is the mould into which Love flows and materializes, and the Ideal determines our success or failure. That Ideal should be no less than perfect. "I the imperfect adore my own perfect," says Emerson, and Kant says, "The execution of his whole duty and the final reaching of the goal placed before him as a work, the command is here—Be ye perfect?' The test of perfection is, that 'You love your neighbor as yourself."

Any thought taken into the Silence that is not born of Love is weakness and writes that weakness in all your expression. Therefore when you love, you fulfill all Law. This is the Law and the Prophets:—"Do unto others as you would that they shall do unto you!" You wish all to act to you in Love of the Beautiful and the Good. By taking thoughts born of these loves into the Silence, by concentrating upon them you prove your love for yourself, and in that love you will love others. Richard Realf, the poet, wished written on his tomb:—

"He loved his friends, their love was sweet!" And Leigh Hunt has for his epitaph:—

"Write me as one who loved his fellowmen!"

Such lives are successes, no matter if the grave covers much that we call error and failure. Soul Unfoldment is at last the standard. Success is attained in perfection only when we come into the Realization that we are one with Infinity. One example remains for us. "I and my Father are one!" This is Loves completeness. This is, as far as earth is concerned—Perfect Success.

When Man shall thus concentrate in Love, then shall be fulfilled the prophecy of Henry Bernard Carpenter:

Man shall not ask his brother any more "Believest thou?" but "Lovest thou?" till all Shall answer at God's altar, "Lord I love!" For Hope may anchor, Faith may steer, but Love, Great Love alone, is Captain of the Soul.

SECTION XXIV.
OPINIONS AND METHODS OF OTHERS.

In order to discover truth we must be truthful ourselves and must welcome those who point out our errors as heartily as those who approve our discoveries. — Max Muller.

Seeking happiness as our aim, we declare knowledge and obedience to that knowledge to be its means, and freedom its condition. The cultivation must receive attention not less than the improvement and equipment of the brain, if our lives are to be worthy, useful and happy. — George Illis.

That you may have the same thought from other points of view I give the following extracts.

This is from the editor of The New Thought Journal, London:

CONCENTRATION

Reserve a special hour each day for cultivation of your ideal. Begin by reading for half an hour or so along the lines you wish to develop. Always use for this purpose the best and most inspiring authority you can find upon the subject, that you may come into rapport with those who have accomplished most in the field you wish to enter. Read that you may be enthused by their enthusiasm and enlightened by their accomplishment. Read slowly and meditate upon each sentence. To meditate is to be still mentally and let the spirit of the writer commune with your spirit, imparting to you the great things which can never be expressed in words alone.

Choose the highest reading on your special line, then "loaf and invite your soul," to absorb what is beyond your present understanding.

After reading and meditating thus until you are mentally and spiritually exalted in the desired realm, lay aside your reading and lie down (if possible) in a comfortable position, taking pains to give the lungs freedom for full breathing. Of course you have your windows well open. Never go into the silence, or go to sleep in a tightly-closed room. The best position for receptive silence is to lie flat on the back without a pillow. Now breathe slowly and deeply through nostrils, filling the lungs comfortably full, beginning at the bottom; hold the breath as long as you can comfortably; then take pains to exhale very slowly and evenly. Breathe thus for six or eight minutes or more, while the Divine Breath flows through you, cleansing and rejuvenating every cell of brain and body. Then begin to picture yourself as developing on this desired special line. Think of all life as a school in which you are getting ready for your career. Think of everything that comes to you as a special lesson which is to be cheerfully learned in order to help in your development. Imagine yourself as making rapid progress. Dwell upon the idea that you are full of quiet, steady enthusiasm, growing enthusiasm, for your work on this line. Never mind how enthusiastic you may feel about it; just keep on imagining and affirming the growing enthusiasm and wisdom and power you wish to feel. Then relax and let the spirit work in and through you for the accomplishment of your special desire. Allow no mental arguments against your desires. Dismiss adverse suggestions and give yourself up to the idea that all you desire is manifesting. Take it all for granted. Get into the silence of it as if it were a game you are playing Silence reason and PLAY. "Play pretend," just as you did when a child. Laugh at your fears and play with a will.

Keep this up daily, allowing nothing to interfere. It is of the utmost importance if you really mean to develop on that special line. Time will prove the value of this practice; you will find yourself growing in that deep, quiet enthusiasm which really accomplishes things.

A THOUGHT FROM TENNYSON.

Poets write in the condition of perfect concentration and fortunately Tennyson, in a letter, tells us how he induces it:

"A kind of waking trance," he says, "I have frequently had, quite up from boyhood, when I have been all alone. This has generally come upon me through repeating my own name two or three times to myself silently, till all at once as it were, out of the intensity of consciousness of individuality, the individuality itself seemed to dissolve and fade away into boundless Being, and this not a confused state, but the clearest of the clearest, the surest of the surest, the wisest of the wisest, utterly beyond words, where death were almost laughable impossibility, the loss of personality (if so it were) seeming but the only true life. I am ashamed of my feeble description. Have I not said the state is utterly beyond words? But in a moment, when I come back to my normal state of 'sanity,' I am ready to fight for mein liebes Ich and hold that it will last for eons." — "Memoire by Hallam Tennyson.

He also gives this same method of concentration, until all consciousness of personality is lost in Principle, through Concentrating upon his own name, in his poem, "The Ancient Sage," putting these words into the discourse of the sage:

For more than once when I

Sat all alone, revolving by myself

The word that is the symbol of myself,

The mortal limit of the Self was loosed.

And past into the Nameless, as a cloud

Melts into heaven. I touched my limbs, the limbs

Were strange, not mine—and yet no shade of doubt,

But utter clearness, and thro' loss of self

The gain of such large life as matched with ours

Were sun to spark—unshadowable in words,

Themselves but shadows of a shadow-world.

EXTRACT FROM "MIND."

There is much of helpful suggestion in the following beautiful extract from an article by Winifred Hathaway in Mind.

You must concentrate. You must first systematically and carefully select and determine upon the subject of your desires. You must be exact in every detail; do not blame results if you have concentrated upon a confused idea. You must then give it your undivided attention. It has been stated that meditation is a lost art. For the masses it is, but for the individual, by constant attention, it will become habit. At first the effort will be a conscious one, objective, but by ceaseless thought it will gradually become subjective; even in sleep the mind will carry on a train of thought. To one accustomed to concentration the object of desire comes almost immediately; but to the no\'ice the time is long; only patience, exhaustless, infinite, can bring about the desired result. By actual experience it has been proved that a full year is necessary to acquire this art; but is it not worth the effort? Once possessed nothing is impossible; realized hopes and dreams; matured plans; are the result. And above all, the knowledge that you are the master of your fate. But remember, that you are responsible for the use of your accomplished desires. If you wish for money you will be held accountable to the last cent; or for fame, 'tis yours to keep untarnished; if for mental attainments, desire also the wisdom to use knowledge, for if one minutest particle fail to fulfill its mission yours is the blame.

ARTIFICIAL AIDS.

The use of artificial means is well explained in this extract from Hudson Tuttle.

The usefulness of all such objects, as a bright coin, a set in a ring, or glass of water, is in fixing and concentrating the mind. A glass of water or a brilliant set, have just as much potency for this purpose as "magic mirrors," "crystals," etc., all duly "magnetized." It must be understood that the "influence" does not come from these objects, but the state which the mind attains by its attention. The object gazed at is secondary and inconsequential. Highly recommended as this method has been it is by no means to be cultivated. It is the process by which the Hindu gains his "wisdom," and becomes the type of passive imbecility and hopeless laziness. The way to receive the highest spiritual gifts is to strive for spiritual strength. The way to become impressible to great thoughts, is to bring the mind up for their reception.

Aliens! through struggles and wars!

The goal that was named cannot be countermanded.

Have the past struggles succeeded?

What has succeeded? yourself? your nation? Nature?

Now understand me well—it is proved in the essence of things that from the fruition of success, no matter what, shall come forth something to make a greater struggle necessary.
—Walt Whitman.

THE PARTING WORD.

Theory, advice, instruction, are comparatively worthless without he who seeks shall use that which he finds. This book has that value for you which you shall determine.

To read and then lay it aside, no matter how much you enjoy it; no matter how much you find in it to admire; will benefit you little. To be of benefit you must adopt the Truth you find here, as the method of living. You must practice it. Demonstration alone is Possession.

Select your season and make sacred promise to yourself that you will keep it as carefully with yourself as if you made it to your dearest friend. When that season comes, be it five minutes, or be it an hour, retire to your ordinary place of relaxing and in your ordinary way of keeping this tryst, keep it— Relax — Concentrate — think.

Keep this up. It will soon become your custom so to retire into the "closet of meditation" whenever any question arises. There you will listen to the "still small voice" which the prophet heard, and as he was led, you will be: "He leadeth me!" will become your constant Affirmation.

I have done all I may. I have told you how I, how many others, have found the way. I have pointed out the road. Now I leave you with the only direction possible for travelling it. Practice! Through practice you will enter the Silence where by Telepathy we shall often meet.

Your friend,
HENRY HARRISON BROWN.
THE END

BOOK THREE
MAN'S GREATEST DISCOVERY
Six Soul Culture Essays

HENRY HARRISON BROWN
MAN'S GREATEST DISCOVERY
Six Soul Culture Essays

FOREWORD

These essays are TRUTH to me. They wrote themselves. I was but the instrument through which thought crystallized. They -welled up from a full heart and were moist with tears of joy. When the significance of the Greatest of all human discoveries dawned upon me, like Saul of Tarsus, I was stricken with the magnitude of the Perception and for several days lived as one in a trance. The sub-conscious life was the only reality. I lived that which I have here written. When the Thought crystallized into the title of this book, like the Greek of old I cried, "Eureka," and paced my room in rapture. I clairvoyantly perceived the wonderful possibilities that lay in the Discovery. Like a mighty spiritual wind, such as the old Hebrew seers felt when they prophesied, was this perception of fulfillment. "The hour now is when men shall no more worship God either in temple or on mount, but shall know themselves almighty and deathless," was the Voice within me.

I saw man as Conscious King of himself, and "I AM POWER" was the Affirmation then realized. In this spirit was the first essay written. Day by day, since that September morning, have I entered more and more into the Realization of the Vision then vouchsafed me. Each succeeding essay has only increased the responsibility which I, as Henry Harrison Brown, have felt, as the instrument for that "which has been from all eternity," as it finds expression in and through me. I am possessed with the desire and purpose to keep my personality behind the curtain and to have Truth for which I stand recognized by the world. This desire is now overruled by this same Perception and Power, and I must say this much that the centuries to come may find it as History. I must also add:— Truth and I are one!

Since Truth is eternal, this book is eternal. The paper on which it is written may perish but the Thought vibrations, never. This generation may pass from sight but MAN will live forever. This generation may have individuals who realize Truth and never die. Generations to come will all so realize and earth will be redeemed from the results of undeveloped human powers. The Potential of Life is IMMORTALITY, and that without pain, sorrow, disease or death.

I know of no other attempt in literature to demonstrate from the position of modern science the Unity of Soul and matter under the thought of a Present Immortality. It being a fact that that the thought of these essays is in accord with that of advanced thinkers along many lines, I have prefaced each one with numerous quotations. Limited in my library advantages, I have given what I found. But finding so many in my limited range of authorities, what must there be to him who has the range of the large libraries denied, by location, to me?

I have only carried their principles and their deductions farther and have done this through the scientific spirit and method, basing all my deductions upon observed phenomena. If my position is false, the physics of the world is also false. The phenomena of Telepathy, Levitation, and Clairvoyance are as familiar tome as that of chemistry to the professors of that science. I have been healed by Thought. I heal by Thought. I send and receive messages by the wireless telegraphy of Mind. By this method I am in communication with those individualities with whom I can establish sympathetic vibration, whether they are in the sphere we call the sense-life or in that we call spirit-life, for these spheres are one to the unfolded Soul.

By means of my Psychometric faculties I read the inner life of man or rock, and know only Soul, as the maker and builder of all external life. Knowing this from over thirty years' experience, I were false to Self, to Truth, to my fellowman did I not write that which I know, that it may be a stimulant to others, helping them to realize that they are not body, but Mind, and are deathless. I can only affirm: that which I am, all men are. The century that now is will see all this phenomena the common life of the advanced races. Telepathy is the promise of that unfoldment of latent power which means for earth the fulfillment of all that poet, priest, and seer have foreseen. Feeling this, I have only let Truth have its way through me. It has clothed itself in the best robes of language it found in the storehouses of my brain. Written first for the columns of my little journal, NOW, these essays, perhaps, have the crudities of the haste of newspaper preparation, but better so than that I take the fire of inspiration from them by the cooling process of criticism. So, oblivious of critic, I put them forth in this form for those who can feel the Truth in them. I thus awaken those vibrations in the Thought ocean, in which all humanity is engulfed, which will find other brains fitted by special training for their manifestation along similar and co-ordinate lines. Thus this little book, the child of my inspiration and love, is set a Bethel-stone to mark the beginning of this Psychic Era that ushers in the Millennial dawn of Perfect Manhood. In the Faith that Love and Truth will soon lead Man to this victory, I am

HENRY HARRISON BROWN.

"NOW" Office, San Francisco, April, 1902.

Ring, bells, in unreal d steeples,
  The joy of unborn peoples.
Sound trumpets far off blown,
Your triumph is my own.
Parcel and part of all,
I keep the festival;
Fore-reach the good to be,
And share the victory.
— WHITTIER.

1
THOUGHT AS POWER.
AN EXPLANATION AND A PROPHECY

Recently, at my class, we tried an experiment, old to me, and yet then and there it burst upon my comprehension that in this experiment lay Power. Later, I saw that this discovery of Power was man's greatest discovery; that more lay in it for the good of the race than in any previous discovery. This revelation grows upon me, and no surer has any scientist been of the worth of his discovery than I am of this. Here is the experiment:—

Five persons were concerned in it. One sat on a stool. Two stood at the side of the person at the knees, two behind the shoulders, all breathed in unison, and all raised their hands together, palms pressing together, all except index fingers closed. As their hands came up the fourth time, the fingers were placed under arms and knees and the person was lifted without any sense of weight. This was also done with a person lying down, and with a table. With a friend, I have lifted a heavy stone thus. I am sure that a few persons, by practice in breathing and moving in unison can in this way practically annihilate, In any given case, the law of gravity.

I call attention to this experiment because I am sure that it means more for the welfare and development of the race than Franklin's discovery, with his kite, of the identity of lightning with the electricity in the Lyden jar, — means more than the discovery of the North pole will mean,—more than the invention of the spinning jenny, the invention of the steam engine or the electric motor; than the discovery of ether, or the marvels of modern surgery have meant in civilization. This is a tremendous claim. But from years of study of the significance of certain allied mental and psychical phenomena, I am free to make the claim and to prophesy that FROM THIS EXPERIMENT WILL COME THE GREATEST SCIENTIFIC APPLICATION OF POWER THE WORLD HAS EVER KNOWN. It may be that in it we have a key to a lost art, that of the Egyptians in transporting their huge stones and the silent building of Solomon's Temple. I can no more tell what it has for the future than Watts, when he toyed with steam and found it force, could foresee the engine of today; or the chemist who first found that there was explosive power in nitre, charcoal and sulphur, could foresee the use of it in modern battleship; or he who first found power in electricity could foresee the present wireless telegraphy. POWER is what a man is seeking. Found, it is to be applied. The first is Discovery; the next is Invention. These two make human progress.

The discoverer of power is the world's benefactor. To apply this is Progress. Every new discovery of power marks an epoch in human history. Fire, wind, water, steed, steam, caloric, electricity, have each marked great epochs of civilization. Of all the past discoveries, the greatest was that of fire. Through fire, man has been enabled to conquer the world of external vibrations, known as the world of matter. Imagine a world where fire should be unknown. Suppose the secret of fire was lost today beyond recovery. What death and desolation would follow. Fire was the beginning of human development. From it, all our science, art, and religion have sprung. Fire is Power. Up to that time, savage man had known only the power of his own brawn. Club and stone were the instruments through which Power within made itself manifest. Ages have passed. Power has been developed; Power has been controlled; Power has been discovered; Power has been harnessed. Through the mastery and application of Power, man has conquered all the Without. He has used external Power. Is there other Power? What is the Power that has thus found, developed, and harnessed, this external Power? Where does it dwell? It is the Power IN man. It is the Power of Ideas. This is recognized. Ideas rule the world. But that they are any kin to these external forces has scarcely been conceived, much less believed, until the last century. The greatest gift that the nineteenth century gave the twentieth, was the demonstration that Thought is a form of Energy. This is the greatest gift of all the centuries. It is Man's Greatest Discovery and marks the beginning of the Psychic Era:—the Dawn of the Millennium. Today it is known, among thinkers and investigators, that Thought is Power. It is THE Power that controls all other Power. THOUGHT is POWER! THOUGHT IS POWER! This is the greatest discovery,—that of fire comes next. This is destined to make as great an advance in human progress as fire made in the ages past. Thought will be consciously used as Power. Its possibilities are unlimited. No imagination can picture what man and his world will be after a century, ten centuries, of the conscious use of Thought. Thought is as tamable as lightning, as easily controlled as steam, and as unerring as gravity.

Let me quote from one of the great books of the last century upon the other great discovery of that century,—Prof. E. L. Youmans' work upon "The Conservation and Correlation of Force," published in 1864. In speaking of the law of Conservation of Force, Prof. Youmans says:— Thus the law characterized by Farady as the highest in physical science which our faculties enable us to perceive, has a far more extended sway; it might well be proclaimed the highest law of all sciences; the most far-reaching principle that adventurous reason has discovered in the Universe. Its stupendous reach spans all orders of existence. Not only does it govern the movements of the heavenly bodies, but it presides over the genesis of constellation; not only does it control those radiant floods of power that fill eternal spaces, bathing, illumining, and vivifying, our planet, but it rules the actions and relations of men and regulates the march of terrestrial affairs. Nor is its domain limited to physical phenomena; it prevails equally in the world of mind, controlling all the faculties and processes of thought and feeling. Star and nerve tissue are parts of the same system—stella and nervous forces are correlated. Nay, more! Sensation awakens thought and kindles emotion, so this wondrous dynamic chain binds into living Unity the realms of matter and mind through limitless amplitudes of space.

Thus early did a far-reaching scientist perceive the fact that has since been demonstrated: — that the realm of Life is one and that it is all Force. Telepathy has verified this statement. It is the link connecting the hitherto divided parts of life, called matter and mind, into one, and making of Nature a Unity. No fact in all the history of human life is more potent than this. Telepathy is the missing link in science. Mind and Matter are by it wed, never to be divorced, and henceforth we shall deal with Mind as we have with matter, and with thought as we have with electricity. We shall learn the power, the laws, of thought, and shall harness it to Human Will and Desire. Thought as Force means the Redemption of the world from all old conditions. Almighty Power lies in thought, and, unlike all other power, it cannot be monopolized.

It is open alike to all men. Its only limit is human ignorance. As the Without has been made to serve man's will through knowledge, so now will the Within become subject to him. The mighty realm of Mind will become the theatre of human activity and all its power be consciously used to bless.

All this lies in that simple experiment. What is the power that lifts the person? It is that which lifts our feet and hands; which is subject to our will in all our conduct:—THOUGHT. It is the first demonstration we have that Thought is not only Force to move through space without visible conductors, but that*Thought is also Force to lift ponderable bodies. We fill up with Thought by unison in breathing and movement. The same thought fills the five persons as five lamps are filled from one dynamo. Thought fills us. We use it as we will and it lifts the man. This simple statement is more eloquent than all rhetoric can be. I cannot think of the greatness of the fact without tears. It means more than all other facts to the race. Thought is force that can be made to affect ponderable matter. "Chalk marks don't draw-cars!" said a railroad man. Chalk marks will draw cars, when thought is put into them to do so. This is the Prophecy:—Thought will in the future become subject to conscious control. We shall yet intelligently do all that the Hindoos are now credited with doing.

Life is subject to will. Thought is a manifestation of Infinite Life. Thought is Infinite.. We know it is Power. It is one with all other forms of power. Its source is limitless. It will flow through us in any required amount. We can direct it to any desired end. This is demonstrated by telepathy; by bodily renovation; by the building of body to will. Thought will be used to control all the lesser forms of force; to direct fire, water, wind, wave, light, electricity and gravity. The fire will cease to burn at command. "The wind and the-wave obey him." Plant and animal life will come at his thought—to him willing servants. Dream! Illusion! Rhapsody! all this may be called. It is only the calm reasoning from present scientific knowledge. Let it stand for future generations to verify. The time is now for us to begin this dominion of Mind over Nature. Beginning with our own body, we will progress until even the largest of our environments is subject to our will.

Would you win? Begin now to control SELF-manifestations by controlling Thought, and by recognizing that it does the work. As you have used in the past other power, now use this. NEVER BEGIN TO DO A THING UNTIL YOU ARE READY. And you are not ready until, like the engine on the track, you are filled with Power. The hasty, the worried, the fearful, the irritable, the impatient, the doubtful, the fault-finding, are all like the engine that has punctures in the boilers, or has no fire. They are not ready. Get ready by first filling up with Thought. As in the experiment, breathe and think. Consider what to do; think of it; and breathe slowly, with this concentrated thought. All calm, patient, concentrated persons do this. All happy, healthful and successful persons do this. It is the secret of their success. Before they move to do, they let the Thought fill them—possess them. The Suggestion and the Affirmation must have time and opportunity to fill the organism with its power. This done, then this Power, his Thought, does the work. Think and breathe before you act! This is the Law of Power.

This is the conquering force in man that will give him dominion over all things. Its scientific demonstration is in the simple experiment given above. I challenge the world upon this. Try it. Learn that by concentration, Thought -will, through the individual, accomplish any Desire. Emerson said this long ago, but we have just learned it: "From within or from behind, a Light shines through man upon things. The man is nothing, but the Light is All."

2

TELEPATHY

THE MISSING LINK

The Power that manifests throughout the Universe distinguished as material, is the same Power which in ourselves dwells up under the form of Consciousness.— Herbert Spencer, in "Principles of Sociology."

Its stupendous span reaches all orders of existence. * * * It rule* the actions and relations of men.— Prof. E. L. Youmans, on the "Law of Conservation and Correlation of Energy." Thought and feeling themselves, which can neither be weighed nor measured, do not admit of being resolved into modes of motion."— John Fiske, in "Through Nature to God." The immortality of our thoughts and actions is a corollary of the doctrine of the conservation of energy.— Peter C. Austin, Ph. D., of the Brooklyn Polytechnic Institute. Mind and matter appear to us as an irreducible quality.— Editorial Review in Popular Science Monthly. That mind and nature must at last be the same, that physical laws and mental laws must be identical, is essentially involved in what has been said as to the relations between matter, force and movement.— Buchner, in "Force and Matter." That one body can act upon another at a distance through a vacuum without the mediation of anything else, by and through which their activity and force may be conveyed, is to me so great an absurdity that I believe that no man who has a capacity for thinking can ever fall into.— Newton, in "Principia." The gulf which separates * * * the organic from the inorganic bodies, is not closed up, and none of our hypotheses help us to bridge the gulf.— Prof. Chon, of Breslan, at a meeting of German physicians.

These extracts not only show that there is to science and philosophy a "missing link," but they also demonstrate that the scientists recognize this and the necessity of supplying it. There is not uniformity among them. The principle of Unity compels Spencer and some others to affirm, with Youmans, the unity of the Law. Fiske recognizes the Law, but illogically denies that thought and feeling come under it.

But among those who see the necessity, the logical fact of unity and the universality of the Law, it is at best with them not a fact, but merely an opinion. No proof do they have except that which should be the most convincing—Perception. This "Gulf" is non-existant.

The fact of this missing link illustrates the limits and the ignorance of science upon this most important subject. In regard to Thought, the investigators are today where scientists were one hundred years ago in regard to special creation. They lack facts upon which to rest the feeling of truth. For all truth begins in feeling. "Thoughts," says Edward Carpenter, "are dying feelings." All truth is self-evident. Men are obliged to reason themselves into errors. Truth is perceived by the Soul—is felt—is self-evident. All men feel Unity. They feel that Law is universal. Because they do not have the necessary facts, they reason from those they have and build up fine, but erroneous, theories.

So built the man who demonstrated, by reason, that steamships could not cross the ocean, and the reverend who, in my boyhood's hearing, reasoned that chloroform could not be possible, because God intended man to suffer pain. In biology, the "missing links" are the dividing lines man has made between the species. Were all the facts in evidence, there would be no species. There would be one unbroken line of development. So here, when all the facts that are at man's disposal shall be allowed to testify, there will be no missing links in Life, no break in Law. There will be one unbroken line of evolution from protoplasm to Love,— one chain from God to rock, and from rock to God again. Lizzie Doten has expressed this beautifully: —

God of the granite and the rose,

Soul of the sparrow and the bee!

The mighty tide of Being flows

Through all its channels, Lord, from Thee!

It springs to life in grass and flowers,

Through every grade of Being runs,

Till from creation's radiant towers,

Its glory flames in stars and suns.

God of the granite and the rose,

Soul of the sparrow and the bee!

The mighty tide of Being flows
Through all its channels back to Thee!
Thus round and round the current runs,
A mighty sea without a shore,
Till men and angels, stars and suns,
Unite to praise thee ever more!

Is this truth or is it mere poetry? Is it feeling or is it reason? I cannot conceive of a person who will not feel that it is Truth. Can you not reason it so? Spencer, Buchner, and others, have so reasoned. But can you prove it? Can it be proven? What will this proof mean? What will the discovery of this link between granite and Soul mean to the race? Where in the list of human achievements will it rank when found?

It will mean, first of all, the abolishing of Death from human thought. It will mean the demonstration of Life forever. It will demonstrate all the hopes of the race to be facts. It will demonstrate as realities, all the desires of the race for continued communication with loved ones who have not died, but who have changed environment. It will mean the demonstration of infinite faculties in Man, and an infinite Life in which to develop them. It will demonstrate that Man is not yet born; that birth is before him; that all these eons he has been gestating in this womb of flesh, awaiting birth. Now he will soon be born and, when born, will not need undertaker, grave nor sorrow. All this past life of man has been filled with premature births; men born out of time,—before time. They have, like five months babes, had to be nurtured in the nurseries of the Spirit till they were able to walk alone. Earth has been a channel house when it should have been a paradise. Ignorance, which is only undevelopment, is cause— a necessary cause—in the evolution of Man. Now he is no longer "coming," he is here—here in the recognition of himself as ONE with that Power which is ALL.

He was the slave of Law until he learned to be its servant. Now he is becoming its Master. Becoming Law! Becoming Conscious Law! And no longer slave, or servant, he is King over himself. Emerson, seeing beyond all other seers, this MAN, exclaimed: "CONSCIOUS LAW IS KING OF KINGS."

This one fact of telepathy accepted, we have the missing link. This will necessitate a complete revolution in obedience to the Law of Evolution— a revolution that will change all present civilization as much as the ancient has been changed by astronomy, magnetic needle, printing press, discovery of coal, application of steam, and the application of electricity. A change as great will be wrought by this fact developed into the Art of Living as has been wrought by all of these, for it will locate ALL POWER within the Man. He can do anything, because he is Conscious Law, and his creative power is Thought. All he has now to learn is how to use Thought intelligently, learn as he has learned to use steam, and he will have "dominion over all things."

This fact, this "missing link," is TELEPATHY-THOUGHT TRANSFERENCE. Telepathy is defined by Prof. Crooks as "the transmission of a thought, or an emotion, from one person to another without visible means of contact." This is a common phenomenon. It has been ignored, denied, feared, considered canny and mysterious, simply because its cause was not known. When once thought is put into the category of vibration, and considered one of the modes of Infinite Energy, then all is clear. Telepathy places it there. This discovery is man's greatest. Things, events, persons, are to be measured by results. Great things require the perspective of centuries. The Law of Conservation and Correlation of Forces, which Prof. Youmans tells us was in 1864 characterized as "the greatest discovery of that half of the century," had then been over half a century in obtaining recognition. Even now it is not fully accepted. Its greatness is not appreciated by even scientists themselves. Every day its far reaching power is being revealed.

So is it with this simple fact—this every day fact— this fact of telepathy, from which has been coined the saying, "The devil is always near when you are talking about him." It is so simple, so common, that it is considered valueless; but, "the stone the builders rejected has become the head of the corner." All the phenomena of the various religions of the world, of the mystics and psychics, of ancient and modern Spiritualism, all the strange and mysterious in life, are made clear when it is seen that Thought is Power; that the Universe is One; that Life is One. Mind acts upon mind, therefore there is no separation. All we have to do is to learn to talk in thought and not in oral speech; to listen to thoughts, and not with the external ear to the slower vibrations called sound. All the intelligences that ever lived are then with us and we with them. As all fishes in the sea, or all birds in the air, are in one common vibratory medium, and can at will converse, so are we in Thought— in the ALL.

But greater than this:— THOUGHT is ALL THE POWER, for all is Mind. Matter never had existence. All is Mind. All is Vibration. All man's power is the Power of Mind. This Power is directed by Conscious thought. It can be directed to do anything. It can literally "move mountains." Telepathy, demonstrating that thought is force, does not stop at the mere transmitting of vibrations between mind and mind, but, since all things are only materialized mind (reduced vibrations when compared with thought), it follows that things feel thought waves, and that we can learn to control things by thought. The Hindoo does this, — we can. Here then is the wisdom, the insight, and the greatness of Professor Dolbear, who makes this remarkable statement, perfectly in harmony with the position taken by this book: —

No one may assume for an instant that the possibilities of other phenomena are limited to such interactions as have heretofore found expression in treatises on physics. Indeed there is evidence which cannot be ignored with safety, that physical phenomena sometimes take place when all ordinary antecedents are absent, when bodies move without touch, electric, or magnetic agencies, movements which are orderly and more or less subject to volition. In addition to this, is still other evidence of competent, critical observers, that the subject matter of thought is directly transferable from one mind to another. Such facts do not invalidate physical laws nor make it needful to modify present statements concerning energy. If such things be true, they are of more importance to philosophy than the whole body of physical knowledge we now have, and of vast importance to humanity. For it gives religion corroborative testimony of the real existence of possibilities for which it has always contended.—"Matter, Ether and Motion," p. 353.

"If?" There is no "if" to one who will seek. Not an hour but the psychometrists, clairvoyants, telepathists, are demonstrating this fact that thought is power and that it is transmitted from mind to mind (as Professor Dolbear, in the preface of an early edition, thinks possible,) through the ether. I demonstrate it daily in my psychometric readings. I receive feelings and read from them the character of the sender. At times, I receive the thoughts. A letter, no matter from whom or where or when written, tells me, as I hold it and listen to it, the character, the mental and physical conditions of the writer and often his past, and his environment; and many times his friends and their thoughts, for it opens to me his thought-world. Here then is the "missing link" which science and philosophy have long needed to unite them in one. The link is telepathy with its demonstration of thought as force. It unites physics and metaphysics, science and philosophy, science and religion, matter and spirit, in one whole. Each of these branches of knowledge is now concerned with some links in the endless chain of Energy to the exclusion of others. The chain is one as God is ONE. Life is One! Energy is One! We are to study Life as One, making no dividing lines where Nature has not. "What God hath joined, let no man put asunder."

3
THE ULTIMATE OF POWER.

The Universe Is. Nor can we venture to speak of Life as one of the varieties or manifestations of energy. — Prof. Wm. Crooks.

All about us, and within us, exist rates of vibration known as forms of energy, some of them forced by man's ingenuity to record themselves by aid of mechanism, others yet waiting this sort of detection. Recording devices to reveal the laws of light, heat, chemical affinity are familiar, but no one yet in a similar manner records thought or gravity. — Wm. J. Martin, in Century Magazine.

Force is not gravity, nor electricity, nor magnetism, nor chemical affinity. But WILL is the typical idea of Force.— Dr. Brown, Dean of Boston University.

It is evident that there will eventually take place an integration by which all orders of phenomena will be combined and recognized as differently conditioned forms of one ultimate fact. — Herbert Spencer.

We know nothing of the ultimate of force. Science is already getting something like a firm hold of the idea that all kinds of motion are but forms of one persistent Force, arising in one fountain head of Power.— Duke of Argyle.

All phenomena are in their ultimate analysis known to us only as facts of consciousness.— Prof. Huxley.

Thoughts and feelings are the fundamental facts from which there is no escaping.— John Fiske.

The laws of thought are the laws of the universe. — Buchner.

Thought is Power.— Victor Hugo.

Great men are they who see that spiritual force is stronger than material force; that thoughts rule the world.— Emerson.

This last quotation, from Emerson, shall be the text of this essay. Science and philosophy have ever sought for the ultimate, for the origin of Power. Religion has ever been the recognition and worship of Power. Theology has been a system of belief in Power. Theology assumes a beginning of things, which is only a beginning of the manifestation of

Power in things or by things or through things. From the earliest theology to the latest, it has been the incarnation of Power that has received praise, thanksgiving, sacrifice, and, where possible, love. Omnipotence is the God of the world. Power has thus been recognized as ONE, even before modern science so decided. The Greek, placing Fate above all the gods, located Power as ONE. Monotheism is the belief in the ONE Power.

Thus Power has been the ONE principle without which no other could be. It has been the ONE-thing without which there was no-thing. With Power—Omnipotence—all things were possible. Hence in the Ideal, Power has been the chief and the prime constituent. To subdue, to create, and to exercise Power, has been man's ambition. For Power is Life and Life manifests in Power. So much Power, so much Life. From child making mud pies, to Edison in his laboratory; from negro voodoo, to Episcopal bishop; from séance, to synod; from club, to dynamite; from water, to gas; from wind, to electricity; from pugilist, to commander-in-chief; from toy boat, to Dewey's fleet; from ward-boss, to king; from money, to magnetism; from medicine, to Mental Science; there has been only one cry, one desire, one hunger. It is the infinite demand for Power, never to be satisfied until man finds and manifests infinity. To meet and to satisfy this God-demand within himself, he has conquered the external forces and made them obey his will, only to find greater desire and greater unrest. He conquered the wild horse and made him his servant. But the power that conquered the horse is greater than the horse.

The horse never yielded to the physical power man exerted. But to .... what? He conquered wind and made it fill his sail and bear him wherever he would. He is more powerful than the wind. He chained the water and fed it with flame, until, harnessed, it became his slave. That which harnessed steam is more powerful than steam. He reached out into space and, grasping the bolts of Jove, taught the gods how to wield their power, as he buckled them to his cars and made the fires of heaven his torches and their dynamic forces his messengers. But the Power that could thus teach the gods is greater than the lightning. Lightning would ever have remained lightning and been self-destructive, had not man—Thought—come to enfold and direct. Man virtually made electricity by converting destructive Power, through direction, to use. In man, then, lies the greater power—the Power that can control all Power, not himself.

Everywhere else is the principle recognized that it takes superior Power to control any form of Power. Why not recognize the same law here? The conqueror comes in some greater form of Power. This principle is admitted and yet, because of present methods of thinking, it will be said:—Man masters because he is man—because he thinks and builds mechanism through which Power may act. True. If Thought can thus direct, is not Thought Power? The very banks of the river are Power. The still car is Power and only superior Power can move it. Nothing can move nothing. Nothing can direct nothing. Only Power can direct Power. Had man any sails until he thought ' 'Sails?" What caused him to think "Sails?" Recognition of, and faith in, external Power. Faith led the way to achievement. As long as man recognizes only external Power, what Emerson calls "Material force," he will have faith in that alone and will use that alone. When he shall recognize interior, "Spiritual," Power, then he will have faith in that form and will learn to use it. He once was used by the "material" forms of force which he now controls. He is now used as a leaf in the Mississippi of Spiritual Thought-Power. He will learn to use it, and then be the Master of Fate. When he thinks of himself as Power, he will use himself as Power and will be Power. Then will all other forms be obedient to him or be useless. Thought is Power. It is the highest form of Power that man, the director of the Omnipotence in himself, can use. He is Thought. He is Power conscious of itself.

Jesus said: "The kingdom of God is within you! " "Kingdom" means, if it means anything, Power. That Power is God. God is Omnipotent and Ever-present. Then it follows that where God is, or where God's kingdom is, there is Omnipotence. He is daily manifesting the Universal Power within himself. He IS Omnipotence. Can Omnipotence be limited? Not by Itself. Man only can limit himself. Self-Limitation is then the only possible limitation to the power of man. This limitation is a thought man places over himself. This thought is born in ignorance. When he knows himself as he is, he will not be limited. The power to limit is equal to the power limited. Man, therefore, as an individual, balances the Absolute. He is the equal in Power to all that is not himself. The Me and the Non-Me are equal. The Universe is ONE. The ultimate seat of power, so long sought, is found. It is in man. The Ultimate Power so long sought is MAN.

As far as Man is concerned, he is all power, and has only to use that which he himself IS. Any power outside himself has influence upon him only so far as he, by recognition of it, has given it power.

He confers upon things their power to harm. He is master, and can still every tempest by his "Peace, be still," when he comes to know himself as Soul. Ignorant of his heir ship to the Crown of Life, he yields himself a slave where he should reign as king. He manifests all his power in those ' 'Fundamental facts" of Fiske,—Thought and Feeling. He can control all that is not himself, and also himself, by those laws that Buchner calls "Laws of the Universe," for they are only the Laws of Thought. Since man can control thought, he is the Master of the Universe and "a Law unto himself." His Universe is his body and his environment. He is as supreme in his individual Universe as God is in the Absolute Universe. That "Will, "of which Dr. Brown speaks, is the persistency of Force, the Law of Crystallization, the Survival of the Fittest, the Descent by Heredity, and all "natural laws" of science and philosophy, to which man now holds himself responsible and to which he will be slave until he shall, as an individual, control, by his Will, the undifferentiated Will that is manifesting through him. That "Integration' ' Spencer prophesies is made a fact by "Man's Greatest Discovery." It is demonstrated daily by the facts of Telepathy and Mental Healing. To assume, as in the common belief, that all man can do is to direct physical force, or to relegate, as does Prof. Crooks, Life to some other origin than that of ordinary force, is to limit man to the use of external force, and this to the neglect of himself as force. It is to shut the gates of the "Kingdom." "Lift up your heads, O ye eternal gates, and the King of Glory shall come in! Who is the King of Glory?" MAN. Man recognizing himself as Power. Religion and Science are now so wed by this discovery that hereafter they are One. One in the recognition of Power, and all Power as One.

Why am I thus positive? Because as surely as the early electricians saw that they were dealing with Power, and felt then all the possibilities it held for the future, so do I realize the possibilities of thought when directed, as it can be, by the Conscious Will. Not long ago I blindfolded a boy and thought to him, "You will go and touch the mantel." Soon his body swayed and, had he not stepped, he would have fallen forward. He was soon touching the mantel. I mentally requested a young man, who did not know that I was going to experiment with him at the time, "Bring me my clock." He went at once to the shelf and brought it to me. Asking the boy why he went, he replied: "I felt pulled that way." The young man said: "I felt impelled to do it." What pulled, what impelled? Thought as Power. It is true that it may be said that I awakened Thought in them. If so, Thought did the work. That which awakens Power is Power. That is all I am now demonstrating. Some form of vibration went from me to them. Accumulate enough of vibration, or of energy, which is the same, and something must move. A lady requested me to treat her daughter by the absent method. I told the girl mentally that she would be well at such a time, and that all pain would leave at such a time; told her to go to sleep, and to awaken at such a time, all of which she did. Thought is Power. Demonstrations similar to these, thousands of teachers and healers are making. Who shall limit the Power of thought? Faith can move mountains. Faith is only Thought united with, and directing, all the Soul forces. Faith is the Self-Suggestion of Power. Faith is a Suggestion of the Conscious man dropped into the Infinity of the Unconscious. Faith is telling the Soul what to manifest. Faith is the Conscious Power of God. Faith is the Power of the Conscious God.

4
LIFE: ITS POTENTIAL AND ITS CONSERVATION

Potential: — Anything that is possible. — Bacon.

Conservation:— The fundamental principle of modern physics:— that the total amount of energy in nature is constant; that it can neither be increased nor diminished.— Century Diet.

Life is not the result of organism, but the reverse. — Haeckel.

Life is only a particular kind of mechanics.— Virchow.

Consciousness: — The common condition of Self-Knowledge. — Sir Wm. Hamilton.

Out of the deeps of Ultimate Being proceeds the outgoing, acting Life. The energy behind all evolution is the progressive consciousness of God. — Bradley, in" Appearance and Reality." Our conscious life is a stream of varying physical states which follow one another quickly, in a perpetual shimmer, with never an instant of rest. The elementary psychical states, indeed lie below consciousness, or, as we may say, they are sub-conscious. We may call these primitive pulsations the psychical molecules out of which are compounded the thoughts and feelings that - well up into the stream of consciousness.— John Fiske, in "Through Nature to God."

There can be no scientific doubt that Life obeys no special or exceptional laws. * * * It must be regarded as the result of a different interaction of chemical and physical forces, or a particular complicated round of mechanical motion.— Buchner, in "Force and Matter."

If my body came from brute, though I sensate from their own, I am here. This is my kingdom. Shall the royal voice be mute? Hold the scepter, Human Soul, and rule thy province of the brute. — Tennyson.

Each Soul is in focus of world * * * For there transformation is wrought, Where forces are changed into Thought. —. W. Powell, "The Soul."

When once the "Great Discovery" was made, through telepathy, that thought is, like heat, sound, light, a mode of motion, identical in principle with all other forms of motion, then was the way open for the study of Life also as a mode of motion. Until then, Life was outside the possibility of study. Its phenomena could be catalogued, but Life itself was an unknown quantity. Thought is Life transformed in accordance with Nature's one unerring law of Conservation. Force is transformable but non-destructible, non-creatable. Thought, being a form of force, had an antecedent form. In this antecedent form, which we term Life, it passes through the brain and becomes thought. As it passes out of the brain, it ceases to be thought. It becomes some other form of Vibration. It is not lost. Though we may not follow it now, we shall sometime do so. It is safe to infer that part of this force is changed to Will, and from Will is changed into the power to do, —into that power which acts in unison with chemical power. By the action of each mode of motion upon each, is caused the phenomena we call the visible conduct of man.

Not yet has the beefsteak been traced by conversion to the thought of the noon. To so attempt to trace thought, would be to trace the origin of the steam in the boiler to the boiler itself. The boiler causes the steam only as one of the many factors at work. Without the boiler, there would be vapor but no steam. We trace steam to water and heat; water and heat to still other forms of force. To trace steam to boiler, would be reasoning in the circle which traces thought to food. Food and some other force must make the phenomena of physical life. We trace water and iron back to the One energy. They are One in the Universal Substance. (One in God, as theology truly says.) Not yet by any process has chemistry been able to convert one into the other, or to trace the change from food to thought, and I do not think it possible. Thought and body are two manifestations of the One. But they are manifestations of two streams of power that start from the One, which, flowing side by side, make by interaction the phenomena of the visible universe. They are never converted, or transformed, into each other. One is ordinarily called matter, the other is called by Science, Ether; by Soul Culture, Spirit. Both are forms of motion. Both flow from the One, the Undifferentiated, the Unconditioned, the Unconscious, the Homogeneous,

"The Undivided Whole

Of which each creature forms a part."

By a series of actions and interactions, the potentialities of the One are manifest. The process is called Evolution.

There is not the slightest -warrant for saying, "thought is the product of the brain;" this is putting the cart before the horse,—putting effect for cause. Before brain was, Life was to build it. After Life has left the brain, brain ceases to be. Life builds brain. Thought is Life transformed. When Life leaves brain, brain decays. We call this death. But decomposition is the result of the same force that was concerned in building brain as constructor under direction of the master,—Life. One of the streams of Eternal Energy departs from body and leaves the other—the Chemical— to work alone. After death only chemical, automatic action is found where had been intelligent, self-directive action. Life is a mode of motion, but it can manifest only through contact with some other mode of motion. Science has heretofore hesitated about calling Life a mode of motion. Many scientists and philosophers have replied, when asked if Life is identical with other forms of force, "No!" All who did believe Life to be motion were called materialists. Even Spencer admits that we must seek a spiritual origin. With the accepted principle of Unity, all thinkers will be forced, before the century ends, through the demonstration of this Greatest Discovery, to recognize Life as one form of the One Energy. And it will not be considered materialistic to do so, for the present distinction of matter and spirit will pass away. All will be, in thought, neither matter nor spirit, but will be the Nameless and Unknown ONE who manifests through these two streams of Motion.

Life is the ultimate power in man. Its absence is death. When Life goes, thought goes. Well says Tennyson:—

Life and Thought have gone away Side by side,

Leaving doors and windows wide: Careless tenants they.

The primal manifestation of Life in man is Consciousness. The primal manifestation of the One to Man, is Life. Be it where it may, in sand-grain or in Cherubim, it is Life. Each phenomenon is the manifestation of the One Life. Like all other forms of motion, Life (Spirit) must Pass through transformations, or it would be only latent, unmanifested Life. Into how many forms Life is transformable, we will not dogmatise, but they must be limitless. Consciousness is one. There are changes in nerve tissue in every act of consciousness. There must be a corresponding change in that which uses chemical force to cause the phenomena of physical life. Thus consciousness is transformed Life. It is the resultant of prior conditions of sensation. Sensation is the result of contact with other forms of force. Sensation is transformed Life. Born of sensation, is Thought. Man says, "I feel." Then he says, "think because I feel." Then he says, "Because I feel and Think, I AM." Thus Life is converted into sensation, then into Thought, and these two make the Conscious Man,—the I AM. In all the change there is no loss of original force. Only a change is given to the direction and, possibly, to the velocity, of atoms, in which the two forms of force lie in potentiality, and this change gives that form of motion we call Life. Thought is Force, therefore Life must be. This has the Great Discovery done for science:— It has discovered Life. Life as a mode of motion is limitless. From simple protoplasmic cell, it manifests through growth. Growth is but the play of these forces in constant change. Life is not change; Life is Power and it manifests through change. Could Life remain constant but the billionth part of a second, it would be annihilated. Eternal motion means eternal change.

Life is a constant stream of power flowing into expression in millions of forms, but all from the One Source. It builds its organism for manifestation by transformation of itself, just as electricity is changed to light by the conservation of force. Light is not electricity. Light is Light, whether from sun, combustion, or electricity. So when thought manifests, it is not Life, but thought. Life is limitless, indestructible, convertible into thought. It is first converted into feeling. This conversion is accomplished by means of the senses. In this word * 'senses, "we have the key to a further analysis of Life's changes.

Sensation is the first change in the transformations of Human Life. Before we felt, we were not individuals. We were only potential power in the One. Feeling is the first step toward individuality. Potentials of Infinity are we still. It will take all eternity to manifest all these possibilities. We are manifesting and, because we are manifesting, we are. By virtue of this recognition of our own existence, we are individuals. Should the Ego ever cease to feel, it would cease to be an Ego. It would become only a possibility in Infinity. Individuality begins with feeling. With feeling, consciousness begins. Individuality becomes perfected with Self-consciousness. When the individual can say, "I am," he has attained perfection as an individual, and has won immortality. Consciousness is only the recognition by the Ego of that which is not itself. This recognition comes from contact with some other force. The Ego responds. It thus knows itself. From sensation come the special senses. These are only varieties of feeling. Feeling is the motion the Ego sends out. Thus we rightly say: an e-motion—an out-motion.

As Life is limitless, so is emotion. The most powerful emotion, we call Love. From emotion, by conservation, comes Thought. Life is thus changed in form, but not in potential. Thought, then, is as limitless as is Life and Emotion. Thought is Life manifest through the cerebrum. Love is Life manifest through all the rest of the nervous system. Thus again do we find Thought as Power. How great the error to call thoughts "things." They are not things, but thought creates things. Things are made out of thought, as one form of power, in union, or combination, with some other form or forms of power. Electricity is not a thing. It is power. When it is in resistance with some other form of power, then we call the resultant things. A thunderbolt is a thing, but it is electricity, plus the resistance and attraction of other forces. No thing is ever formed from one form of force alone. Thought enters into combination with other forms of force and builds body; then, through hands, it builds whatever it wills. It is silently building, in union with silent forces, still other things as yet unrecognized. Thus Life and Thought are no longer unknown forces. As we know electricity, we know them. We will learn to use thought in carrying out our desires, as we now use electricity and chemical force in telegraph and cannon to carry out our purposes in other fields of activity.

Thought is Love transformed. Like Thought and Life, Love is limitless. It is the e-motion of the Ego. There is but one possible out-motion, therefore Love is the only possible emotion. As it is not Life and death, but more or less Life, so it is not Love and hate, but more or less Love. Love is the Master Passion. We are in the habit of so naming only those states of intense passion, but this is naming only a degree, and not the emotion. The one motion from the Soul is directed and controlled by different thoughts. It is the thought accompaniment that differs and is named, and not the emotion. There is one Love. Wherever is the most perfect manifestation of the Indwelling God, there is the most perfect manifestation of Love. Conversely, where there is the most perfect manifestation of Love, there is the most perfect manifestation of Life. For Life and Love are one. Love is only Life in expression. Let Life manifest in Love, and there is health. People are sick and die because they do not love enough. The streets are filled with dead and dying persons, dying because they will not let Life flow through them into expression. Repression is death. Were it not for Love, there would be no reproduction of the species. But for Love, no daily reproduction of the body. Love is the measure of life. Corollary:—To be in health and enjoy life, we must be loving. Whenever we give any lesser degree of Love than normal, then cells created by the larger degrees die. This decay causes poison and disease is the result. Cure:—More Love. Here, in a nutshell, is the whole of mental science. Here, in the same shell, is the whole of Professor Elmer Gates' chemical discovery regarding the effects of emotions upon health. Have no ill-feelings, no ill-thoughts, would you have health. Be happy and you will be healthy. It is happiness that creates health. The rule of science is that of Jesus: "Love the Lord (within) with all thy heart, soul and mind. Love thy neighbor as thyself." Hereon hang all the mental and physical sciences. But when Love passes through the brain it becomes thought. Thought is limitless. Life and Thought are one. To think is to live. Only as we think, we live. The measure of our thought is the measure of our life. The thinker is a healthful person. But do not confound the thinker with the reasoner. Thinking is the spontaneous action of the mind. It is Life in activity. It is spiritual activity. Reasoning is mere intellectual activity. It is not thinking. It is arranging Thoughts that are dead; they have an objective value, but are spiritually dead. Reason is for the objective life. The Soul knows. It perceives Truth. The intellect applies Truth thus perceived to the needs of the objective life. But to try to live by reason is like man trying to live off of stones for bread. Man does not live by material food, but by every thought that cometh from the Sub-conscious (The Inner God) into the conscious life.

Love and Thought, by the conversion of energy, are only transformed Life. Therefore, to think, and to love, is the all of Life.

When the Human Soul came to say, "I think and I feel," then, because it had power to decide upon its manifestations and to choose pleasure from pain, it became Self-conscious. Through this choice, it became self-creative. It therefore cannot die. Every act of self-consciousness is an act of re-creation. It may change its environment; may, through this Law of Conservation, change the manner of manifestation, but "I" must henceforth ever be "I," because it must ever know that it is not something else. Thus has Telepathy solved the problem of immortality, solved it by the same law that has solved the indestructibility of force. The greatest of all discoveries has demonstrated the necessity of immortality, through the transformation of unconscious, undifferentiated, force, into differentiated and conscious forms of force, and these again into individualized and self-conscious forms. From Motion, Self-conscious motion has been evolved, and the purpose of the Absolute is accomplished. Henceforth with this Self-conscious form which we call Ego, the Absolute has no place as master. Life is subject to the Self-conscious One—MAN. The steps of this evolution are easily traced in the slower vibrations we call matter by biology. Here we have traced them in the higher vibrations of spirit. The missing links in the chain of evidence, that Prof. Dolbear says are wanting, are found.

If it could be shown that Life itself and the mind of man were in some way associated with atoms of some sort * * * the hopes and longings, cherished by mankind, for a continuous existence would give way to convictions as strong as one has in any physical phenomena.— Prof. E. A. Dolbear, in "Matter, Ether, and Motion."

5
VIBRATIONS

The Soul is a harp, I remember,

Where vibrating cords are of Consciousness strung,

And Cosmos forever is harper,

Who strolled down the ages measured by sun

With songs of the mighty Becoming. —Prof. W.J. Powell, in "The Monist."

It nettles one that Truth should be so simple.— Goethe.

There is no speech; there are no words; their voice is not heard; but their melody extendeth through all the world.— Lesser's translation of the Psalms.

The language of tone is the language of the spheres; it is the language of the universal world; it is the language of the angels.— Dr. C. W. Emerson.

The whole fabric of human thought and human emotion is built up of likeness and unlikeness just as much as the material world, in all its beauty, is built up out of undulations among invisible molecules.—; John Fiske, in "Through Nature to God." The atoms of the indifferent molecules are held together with varying degrees of tightness—they are tuned, as it were, to notes of different pitch.— Prof. Tyndall.

Thirty-two vibrations per second equal the lowest tone ear can catch; 32,768 vibrations the highest. * * * The vibrations of the red ray are 450 thousand millions per second; those of the violet are 750 thousand millions per second.— Prof. Crooks. The lowest tone perceived by the human ear is a vibration of 24 per second; the highest is 4,700 per second. The lowest note of the piano is 24 per second, too low to be perceived as tone. The highest key is 3,500. Highest on the piccolo is 5,700. Highest pitch of man's voice.is 64; of woman's, 1,044. --Sydney Lanier.

From the extreme red to the extreme violet, between which are embraced all the colors visible to the human eye, the rapidity of vibrations steadily increases, the length of the other waves produced by these vibrations diminishing in the same proportions. I say, "Visible to the human eye," because there may be eyes capable of receiving visual impressions that do not affect ours. There is a vast store of rays, or more correctly waves, beyond the red, and also beyond the violet, which are incompetent to excite our vision; so that, could the whole length of the spectrum, visible and invisible, be seen by the same eye, its length would be vastly augmented.— Prof. Tyndall, in "The New Fragments."

Particles in vibration strike our nerve points in one way and we see light, or color; in another way and we feel heat. Our nerves and brains transmute the motions into forms of sensation. The brain is the translator of motion into images; of sensation into ideas. There is no reason why there should be any limit to the modes of molecular or etherial motion; but our senses, as we call our translators, are but few in number, hence we recognize but few of them.— Peter C. Austin, Ph. D. P. C. S., in Christian Register.

Lord Kelvin, the greatest physicist in the world, has this year come out with a paper which casts a doubt on the prevailing molecular and ether theories. He thinks there is no definite limit to the universe. He says that the dynamic theory which asserts that light and heat are modes of motion, is at present obscured by two clouds.— Prof. John Towbridge, of Harvard University, in San Francisco Examiner.

Since, through Telepathy, thought is demonstrated to be a mode of motion, it follows that whatever we have found to be true of one mode, must be true of all modes, for these modes are only different rates of speed; or, what is the same thing, are of different pitch. Thought is subject to the same laws, to the same regularity, to the same methods of control, and the same methods of study, as are light and sound. Of these two modes of motion, we know the most. Music is the most perfect of the methods we have of studying motion. Sound is slow enough to measure. It can easily be handled by the human will.

Through the study of light and tone, we find that vibrations pass through octaves. There is a regularity and a system, and that order can be understood and followed in composition. He who follows that order, wins by touching the human Soul. When the right combinations are made, the Soul is touched; that is, it vibrates in response. Sympathetic vibration is established. Here we have the key to the practice of Mental Healing; to the power of the orator; to the power of song, cantata, picture, statue, storm, fire, and whatever in the external starts a vibration, an emotion, within.

Thought being a form of force, it passes in vibrations or, in better terms, in undulatory waves from brain to brain. Feeling being also a mode of motion, it passes in similar waves from soul to soul. The difference in the two is similar to the difference between sound and light. Both are ONE in origin, but differ in speed. Thus Emotion and Thought differ. The merely mental healer cures by the force of thought, which awakens sympathetic vibration in the brain of the patient, just as striking C in one octave on the piano causes the C in the other octaves to vibrate, or as the violin on the table vibrates when certain cords are played upon the piano. But the spiritual healer cures by awakening the same sympathetic vibration in the Soul, through love. When the love nature is awakened and Thought, by Suggestion, directs it, then is the healing power, strongest. This can be a fact only in those most highly developed spiritually. In these it is limitless in its power for good. It is typified in Jesus, who spent his whole life in doing good; loving so much, that those who came into His presence were healed. This development is possible to all. We have only to raise the pitch of our radiations from those we now have to those of a higher octave. Love will develop this. If we Love enough, we shall not only be whole ourselves but will be wholesome to all who meet us,—to all of whom we think.

As the vibrations of electricity pass where sound will not, so will thought go where electricity will not, and love will go where thought will not. Sound-waves will not pass long distances over the wire. Electricity will. So man loads the electric-wave with a sound-wave of his choice, and electricity, which was ready to go that way, carries it. Thought and Love work together in the same ways. Love goes, but it must carry the Thought-wave to produce the conscious and the chosen effect. Love alone would never cure without a thought of health accompanying it. It would intensify the activity of the soul in the way it was going. Love is help in the way of power, but it is not directive. Thought—the will of the conscious man—must come in to give direction. Suggestion must be that the chosen activity can be. Otherwise there will be activity, without self-direction. The Force that directs individual expression is Thought. The Force that is directed is Love. The time will come when, through the demonstrations of Telepathy and the study of Suggestion, man will study Thought and Love, as he now studies light and sound. He will formulate his knowledge of these into science and develop an Art of Thinking and Loving. The promise and the prophecy of this is herein the present schools of Mental Science, and in the fast developing Art of Suggestion.

Thus do the phenomena of Telepathy contain within them more for the good of the race, contain more promise for the future of man than all the previous facts he has gathered. Thus is it that when man demonstrated Thought to be a form of Force, to be a mode of motion, he made his Greatest Discovery.

All that we know of Vibration is true of Thought and Love as forms of Vibration. As other forms of motion have been studied, so can these two, which we now throw into the category of force, be studied. As all lesser forces are less only -when compared with some other forms of lower pitch, and as all lesser forms are subject to the greater, it follows logically and scientifically that all other forms of force are subject to the greatest form, Thought. They will obey human will. Thus is Thought master of all the other forms of the One Universal Energy. Love and Thought being ONE in Man, it follows that Love is the only manifestation of the Absolute. Thought is the Individual expression; Love, the Absolute expression. The design of evolution being to bring the Individual into supremacy, to bring Man into "the Kingdom," it follows that Love, which is the highest mode of motion in the ONE, should thus be subject to the only form of individual, self-directed motion, Thought. Love must be thought-directed. In his Thought, each man differs from all other men. His individual stamp is placed upon his perception of Absolute Truth. But Love is in each individual, one and the same. Thus does Individuality consist only in the pitch, or in the octave of thought in which each individual moves. As these octaves are limitless and as there is no limit to the possible range of pitch, it follows that there is no limit to the variety of Human Life. ONE in origin, ONE in substance, ONE in possibility, ONE in the Absolute Truth, we are Individuals only in the sphere of Thought. Only to the degree that a person thinks for himself does he attain Individuality. To Think is to be an Individual. To Love is to Live. Love is the primal energy; Thought is the Human. Thought can raise or lower the pitch of life. Love can keep life in the animal scale, or octave, where man started, or it can raise it daily in pitch toward the Ideal Man, as typified in Jesus and other seers. Through Telepathy, this is demonstrated. It demonstrates that each person has the power, by his thought, to depress or raise the dominant note of his life; that each person can raise or lower the pitch of his expression; that he can control himself in all his being, thus becoming self-controlled.

The possibilities of this Discovery cannot as yet be dreamed, but that it is the Greatest of all human discoveries, the century will demonstrate. Thought -will yet control, where now we use the lesser forces. Nature's finer forces will need no crude machinery; will need no dynamos, no locomotives, no wires. The only dynamo is the Human Soul; its wires and tracks will be Thoughts. But the material world will be the playground of the Conscious Life in Man, and he, because he is "Conscious Law," be "King of Kings."

6

THE VICTORY OVER DEATHS

LEVITATION, MATERIALIZATION, AND DE-MATERIALIZATION

The final enthronement of man over all material things and ·conditions, is the very end or purpose of creation, or of the culmination of life in this world.— Dr. J. H. Dewey, in "The New Age Gospel."

Thou hast made him a little lower than thyself and hast crowned him with glory and honor; thou madest him to have dominion over the works of thy hands; thou hast put all things under his feet.— Psalmist.

This fact (Telepathy) has a more tremendous import than any discovery of the age.— Shelton, in Christian. This new science (Telepathy) is yet in its formative stage, but in its possible applications in the realm of psychology and mental development, it promises to vastly transcend in its emancipating and revolutionizing results, even those of electrical science in the realm of physics.—Dr. Dewey, in Christian. The movements of heavy objects without any possible contact, by Slade, was of common occurrence.— Prof. Zollner, in "Transcendental Physics."

Slade laid a book and a bit of pencil on the slate. * * * The book vanished and, after having been looked for everywhere, it fell several times from the ceiling.— Baron Hellenbach, in "Letter in Transcendental Physics"

She at times saw him (D. D. Home) while he was reading, suspended in the air some 3 or 4 feet over the chair in which he had been sitting.— Bulwer Lytton, in "All the Year Round." On one occasion, when a number of friends were present, Home desired the windows to be opened and he floated out of one and into another, 70 feet above the ground.—Report by Lord Lindsey of a séance at Lord Amberley's castle. The vase was a large one of stone, holding some six "gallons of water, yet as the Fakeer's knotted staff was pointed toward it, it began to slide along the court, reached the open glass doors which divided the apartment * * * There it paused, then, as if reflection had ensued, it slowly floated up a foot from the ground, came in through the glass doors, then gently subsided to the ground and still slid on, until it stopped at the Fakeer's feet.—"Art Magic."

If such things (thought transference and movements of physical bodies without physical contact) are, they are of more importance to philosophy than the whole body of physical knowledge we now have, and of vast importance to humanity.— Prof. A. E. Dolbear, in "Matter, Ether and Motion."

I predict that, when once he has found the way, he will have no use for all the cumbrous machinery called science, nor for much of the present mechanical or motive power. Occult manifestations of the One Power will do all that is now done, and more, with less labor, cost or friction, than is possible even with liquid air. "Chalk marks don't draw cars," once said a railroad man. But we are much nearer that time when some manifestation of force less tangible than chalk marks will draw cars than was the possibility of lightning drawing them when Franklin drew it from the clouds.— Henry Harrison Brown, in "How to Control Fate through Suggestion."

The laws of the Conservation of energy, evolution, etc., which express the Unity of Nature, are at present dead laws and statements, being merely intellectual; but when man comes to feel, as a distinct sensation, his continuity with external objects and his absolute inward unity with all grades of creatures,— man, animals, plants, etc.,—Nature One, namely Self—then those laws, or facts, will have their right and everlasting place in his cosmos, the outer or intellectual form will drop off, but the facts themselves—the feelings—will be found to be eternal. — Edward Carpenter, in "Modern Science."

Thought is Power! Where is the limit to Power? What is the limit to Power? When these questions are answered, the limit to Thought is found. Power in every manifestation is limitless. Limitation is in the form of manifestation; in Power, never. All is Motion! One Energy! One Motion! One Power! One God! These affirmations are synonymous. Manifestations differ: Cause is One. * 'Differences of administration, but the same Lord," said Paul, with rare insight. "Diversities of operation, but it is the same God," he says again. Again he says, showing that the words had to him the same variety of meaning that we give to Energy, Motion, and Spirit: "All these worketh that one and selfsame Spirit." It has taken two thousand years for man to attain the scientific perception of the fact which Paul perceived intuitively. The discovery of the Law of Conservation of Force enabled man, sixty years ago, to say: "All Energy is One." Man's Greatest Discovery enables him now to say: Thought is a form of Energy! The Universe is one Substance, whose manifestation is Motion.

"One God, one Law, one Element,

And one divine, far off event,

Toward which the whole creation moves,"

says a later poet than Paul, from the same intuition.

What is the limit of Power?

The limit of wind, wave, water, steam, electric power? What is the limit of light, magnetism, X-ray, heat, and gravity? They are limitless.

By the use of musical tones, Keely raised a power he could not control. It destroyed his every machine, softening Bessemer steel to the consistency of putty. He no more knew the Power he had evoked, than did Franklin know that which he drew from the cloud to make chips and straws dance between his key and the ground. Where is the limit to Electricity? There is none. What is the limit to its application? Human ignorance! All limitations to Power in any direction are those imposed by man. Nature in one form of motion is as limitless as in any other. Behind each manifestation of Power lies Infinity. Deep and enduring as the glacial marks on the granite ledge, let this truth be etched upon your intellect, then you will have no trouble with my thought. All is One and that One is Omnipresent; not omnipresent in any one manifestation of Power, but in all. The possibility of Infinity lies behind every manifestation. There is no limit to Ever-present Power.

Beyond all dream of man, is the possibility of the One. As sand-grain to a world, is any dream of achievement compared to the Possible. Beyond the possibilities which man has found in the lower pitched vibrations, lie those which he now dimly sees in the vibrations of Thought and Love. To know Power, to apply Power is the whole possible endeavor of man. From cave to "White City," he has only learned how to apply Power. What Power can do, he can do, for he is Power! Until now, he has sought and used Power outside himself. Now, through his Greatest Discovery,— Thought is Power! Love is Power! Life is Power!—

he realizes that the soul is only a CENTER OF POWER IN POWER. He has within himself all Power. Thus Man has, whenever he will take it, Dominion over all other manifestations of Power. Man has just awakened to a knowledge of his place in Unity. He is entering his "kingdom." Where Law heretofore ruled him, he will now, as Conscious Law, rule Law, and thus BE Law. O, the grandeur, beauty, glory, and the Almightiness of this Discovery! Lift up your heads, ye eternal gates and the king of glory shall come in! Who is this king of glory? The Lord strong and mighty! But that Lord is Man, coming to consciousness of his Power.

Among the possibilities that lie within the Power of Thought are those already mentioned and others hinted at, in the excerpts that introduce this essay. Knowledge is but the recognition of Power. Classified knowledge is Science. Science applied is Art. There is as yet no Science of Thought, and but very little knowledge of it. The Art of Thinking is almost unknown. It is the glory of the new century that it starts with the glimmerings of the Light which will yet illumine all mankind. That will make Illuminati of every one. That this Light is now unknown, "rejected of men," was to be expected. That many who have seen this Star in the West are blinded by its Light, is necessary to their evolution. But in the movements called "Spiritualism," Christian Science," " Divine Science," " Mental Science," there is born today the Savior that was to come. Christ in Its second coming is here! The Advent already IS. Light has broken through the vestments of mortality and Immortality has come to light in the discovery of Thought as Power. The Science of Thought has begun. The Art of Thinking is at hand. Man is learning How to think and What to think. When he thinks as he can and will think, there will be no sickness, disease, poverty, accident, suffering, or want. This is as scientific a prophecy as was ever made in a chemical laboratory. "When I know how to harness steam," said Watt. When any one knows how to harness thought to his desire, then will he not only master all environment, but he will fulfill the prophecy of Paul: "The last enemy to be destroyed is Death." Bodies are Thought-builded. They are Thought-destroyed. What Thought does unconsciously under Law, Thought can do consciously under Law. Thought under Law builds diseased bodies. Thought under Conscious Law will build imperishable bodies. Thought under Law destroys bodies. Thought under Conscious Law will regenerate bodies, will purify them, will refine them, will lift them in their pitch until hands that feel only, and eyes that see only, on the plane of the senses, will also see and feel, at will, bodies that are still here but unseen. The bodies in which men live, when made under Conscious Law will be made and unmade at pleasure, as the possessor shall raise or lower them in pitch, just as the musician changes the pitch of his instrument. This Jesus did. "I -will lay down my life and I will take it up again," he said. He laid his body in the tomb. He took it up again. He passed through closed doors at will. He ascended in the scale of vibrations until he "passed out of sight" of the gazers, but is here still. This is within the Power of Thought. All can and all will do this when they THINK ARIGHT.

Some of the possibilities of Thought are shown in the transference of messages from mind to mind, the transference of pictures by Clairvoyance or of individuality by Psychometry. When I hold the letter of an absent person, a stranger, and once come into sympathetic vibration with him, I become him for the time being. I feel as he feels, I think as he thinks, I act as he acts, for I LET his thought act through me and I become transformed for the time being into his image. Mental Healing, which is only Thought and Love transference, is a fact, testified to by thousands. Healing by Suggestion is testified to by other thousands; Magnetic Healing, by millions. Success in every walk of life, born from Right Thinking, is testified to by thousands more. Success by dollars, books and arms is giving -way to Success by Thought alone.

Horse and lion tamer and serpent charmer succeed by the Power of Thought alone. Flora Paris Howard tells in her book, "Idols Dethroned," of clearing a fruit garden of insects by concentrating thought upon them. Mr. Boucher, whose article appears in the "Addenda" to this book, controls the rattlesnake on the prairie by thinking to it. Many persons tell me of gaining in this way immunity from flies, fleas and mosquitoes. Why not? As the Mississippi carries driftwood, so -will the strong radiations from an individual as a center of Power carry away all undesirable things, from bacillus to man.

Facts are easily found by him who seeks them, that testify to the Power of Thought to move bodies without physical contact. Some things seem moved by persons who are in bodies we do not see. Wherever they are, they are human still. They can only use Power that is open to all. When these facts of Telepathy and Levitation are known, the observer can well say, with Professor Dolbear of Tufft's College, that they mean more for the future of mankind than the whole body of phenomena with which science at present deals. Soon will scientists see that all present knowledge is primary and has its value only as the first rung in the ladder leading from the cave of matter to the plain of Motion, from the darkness of body to the sunlight of Spirit.

As Power is unlimited, and as manifestations differ only in the pitch of vibrations, we may learn to so raise the pitch in which we manifest that we may become invisible to those who can manifest only upon the Lower-Octaves-of-Humanity. That this is possible, that it is scientific, note what Art is already doing. The solid iron becomes liquid when man, by applying heat, raises its pitch. Applying still more heat, it is so raised in its vibrations that it passes from sight. But it is not destroyed. It still IS.

The Human Intellect cannot yet trace it, but it exists as something in higher octaves. Why may it not be the foundation upon which man, in his higher octaves, may stand? When I go into a chemical laboratory, if I do not become positive to the atmosphere, I see that whole interior of the room as a transparent, irridescent solid. It is as real to me as is the spectrum the Professor throws from the prism. He sees but the spectrum. I see both the spectrum and the vibrations that are above the range of the spectrum. Because I so see, the professor thinks me "a little off," if he does not say something more strongly indicative of his belief in my insanity. Apply this fact logically. Here is the demonstration of the claims so many make for physical immortality. The question is not, Will Mrs. Eddy or Mrs. Wilmans live forever without passing the change we call death? The question is, Is death a necessity?

They are teaching Truth. They may fail to demonstrate, but that failure will only be the failure of those who failed -where Marconi succeeded. If others had not tried and failed, he would never have succeeded. So, sometime it will be demonstrated that Death is an unnecessary procedure on the part of any person; then the Ego will pass to the higher vibrations without it. As iron is lifted, by the intensifying of its vibrations, from solid to gaseous, so will man lift himself. He is lifted now by sudden transition, by LAW. He will lift himself as Conscious Law, gradually. By Law he now goes through Death to other octaves of life by chemical action. By Conscious Law he will go without Death, by Thought action. While he located Life, Cause and God outside himself, he was subject to the Unconscious Law that controlled the without. When he locates Cause and God, as he does Life, within himself, then will he BE law. Since he is "Spirit conscious of itself," since he says, "I AM!" he must become Conscious Law and, as such, he passes at will up and down the scale of vibrations.

All who once had these coarse bodies we call mortal, are now somewhere on the infinite scale of vibrations. They are bodies still. They who made themselves Light before the change, are now centers of Light; are not in bodies, but are bodies of Light. Those who did not so develop while in these mortal bodies, are now centers of less radiation, and are bodies of the grays, merging into the blacks, until at last they, who lived most carnally, are in blackness, lost even to clairvoyant vision. The only difference between the Caffir Negro and the saintly mother is the place each occupies in the infinite scale of radiations. Each person is "sensible" to us if he is within the limit of our perception. If he is without the limit of our recognition of vibrations, he does not exist for us. All the difference between the caveman and the scientist who finds his bones, is the pitch of the radiations that come from each as a center of power. The modern scientist sees and knows more than he knew who left the Neanderthall skull. It would have been natural for the cave-dweller to deny the knowledge of Darwin, but it is insanity for the Darwins of today to deny the phenomena of thought as presented by Mental Science. They who will not accept these facts are mental cave-dwellers. They are living in matter—are dwelling in the cave of the body. They will seem to the reader of this book in the year 2000 as the Mound Builders seem to us.

The range of vibration is limitless. Evolution is but the passing from octave to octave of Life—God —and making It, or Him, manifest to sense. By Right Thinking, we may pass thus to immortality as easily as we have passed from post horse to electric motor.

This possibility has been prophesied by seer and metaphysician. But it is the claim of the author that this is the first time that the prophecy of Jesus and Paul has been scientifically demonstrated. No scientific demonstration was possible until thought had been demonstrated as a Mode of Motion. That once determined, all the rest follows with the certainty that invention followed the discovery of the Law of Conservation. By right thinking, we may develop our sight so that -we can see beyond the range of telescope. In the same way, we may learn to live above the plane of the senses.

Mrs. Eddy, Mrs. Wilmans, T. J. Shelton and others have seen this from intuition and have verified it from metaphysics. Their vision is true. These essays upon "Man's Greatest Discovery" is the first attempt to bring Immortality without death into harmony with physical science, and to make Thinking, Living, and Immortality parts of a Universal Science, whose primary chapter is Physics, and the last is Soul.

ALL those who are today believing and teaching "The Conquest of Death" are Johns in the wilderness of materiality, crying: "Repent! turn in your thought, and live above the sense life, and you shall never die. Think, 'Live forever' and you will live forever!"

This is no new thought to me. By intuition, I saw it in 1870. I began to lecture in 1873 upon "The Victory over Death," in which I prophesied death would be no more. It was then only a logical conclusion. For these thirty years, I have been seeking and waiting for the scientific evidence. Not till the writing of these essays did I find it. In doing so, I have found it for all humanity. The seer comes first, with his vision; the philosopher next, with his reason; the scientist last, with his Law. In these essays is given the Law. They are more important to humanity than any ever before given the press. I know this is an extraordinary claim. But it is the importance of the Truth presented and not the man who writes, nor the way in which they are given. These essays are a center of Thought Vibrations that will shed Light when I am forgotten. I am the instrument for Truth.

I wish no credit for them—they wrote themselves. They have opened to me a new world. They have lifted me into the seventh heaven with Paul. I KNOW them truth. That is enough. This is the first time I have thrust my personality upon my readers. As evidence as to the instrument through whose hand Truth wrote "Man's Greatest Discovery," this must, for future generations, go on the record. So let it be!

"Man's Greatest Discovery," Telepathy, banished death from the world. It fulfills the promises of the Ages. It opens the door for the new century to usher in the Millennium. * 'Death is swallowed up in Victory." But greater than this is the prophecy of Human Power given us by the Greatest of Seers. His matchless line, that is at once perfect poetry and perfect science, that is religion and fact, shall close this series of essays, written from the Illuminated I AM, and for the generations that are capable of hearing the Word,

"And Conscious Law is King of kings."

A Successful Experiment in Levitation.

I requested a warm personal friend and an ex-pupil -who possessed a power of concentration I have never seen surpassed, one who in his youth became a most successful operator in the Art of Suggestion, and who is now a most successful healer, to write for NOW an account of an experiment which he once related to me. He has kindly done so. It comes as a demonstration of the truth in "Man's Greatest Discovery." Here is his letter:

ABILENE, KAN.

Dear Mr. Brown:

You ask me to relate the experiment in Suggestion in which I caused a subject to float. It was during the year of the wonderful experiments in Hypnotism and Occult Forces that attracted the attention of my friends and the public—1896. Having spent much time and study upon the Science of Hypnotism and the Art of Healing, my principle-; teachers being Prof. A. W. Connett and Henry Harrison Brown, I attained quite a notoriety by my public work. Among the many experiments that seemed to border on the miraculous, and yet are only a demonstration of the power of the mind over the matter, were some that cause us to believe that someday we shall counteract gravitation by mental concentration. My experiment was as follows:—

My subject was a physically strong gentleman, weighing about one hundred and fifty pounds He had been with me a number of years and I had experimented with him from my first lessons. He was a perfect sensitive. Having never failed in any experiment, and believing that all things are possible to him who knows the law, I decided to try to counteract the action of gravity, had him lie on his back upon a carpeted floor. I determined that I would raise him from the floor without any physical aid. I believed this possible from the fact that arms and limbs could be raised by my simply making passes over them and willing them to move.

I then placed him in a cataleptic condition, causing his muscles to become perfectly rigid. At the same time, I suggested to him that he would be raised from the floor simply by my Suggestion. I made passes from his head to his feet, as if I was charging his body with my magnetic force, all the while orally Suggesting, and concentrating my own mind on this thought: "Now you are in a perfectly susceptible condition and will receive every word I give you. You cannot hear nor think of anything but what I allow you to think. My thoughts are your thoughts and my will is your Law. Your body is becoming lighter. It is losing weight. As I charge it with my magnetism, I take away all resisting force and your body becomes lighter than a feather. The least wind will blow you away. Now you are getting lighter, lighter, lighter, and you soon will float. You are now gradually rising; you are floating, floating. You are floating."

As I gave the last suggestions, after making the long passes from head to feet, I placed my hands over his breast and raised them as if to raise him with them. As I did so, his body lifted clear from the floor with the exception of his feet. I passed my hand along under him until I reached his feet, so that 1 know his body was several inches from the floor. It was thus suspended for at least one minute, then it gradually settled down. He relaxed and awoke.

The experiment produced a peculiar effect upon the subject. For several days afterwards he said that he felt as if he was walking in the air and was light-headed. He refused to experiment farther.

I firmly believe that, with repeated trials, his body could have been made to float. Yours for Love and Truth,

OTIS L. BOUCHER, D. M.

Verifications of the Position of the Author,

In the thought of this Discovery, attention is called to "Mack, the Boy Wonder," and his feats of overcoming gravity. The editor of the Magazine of Mysteries says: "We have closely questioned him as to the cause of his strange power. 'Years of steadfast concentration,' was his reply."

Dr. L. Miller of Duluth, Minn., sends an interesting letter. He says:

The articles upon "Man's Greatest Discovery" and "The Missing Link," are bringing together-what should have long ago been summarized, for Thought is Omnipotent Creator. I am sure that a great truth is connected with breathing the "Breath of Life" with simultaneous physical effort. Mack, the Boy Wonder, was in my office yesterday. He claims that he does not breathe deeply to perform levitation of the body while some one lifts it from the waist, but he simply concentrates his mind and his body is easily lifted up to the height of the lifter's head. On the other hand, when he concentrates against being lifted, a man has great trouble in raising him from the floor. Asked for an explanation of this gift, he says it is psychic; and indeed this seems the only shadow of explanation. He says he is nervous, and thinks his power may in time leave him. He can also increase his weight on the scales.

So writes Dr. Miller. "Psychic" names, but explains nothing. What do you mean by it? How do you do it? What is the Power? We are after this. I claim it is THOUGHT. Methods may be numbered by millions. It is "concentration," but concentration of what? Concentration of some Power? What is the power?

As to the nervousness, that would come from the excitement and from the life led as an exhibitor; also from ignorance in using the Power, not to manifest health and intelligence, but simply to show what he can do. When he shall think of Use and Health with his exhibitions, he will neither be nervous nor fear loss. If there be loss, it will be because he fears it.

From another source, I find this statement about Mack:

On the scales he can vary his weight (123 lbs.), tipping the scales at 800 or at 98. In the Chicago American office, he defied the strongest person there to lift him from the ground, and no amount of energy seemed able to raise him.

Scientists have studied him and can give no clear explanation. One great Professor thinks it a form of "nerve resistance." Which is as clear as a fog to obscure but not to reveal. Try THOUGHT, Professors, and declare your theories of gravity false and weight to be merely a sensation that one need not feel when he will not.

Similar reports of the Power of Thought through concentration come to us concerning Viggo Lerche of Alto Pass, Ill. This is the press report of his manifestations:

He used an iron poker, several feet long and quite heavy. Standing it against the wall at an angle of 45 degrees, he seated himself a few feet distant and focused his eyes on the top of the poker. Within a few seconds, it began trembling, then gradually rose to a perpendicular position. After standing a moment, it moved toward him in short jumps.

Mr. Lerche can affect any wood or metal object, such as umbrellas or canes, in the same way. He can be induced to exert his strange mental power only a short time before going to bed, as he says it makes him deathly sick unless he can take refuge in sleep.

While attending a Copenhagen college several years ago, he accidentally discovered his power. He was sitting on the lawn with his face in his hands and his eyes on a small stick at his feet, lamenting a quarrel he had had with a schoolmate, when suddenly he noticed the stick wriggling. Wondering if he had gone crazy, he rubbed his eyes, took his bearings, and again looked at the stick. Again it showed signs of life. Then he realized that he had been endowed with a wonderful gift.

Helen Wilmans says of this in Freedom: Of course I cannot be sure that what is told of Viggo Lerche is true, but from what I know of the power of thought and of the power of the individual to transmit his thought to another person, it would not surprise me to know that the statement is positively true.

It has been noticed that in treating a patient, even though the healer addresses the mind of the patient,—the thinking part of him—that the thought he sends out seems to enter the patient's body first; that it seems to make its impression there even before the patient's brain perceives that the impression has been made.

In lull accord with the position assumed in "Man's Greatest Discovery," that man will use Thought, or Life, as a motive power, is this extract from an article in St. Louis Post-Dispatch:

Dr. Charles Tuckett, a retired St. Louis Doctor, is exhibiting-in his home, at 4563 North Market street, the most extraordinary little railway in the city—a railroad whose motive power is the nervous energy of the human body.

Dr. Tuckett believes a time is coming when science will so confine the energy in the human system that, by grasping a lever, a man may run his automobile with the life force that is in him. To illustrate his discovery of nervous energy as a motive power, Dr. Tuckett has strung a copper wire in his home and has placed upon this a tiny truck. By rubbing his hand on a piece of paper and hanging it on the truck, he can pull the car forward, or back it, across the room by holding his hand a few feet away, the principle being that of the magnet.

Experiments.

From the many reports of experiments, the following reports are selected:— Mrs. M. A. Winans, of Kansas, writes:

I have helped to perform that experiment in September NOW many years ago, but did not realize where the power lay. Four girls could lift a heavy man with ease when properly done. That is, there must be no foolishness nor laughing mixed with it.

C. H. Doty of Juniata, Neb., writes:

When I was a boy, somewhere from 1837 to 1840, we performed the experiment of "blowing each other up." One would lie on his back on a table or counter. Several, say four or eight, would stand on each side of him with one finger extended under him. Then all were to blow a long, steady, continuous breath upon his breast until we felt somewhat lightheaded. Then we raised our fingers and he would come up with us. I would like your explanation.

Here is the explanation: THOUGHT IS POWER. Power can be applied in millions of ways. Onfa, of New Mexico, writes:

A sea captain, at an evening party in San Francisco, gave an illustration of what he termed an "Oriental Trick." He selected six young ladies, then placed himself upon the floor in a rigid condition, and placed the ladies, one at his head, one at feet, and two on each side—one at elbow and knee. They were then commanded to lean over, each placing the index finger of the right hand under the points mentioned. The order was given to breathe in unison and to lift with the finger with the first breath. At first breath the ladies raised the captain level with their heads, and then with the second lifted him above their heads and lowered him to an upright position by first removing the finger from the feet, then from the knees, balancing him for a moment on his elbows ere his feet reached the floor. This story was told me by one of the ladies who took part in the experiment.

I quote from Edward Everett Kale's book, "Lowell and His Friends," page 190, this remarkable reliable case of Telepathy:

The person who was the recipient of the message tells it thus: I spent the night before Commencement on a lounge in Hollis 21. I could not afterwards remember dreaming of anything in particular; but as I woke I heard

"And what they dare to dream of, dare to die for." Rather good sentiment," I said to myself; "it seems appropriate to the day"—then just dawning. And so I dropped off again.

The dinner was spread in the green. "My seat was just about the middle. Mr. Lowell was about under the window of Hollis 21. When he arose he waited until all was quiet before he commenced reading. (It was his masterpiece, "The Harvard Commemoration Ode.") As he came to the words,

"Their higher instincts knew Those love her best,"—

I began to feel, not that I had heard this before, but that something was coming that was familiar.

"Who to themselves are true," went on the reader.

"Hullo!" I said to myself, "I ought to know the next line."

"And what they dare"—

"Yes, but it isn't going to rhyme," and this without distinctly repeating the rest of the line.

But when he observed, "to die for," would not rhyme with "True," Lowell came to his relief by saying:

"And what they dare to dream of, dare to do."

Says Mr. Hale: "So well authenticated a story of sympathy and telepathy seems worth repeating."

THE END.

BOOK FOUR

NEW THOUGHT PRIMER

ORIGIN, HISTORY AND PRINCIPLES OF NEW THOUGHT TO
THE MEMORY AND OMNIPRESENCE OF

All who, by thought, word, or deed, have contributed to the present freedom of Sow.

FOREWORD

I purpose but an outline of the origin, development, principles and purpose of the widespread and ever widening movement comprehended under the term, "New Thought." The term has no definite meaning. It covers a movement at present heterogeneous and embracing many minor fields. Its limits cannot be mapped. Each person is to draw his own lines. In this Primer, I have intended to make the definition as broad as justice and the Principle of Evolution would let me. I have tried to be as impartial as truth, and to look upon every side of the question only as a reporter. The charge of partiality may be brought in my attention to my own position, but here I feel I have the right to be personal and positive.

TRUTH alone is our aim. I have consecrated myself to Truth and my life is now in her service. I can afford to be true only to her, and in love, just to my fellows. The reader will find in this that which will help him to an understanding of this mighty movement and will also find hints that will direct his future study.

Truth is so lovely that the Truth-seeker soon becomes the Truth-lover. I am glad of the privilege of lifting for a moment her veil, knowing that all who see will follow her. In Love and Truth,

Truly your friend,

HENRY HARRISON BROWN

ORIGIN, HISTORY AND PRINCIPLES OF NEW THOUGHT

HEREDITY.

Under the law of Heredity science traces evolution from parent to child and thus finds tendencies, faculties and conditions, that appear in parent, are transmitted to offspring. There is no human condition that is not the child of a preceding one. Variations occur and under the Law of Variation, Nature unfolds. This law of evolution, of continuity, of method, and purpose is a constant one. Ideas also have their heredity. All movements in human thought obey these laws of Heredity and Variation. I purpose to trace in outline the Heredity of the New Thought movement. I will give information sufficient to enable the curious reader to easily fill in additional details. Desiring to deal justly with each form of the movement, I will correct any reported injustice in subsequent editions.

PAST EVOLUTION,

Human progress is the gradual unfoldment of that which is eternally in man. Life in man is germinal; time is the unfolder. Each condition is but a slight change upon some earlier one. Effects are the result of some cause which is but the effect of some anterior cause, which is also the effect of a still more remote cause, so that when one seeks a beginning of any movement he is compelled to answer: "The beginning is in Ultimate Cause." Therefore to trace the beginnings of New Thought we should have to trace the beginnings of history. From earliest historic periods we can trace many of the ideas of this movement. Thought is a wave that flows like those of the ocean from shore to shore. Every age and people is a manifestation of this movement. A wave once started in ocean never stops till it reaches the limit of the ocean, so a thought once started will never stop, for there is no limit to the medium in which it is a wave. That medium is variously called: Energy, Spirit, Soul, God. Truth is one with Ultimate Cause. Truth is ever unfolding. Well says Lowell: —

God sends his teachers unto every age, To every clime, and every race of men, With revelations fitted to their growth And shape of mind, nor gives the realm of Truth Unto the selfish rule of one sole race. Individual perceptions and expressions differ and often some old thought, which is the common possession of the race, is given forth by some earnest soul as a supposed new revelation. The student of comparative religions, finds that all these varying systems are based upon the same conceptions. Max Muller tells us that three ideas form the foundations of all religions, viz: 1st—Sense of some over-ruling Power; 2d—His demands on us, out of which grow systems of worship; 3d—The recognition of human duties, out of -which grow regulations of the conduct of man to man. Jesus announced the same in his condensation of Hebrew Law and Prophets: 1st—Love the Lord, thy God. 2d— With all thy soul, heart and mind. 3d—And love thy neighbor as thyself.

No matter what the religion or philosophical belief, it is based upon these. From the conception of primitive man to the present time, there has been but an evolution of human thought concerning the Power that is. New Thought is but a later conception of this One Power. It is an evolution of that conception into a conscious reality. Soul Culture has made this primitive thought of Power an actuality in daily life by methods of spiritual unfoldment.

ANCIENT IDEAS.

The nations of antiquity, as evidenced by their relics, and notably- by their clay tablets, held many of our present conceptions. Have not these conceptions come down to us with the life they transmitted? The Hindoo Scriptures contain many conceptions of God, Man and Duty that are familiar to us. Did they not come down to us with the stock of Aryan words?

From Hebrew Scriptures and the New Testament we have derived much of present conceptions of Truth. Why have all these conceptions survived? By reason of Nature's law: The Survival of the Fittest. That which nearest expresses absolute Truth, that which most completely satisfies the Soul, is not allowed to pass into oblivion. "Old ideas revised and improved, "could be written above every theologic, scientific, economic, social and artistic creed and above every invention. " Improvements," we call them. They are only enlarged conceptions of the truth that our fathers held. Truth is one. The most any age or race can do is to develop somewhat some phase of Truth by making some distinctive change in the method of expression. Through this Unity of Truth and Unity of Unfoldment, we are connected with all the past and with all mankind. It is thus that the thinker in every age becomes one of the " choir invisible."

THE CHRISTIAN ERA.

Present civilization has been most effected by Greek Ideas as they came to us through the New Testament. It is to Paul that we are indebted for this. He was steeped in the Logos Philosophy of the Greek which he Hebraized, and through the impetus of the early church they have been sent down to us. Jesus marks one of the great eras of unfoldment in the conception of Omnipotence. He placed the emphasis upon Fatherhood and that Fatherhood made Deity, Human. The Love Principle had been but dimly perceived before him. He said " Our Father. 7 ' Prior to this it had been " Heaven-Father." Max Muller tells us that "Heaven-Father" is the term for Omnipotence in every religion. "Heaven-Father" embodies conceptions of Power and Creation; "Our Father," those of Love and Providence.

Jesus also developed the idea of duty into that of brotherhood, and this lifted the worship of Omnipotence from mere external ceremony and manifestations of fear to worship through Love. He applied the Love principle also to human conduct in the "New Commandment" —"That ye love one another." Thus may Jesus rightly be termed the founder of New Thought, as it appears during nineteen centuries of human evolution.

MEDIEVAL THOUGHT.

During the Middle Ages many thinkers arose whose teachings gave birth to what is known as " mysticism," systems that have much in common with the idea of Omnipresence, and the conception of Realization as held by New Thought teachers. Mysticism is a recognition of unity between the Soul and its Divine origin. It is the practical side of the saying of Jesus: "My father and I are one." This phase of thought came into existence at the close of the third century. It developed later into the form one may find in Thomas a' Kempis and Madame Guyon. It is a condition of most ardent piety, and so warm was it at times that Jesus and the church were thought of as one thinks of wife or mistress.

GERMAN PHILOSOPHERS.

The Mysticism of the Middle Ages developed in Germany into a philosophy which changed at that time the current of thought, and moulded the opinions of the present. One who desires to become familiar with these authors are recommended to read Kant, Hegel, Shelling, Fichte, Schopenhauer, and especially Goethe and the poet

Schiller. In these can be found many of the ideas of New Thought teachers.

IDEALISM.

But in the English philosopher Berkeley do we find the greatest resemblance. Christian Science in an imperfect reflection of the Idealism of Berkeley. Berkeley, Locke, Descartes, Spinoza and Leibnitz revived the Idealism of Plato. Zeno, before Plato, fundamentally taught the same. Idealism holds that Ideas are All. The external universe exists only as it is reflected in the mind. Matter is part of that which is not the Ego. According to Fichte this non-Ego is but a creation, or an idea of the mind of the Ego. Hegel finds the only reality in the relation that exists between the Ego and the non-Ego. The speculative truth that lies underneath this philosophy is realized Truth in New Thought. What they intellectual perceived is now a constant reality in the lives of thousands. All interested in tracing Idealism farther can find in any encyclopedia enough to make clear our indebtedness to these philosophers. Rev. F. W. Evans, in his works upon Mental Science, shows, by his quotations, how great was his indebtedness to them, and I here most gladly acknowledge my own philosophic debt to this most lucid, strong, and able of our New Thought teachers.

THE NINETEENTH CENTURY.

I will trace only the last century history of Thought evolution. I have briefly shown how that century was the culmination of all the thought of the past. This new century is the child of the old. New Thought came legitimately from the loins of the Thought with which the nineteenth century and the new nation opened. The new American nation was to a great extent the child of French liberalism. Liberal ideas at the beginning of the Nineteenth Century were permeating every channel of the national life. The national birth but twenty-four years previous had stimulated thought in all directions. In politics, religion, and social life, there was a decided American atmosphere. The discontent with the old had culminated in Thomas Paine's "Age of Reason," a most thought provoking and stimulating book. All who are today emancipated from the rigid theology of that period owe a great debt to him. Political liberty, won in the eighteenth century, opened the way for the intellectual liberty which the nineteenth century won. Now comes the last, and the perfect liberty knocking at the door of the 20th century. This liberty is Spiritual

Liberty, a liberty that belongs to each, as a child of the universe, as a son of the one power; or as John has it, "The liberty of the sons of God." It is for this liberty that New Thought stands.

ABOLITIONISM.

Out of the awakened conscience and intellectual perceptions of Truth that were prevalent at the beginning of the nineteenth century came later the abolition of physical slavery, and with it the emancipation of the masses from the stern and unyielding theology which our fathers left us. Whenever the prophet is needed he comes. He has come. He has had many names. Only a few of these names can I mention. To give them all would be to trace the mental unfoldment and progress of the century. I can only follow our special thought. The history of a nation is the history of its few thinkers.

CHANNING.

William Ellery Channing gave in Baltimore in 1818 his great address, which later caused a split in the Calvinistic churches, dividing them into the Unitarian and Trinitarian.

This movement lifted the theologic thought from that of Justice, which Calvinism emphasized, to that of Love, which Channing emphasizes. "God is Love,"-was his shibboleth. It made as great a change in the popular thought as that which the affirmation, "All is good," makes today.

ELIAS HICKS.

Quakerism had been an important factor during the 18th century and did noble work in preparing the colonies for their liberty. In the 19th century Elias Hicks came, and with his new vision helped on emancipation, and gave opportunity for still other visions that are culminated in the present awakening.

UNIVERSALISM.

John Murray, through his doctrine of Universal Salvation, started another progressive movement in the theological field which, though of importance, was limited, because he held to Revelation, and as Dr. Livermore of Meadville Theological School taught us, "Murray's was not a change in principle from Calvinism. Calvin taught that all were born to be damned, while Murray taught that all are born to be saved." To an age that believed in "Eternal Damnation" Murray was an important reaction, and no student of the history of New Thought can afford to omit his life.

EMERSON.

In 1838 Emerson gave his address before the divinity students of Harvard College. That address marks an era in the intellectual life of America. It did not seem important then, but from the vantage ground of today it is seen as the turning of the wheel that set the ship of progress on a new tack. Emerson was at the center of intellectual culture of the United States, and there started a discussion that is responsible, more than any other factor, for present liberal conditions. He lifted mankind onto the plane with Jesus by declaring that which Jesus was, all men are. This removed the barrier to human aspiration and opened divine expression as a possibility for all men. He did in this the greatest work of any one person in the whole century. In this declaration he made all subsequent growth possible. For this reason I attribute to Emerson, more than to any other source, the credit of the New Thought movement. Two years before this he had written " Nature" in which the Idealism of Berkeley, the mysticism of the middle ages, the obtuse and speculative doctrines of the ancients, were all winnowed, and the pure wheat stored for present sowing. From that time until his death he taught along the lines be therein laid down. His writings are a source to -which can be traced all phases of New Thought. Christian Science is an exaggerated and contorted exposition of the clear and pure thought of Emerson. Would my reader drink at the original fount, I advise him to read Emerson. It matters little where he begins; but if he starts with the essays upon "Self-Reliance" and "Compensation," and "Over Soul," he will drink so deeply that all other authors will seem tame commentaries upon him.

PARKER.

Following Emerson came Theodore Parker, His contribution was the placing of all phenomena under law. As Emerson humanized Jesus, Parker rationalized the miracles. He did for theology what Humboldt did for Philosophy. Said Humboldt: " The Universe is governed by Law." Parker forced the theologians to accept this and placed the so-called Bible Miracles under Natural Law. His sermon upon the " Permanent and the Transient in Christianity" had an effect second only to Emerson's Divinity School address.

LAW OF CONSERVATION AND CORRELATION OF FORCE.

During the last century-, Science and Philosophy made great strides. The most important contribution during the first half was the acceptance of the Law of the Conservation of Force. The Law is: All Force (or Energy) is one; is fixed in quantity, cannot be destroyed; but it can be, and /s, changed from one mode of manifestation to another . Following this, came the Principle of Evolution, for which in its present clear understanding we must thank Spencer and Darwin, though at about the same time (1845) Andrew Jackson Davis independently gave, in Principle, the same in "Nature's Divine Revelations," though he used the term "Progression." Upon this, the Principle of Evolution and the Law of Conservation of Force, rests all future thought progress. In harmony with these, we are beginning a Science of Man as Mind, and developing an art of Mental Healing.

INVENTIONS

There was never a century within the historic period so prolific in invention as the last. Each improved tool, each new machine, each change for the better in ways of living, creates a new environment, and thus, by Suggestion, causes new thoughts and thoughts create the man. The son who uses an improved plow cannot think the same thoughts nor live the same life his father did. Inventions and dis-discoveries created conditions for the present New Thought.

INFLUENCE OF GERMAN THOUGHT.

A great impetus was given to American thought at the beginning of the latter part of the last century by the introduction of German Philosophy. The initiative was taken by Rev. Frederick W. Hedges, who introduced Kant and other German Philosophers. Margaret Fuller brought Goethe to notice of American thinkers, and Emerson caused Carlyle's "Sartor Resartus" to be re-published here. Out of the interest these awakened, arose the "Transcendental Movement" which movement was, in reality, the birth of the present various movements in the liberal thought world, and in Transcendentalism we may properly locate the birth of New Thought.

TRANSCENDENTALISM.

"In the second quarter of the Nineteenth Century, there was a very general feeling of unrest in religious circles. This was particularly observable in the Eastern States. Groups of individuals here and there broke away from former beliefs and associations, in the confidence and purpose of a living faith that rested on a better foundation. It seems hardly possible for the American mind to hold mere opinions without carrying them into practice with all sincerity. These uprisings often took place around the places of learning, but oftener at places remote from centers and among the unlettered, who knew only the Bible and the avocation which they followed." This gave rise to many peculiar religious sects. The only one of which now active is that of the Second Advents. "It was among the cultured men and women, many of whom had been educated at Harvard, that a movement began which represented this unrest and gave it somewhat of form and consistency. Unitarianism had opened the avenues for freedom of thought, and now naturally arose the Transcendentalists with an ideal philosophy which they were to promote as the inspiration and prevailing principle of everyday life. Bright stars were those in the intellectual sky who started the movement. They lighted the way to profounder thought, more conscientious activity, and more general usefulness. The names of Emerson, Alcott, The Channings, Ripley, Margaret Fuller, Frothingham, Thoreau, and their associates, gave to the American public a higher conception of life, its nature and aims. They placed a leaven therein that was destined to continue its work till it transformed the whole mass of American Society. Before this Transcendental movement, America had no literature that was more than local and a copy of foreign models. From this, America derived a literature that was a new creation, indigenous to our soil." Here are some names rightly credited to that movement, as their thought is the transcendental thought: Lowell, Alcott, Thoreau, Margaret Fuller, C. P. Cranch, William Henry Channing, Charles A. Dana, George William Curtis, Theodore Parker, David A. Wasson, John Weiss, T. W. Higginson, Julia Ward Howe, Jones Very, Edna D. Cheney, Frank B. Sanborn, and Horace Greeley. The Transcendental period was the formative period in American thought-life. To it we may trace New Thought.

BROOK FARM

Out of Transcendentalism arose the attempt at community life, known as Brook Farm. Here met great thinkers, and what if the experiment failed for want of financial support? It was, in its scattering, a ripened boll. Its harvest of success has come in the lives of those who today have found in another manner an application of the Truth they held. The reader is referred to the "History of the Brook Farm," by John Thomas Codman, and to C. B. Frothingham's "History of Transcendentalism," for further particulars upon one of the most interesting attempts to actualize the Principal of Brotherhood.

COMMUNITIES.

Whoever would understand thoroughly the sources of present thought, and would trace the evolution of ideas, needs to become more or less familiar with community life in the United States. It is without the province of this essay to detail that history. It covers the Shakers and the Oneida Communists, two of the successful. Many others started and many, judged by the world's business standards, were successful; and all are steps toward more perfect realization of the Principle of Brotherhood. This Principle is now finding expression in Trades Unions, Co-operative Associations, Colonies, Profit Sharing, Fraternal Societies, and Fraternal Insurance Companies. Perceptions of this Principle is also stirring the world tinder the many phases-of New Thought.

UNITARIANISM

Unitarianism, because of its organization, its persistence, its great men, its liberality, and its truth, is the great intellectual fountain from whence has flowed into everyday life the latest thought along all lines of investigation. It is the cultured source that has kept sweet and clean the progress of theological thought. Despite its too coldly intellectual attitude, it has held the religious life of the people poised and harmonious, and kept the church in touch with science and philosophy. It has been the balance wheel in the mental workshop, conserving all that was good and true in all movements, and protecting the national life in the excitement of fads and speculations which arise on the one hand and the advance of skepticism and materialism that threatens on the other.

In Unitarianism, we find the nearest approach on the intellectual side to the present New Thought. The fundamental principle of Unitarianism is the right of private judgment. It has no creed. Each person is expected to teach that which to him is truth. It proclaims the fundamental propositions of Mental Science and Soul Culture in its affirmations of "The Indwelling God" and "Divine Nature of Man." "Man is not a fallen but a rising creature," is one of its favorite maxims. "Upon every thing write, for the service of man," says James Freeman Clark. This denomination is not sectarian. From Channing's time to the present, it has stood for all that is free, beautiful, and serviceable in life. Western Unitarianism proclaims itself for "Freedom, Fellowship, and Character, in religion." There is in Truth no break between the teachers of Mental Science and Unitarianism. Every Unitarian Society intellectually is New-Thought. The two movements differ only in the application of Truth to life. Unitarians follow the old method:—preach and educate. New Thought teaches: Demonstrate by Living. I preached in the Unitarian pulpit, taught on the Spiritualist platform, the same perceptions of Truth I now preach under "Soul Culture," but there is as much difference between my then and my now, as there is between a student who reads his books on astronomy, and never looks at the stars; one who reads chemistry, and never goes to the laboratory; or one who studies mathematics, and never calculates the price of material at so much per pound. It is the difference between knowing one is a Son of God, and being a Son of God. I preached the "Indwelling God," and grew sick and broken down in body. I preached, "The kingdom of heaven is within you," and created within myself the kingdom of disease, pain, worry, anxiety, fear, and heart-hunger. Honest and believing, and I then thought I was faithful. But amid my pain, and on the verge of the grave, suddenly there came in my mind this question: "If God "dwells in you, why are you sick and in pain?" As soon as I could straighten out my affairs, or better, as soon as, through suffering, the Indwelling God straightened them out, I put myself into His hands, and to the only Living God, I said: "Now, God, you dwell in we and I expect you to take care of me. I will take no more thought for my body than I did when I was a babe. You cared for it then; you will care for it now. I thought I knew what my body wanted. I find I do not know how to take care of it. I surrender it to you. I let you have perfect control of my life, because I have perfect faith in you " It took me some time to outgrow old habits of thought. Old doubt and old conditions would come back. But I persevered and gradually my body assumed the conditions of health. "God knows his business," I would say to myself when things seemed to go wrong. In time, I left all things to Him. I have never faltered in this surrender. He became "My Silent Partner!" We are one in all Life's manifestations. He attends to the subconscious; I to the conscious. He attends to the subjective; I to the objective life. All is thus ever well with me. Yet, I have not changed the idea which I had of God while in pulpit or on platform. I have not changed my ideas of man as Spirit. I have simply learned to make practical what I then intellectually held. God is in me "an ever present help." Where once I felt trouble, or pain, or fear, I now know only peace: "For Thou art with me; Thy rod and Thy staff they comfort me." I trust, as the child the parent, the One "in whom I live and have my being." I know that "The Lord is my shepherd, "and I do not want. I cannot want with Him as provider. This position is one which the faithful ones in every religious belief have taken in all ages.

We have different thoughts, but we live the same life. New Thought is the "Old Faith" intellectually applied to daily thought and activity.

NEW THOUGHT.

New Thought is logically carrying into daily life the faith of the church. It is consciously applying Truth which man has unconsciously applied during all his past. Unitarianism has the most nearly approached an understanding of Truth. New Thought is a method of living in the conscious thought of Divinity with the same spirit of faith which consecrated the martyrs of old. All is good. " Though he slave me, yet will I trust in him." " I will fear no evil." These axioms are to us as clearly self-evident truth and as easily applied to daily life as are those of mathematics or chemistry. When the history of the Emancipation of the Soul from fetters of fear, authority, and reason, and its initiation into the pure air of spirit is written, many names on the role of Unitarian teachers will be among those whom posterity will delight to honor as intellectual and noble pioneers, who by thought and life ushered in the day of our Redemption, for that day came through demonstration by living the truth, which they proclaimed. •

FREE RELIGIOUS ASSOCIATIONS.

Between 1865 and 1870 a Free Religious Society was formed in Boston with which many progressive thinkers and scholars of the nation were associated. Emerson was a member. Among the most active members were O. B. Frothingham, Francis Ellingwood Abbott, Edna D.

Cheney, Lucretia Mott, Wm. H. and Celia Burleigh, and others whose names were then power in the intellectual world.

Its organ was The Index, which has, in power and ability, found no superior among liberal papers. As a seed sower, as a movement that made conditions for the present New Thought awakening, this was very important. Its literature teems with thoughts which are now the common property of all progressive men and women. Its limitations lay where the Unitarian, Universalist, Liberal League, and Free Thinkers all are limited; not in thought, but in demonstration. The Mental and Christian Scientists and all other phases of New Thought have added little to the intellectual perceptions which were already the stock of the race and which emanated from multitudes of reformers and reform movements prior to them, but these latter movements have put a soul into the intellectual mummy, and we live what they 7 thought. The twentieth century uses the force previous centuries discovered. We now use Truth as Power, just as the nineteenth century used steam. The Free Religious movement was a spring far up the mountain; its many streams of thought have found the sea of daily life, and are now an important part of the mightiest movement the race has ever experienced. A movement that means the abolition of pain, poverty, disease and death.

RELIGIOUS AWAKENINGS.

The nineteenth century saw many religious awakenings. Many prophets sprang up declaring these were "the last days." Miller-ism was the most important of these. Out of that has come the Second Advent sect. Then came Mormonism. Revivals were frequent, all led by many powerful teachers. Those who proclaimed the "end of the world" felt the oncoming power, that silent growth of Soul which would ultimately break the limitations of sense. They interpreted this feeling according to their intellectual and theological training. Psychometry solves these riddles of feeling. Coming events are realities of Spirit. The sensitive feels them, and must interpret them according to his intelligence, just as Sweedenborg interpreted his visions. Emerson says that Swedenborg "was hampered by theological limitations." Andrew Jackson Davis was free from limitations of education and theology, he had never read a book when he gave the world "Nature, and her Divine Revelations." This freedom preserved Modern Spiritualism from having a "founder." According to education and predeliction of each prophet, have been interpreted the millions of communications from the decarnate and from the sub-conscious. In like manner came visions, inspirations and interpretations of theologians and sectarians during the last century. From the vantage ground of the present we readily see that these awakenings were but a throe in the old order, giving birth to the New. "The Second Coming of Christ," and "The End of the World," are now realities through this application, under the common sense and scientific habits of a developed race, of ancient thought of God in man. Questions that for centuries have disturbed the minds of men concerning their Soul and the future, are now settled scientifically, as have been those concerning the world, man, and his origin. Every religious awakening takes its place as a factor, preparing for this present movement. Each new sect, each new teacher, each new interpretation of the Bible, each new convert in a revival, has helped it on.

SALVATION ARMY*

This denomination was of great help during the last years of the closing century in developing the Spirit of Equality and Brotherhood. Its freedom from the virus of respectability, its spirit of helpfulness, are a protest against the exclusiveness and heartlessness of wealth and culture. It has done much to bring light to the slums of society. The spirit of New Thought is one with theirs.

HIGHER CRITICISM*

While many teachers, authors and editors in various lines of New Thought are woefully ignorant of the results of Higher Criticism, and evince this by their use of, and by new interpretations of, the Bible, the public mind has been prepared for rational use and interpretation, by the emancipation that has come to it through the labor of scholars in unearthing its history. Today more is known of the origin of the books of the Old Testament, and we are better posted on ancient Jewish history than were the Rabbis at the time of Jesus; while in the history of contemporaneous, and still more ancient nations, we are intelligent where they were totally ignorant. Suffice it to say that did the hundreds who are today basing their teachings upon Biblical interpretations, know the real place and origin of the Bible, they would turn their attention to more profitable discussions. The Bible is valuable as literature; valuable as a record of the religious development of a peculiar people; valuable for the inspiration of in its beautiful passages, and as a vehicle through which the aspiring soul may find expression. The Psalms, the Prophets, the Gospels, will live as long as the human heart is human, not because they are special revelations, but because they are common revelation. They are the daily expressions of millions, and will ultimately be the expression of every soul. As Homer, and Shakespeare, as Burns and Whittier, will live wherever they voice a common human need, so lives the winnowed literature of the past. The Bible so lives.

The higher criticism will have conferred its greatest benefit, when those who, under the impetus of an unfolding soul, have thrown off limitations of authority and use the Bible, and all literature as means of expressing the faith of a common humanity, and of one God in that humanity'.

POLITICAL LIBERTY* ABOLITION MOVEMENT.

The growth of Personal Liberty, as manifested in the weakening of sectarian fetters, is also manifest in the breaking of party fetters. When I was a lad Whigs and Democrats were born. For a boy to vote a different ticket from his father and grandfather was to brand him a " turn coat," and often caused him to be disinherited. The Abolition Movement was the first great disintegrating political factor. It virtually broke up the Whig party through the Free Soil movement. Ultimately, out of many fragments of old parties, the Republican party was organized. This liberty of political action was necessary before we could be free today to advocate our principle of Emancipation from all authority and the right to follow the individual conscience. Luther proclaimed freedom of conscience as a principle, but stopped at his limit. Garrison proclaimed it and stopped at his limit. Mrs. Eddy proclaimed it, but limits it to her revelation. But the Soul goes marching on, and now its cry is " Truth for Authority, but no authority for Truth." Its shibboleth: —I AM TRUTH. Every civil, theological, sectarian, social, political fetter that has been broken and was a step on the way to this New Thought affirmation. The various phases of New Thought are other steps toward unified, scientific and practical study and culture of the Soul. Soul Culture comes as the fruit on the tree of intellectual development. Man knows he IS, not has a Soul. As body, intellect, and aesthetic ability have been systematically trained, so this century will see spiritual faculties cultivated. Man, as Soul, will pass beyond disease, poverty, property and death; will learn to live the immortal life here and now. Will never think of any other condition than that which he can enjoy while living in a body as sensible as that he now has. No matter of what vibrations composed, he will not die to possess that body.

ANIMAL MAGNETISM.

Early in the last century there was an increased interest in the discoveries of Mesmer who, during the last quarter pi the preceding century, had found that certain persons could be effected by what he, at first, thought were forces from the magnet, but which later he thought were magnetic forces of the operator. Later investigation has proven the power he and his contemporaries called " Animal Magnetism "to be but the power of Suggestion. All that was included in past investigation under the terms " Mesmerism," "Animal Magnetism," "Magnetic Healing," "ElectroBiology,"'; "Statuvolence," and "Psychology," is now included under the term "Suggestion."

THE LAW OF SUGGESTION.

Man has made no more important discovery than this law. It opens an era in human progress that presages the realization of that New Civilization which prophets have foreseen and sages foretold. This Law is the one Principle, present in every New Thought movement. The Law is stated thus—I AM THAT WHICH I THINK I AM. Every person is controlled by his thoughts. The mental attitude determines conditions of body and environment. The secret of all inspiration, instruction and healing, lies in knowing how to cause friend, patient or pupil to think that which will in him produce desired conditions. When one has caused a change in the mental attitude of another he has done all he can do for him. That other will manifest in conduct that which he has mentally accepted. Suggestion gives the key to the religious, political, social, medical and industrial phenomena of life. Literature is plenteous upon this subject; to it I refer the reader. I especially recommend my books as containing an up-to-date explanation of the Law and its operation. From the study of Suggestion under other names has sprung every phase of New Thought. Though it is just to say that few teachers are aware of the fundamental Principle or know the secret of their success.

PROGRESSIVE FRIENDS.

These were of set of "come-outers" from the Quakers who held yearly meetings in West Chester, Pa. They comprised a body' of free-thinking, progressive people, who were a great leaven in American thought and a factor of power in that evolution which ultimated in New Thought.

THE CIVIL Next to Emerson, Unitarianism, and Spiritualism, the Civil War was the most potent power in breaking down partition walls between the sects and giving a free field to thought. This war was the culmination of a long struggle, closing with the emancipation of the black slave; it also freed the masses from the prejudices of sect and section. Suffering in a common love of country made each person more tolerant of others' opinions and made more real that Ideal of Brotherhood lying in the Declaration and the first three words of the Constitution: WE, THE PEOPLE. Like a fire over a wood lot, the war burned rubbish and left a soil ready for the sprouting of new seeds. The returning soldier brought home that tolerance which comes only from comradeship in danger.

VASTNESS OF OUR COUNTRY AND ITS NEW SETTLEMENTS Nowhere, save in the United States, could the movements which preceded New Thought have been possible. The breaking of old associations by removal as pioneers, produced a mental condition ripe to impulses that arise in the sub-conscious; consequent we find every new settlement fertile in new ideas. Constant movement westward kept public sentiment pliable. New problems were ever arising for social and political solution. This gave an intellectual impetus to the new nation, and such men as Lincoln and Douglass, and hundreds of others, were developed as were the orators and artists of Greece, for these can flourish only under spontaneous action of the Soul such as Greece had when she was emerging from barbarism to civilization. Conformity kills spontaneity and inspiration. In the new settlements, this spontaneity was active. Now that the tide of emigration has been stopped by the Pacific, Soul still marches on, and backward goes the tide; the new century sees the breaking of new soil for Liberty. A new exodus is necessary and it comes. Liberty of Spirit comes in the twentieth century- as liberty of thought came in the nineteenth. To every pioneer from Plymouth Rock to Golden Gate, we, as spiritual pioneers, owe a debt of gratitude for that condition of race—thought and public opinion that makes our New Thought acceptable. All is Mind, and All is Good.

THEOSOPHY

This phase of thought cannot rightly be termed a part of the New Thought movement. It is more of a side track for those who, under the impetus of the age, have reacted from the stress of modern scientific investigation and, from desire to rest upon something, are seeking that old staff:—Authority. It is an attempt to graft upon the thought and life of this era the childish speculations of an early people, in regard to the origin and destiny of man.

While the theosophists have much in common with all forms of liberal thought their peculiar dogmas of Reincarnation and Karma distinctly isolate them from every other phase and make of them a distinctive class, which may well be called a sect. Their teachers make too great a claim for the movement, by making it cover the work of early liberals and especially that done by the Unitarians. Their doctrine of Reincarnation is a speculation based upon unproved premises. It is the easiest way to account for much of the phenomena of existence, but they who first taught it, also accounted in the same easy way for the movement of the heavenly bodies and for the origin of earth and man. As these phases of speculation have been outgrown this should be. Karma is also a childish way of righting the seeming injustice of life. Its error lies in the claim that justice is not done here and now. Simultaneously with every thought comes its effect. The Law of Causation, which lies at the root of all scientific investigation, is not the law of Karma, for that delays effect to a future reincarnation. To modern thought, Cause and Effect are, in the words of Emerson, "Two sides of one fact." He also calls them " Chancellors of God." They cannot be separated in time the one millionth part of a second. The difference between Theosophy and New Thought is that the latter deals in Demonstrated Truth, while former is based on Speculative Philosophy. New Thought deals with the now; Theosophy with unthinkable duration, both past and future. New Thought is practical and teaches one to live now, to make heaven now, and inspires man to be now all that it is possible for him to be by teaching him that he is a free agent in shaping his life.

Despite the fact that there is much in common between these two, and that many of New Thought teachers accept these speculations, it is safe to say that Reincarnation and Karma will never be the accepted solution of the problems of life by scientific minds nor become part of the future Science of Mind. Every known fact and every principle of the evolution philosophy disproves them. Theosophy cannot rightly be credited with giving any great impetus to liberal thought in America. It has proven itself a ratchet upon the mental machinery of the nation, by compelling that which might have been a too rapid progress in the realm of ideas to modify its speed, thus giving time for reconsideration and correction. It has furnished a resting place for the leaner upon Author; for the conservative and the timid. Beyond this, it is more of a fad than a faith. It can never become the faith of the warm hearted and religious, nor meet the demand of modern mind for clearness and practicability.

I am aware of the claims made for its numbers and power which, if true, does not count; for one with truth is more than millions repeating ancient error. Remove from it these two dogmas and its peculiar nomenclature for common mental states and common phenomena and we find but the commonplace thought of all liberal teachers.

PHRENOLOGY.

This phase of thought has an important place in the development of the present movement. It cannot yet rightly pose as a science, but it has important data for the Builder of the future. It is a fine study of Mind, based upon, as yet, non-established theories. Behind all its claims however rests the fact that size and texture of brain accompany certain human tendencies. Its principal error lies in giving too much power to matter. When asked if I do not believe in phrenology I answer: " Yes, in so far as it recognizes that I build my head and can control it. In so far as it tells me that I am controlled by my head, I deny it. I build my head, and it, like every other organ of my body, is subject to my will and desire. I, the Ego, made, and I, the Ego, may control the head, even to changing, first, the texture of brain, and next, the shape of the skull in which I carry my brain." Phrenology is a great advance upon earlier theories. It has been and will continue to be a great help to Mental Science. To Spurzheim and Gall the world owes a great debt, and it is also deeply indebted to the travelling phrenologist who has been preparing the field for New Thought, by giving the common mind a nomenclature through which the present teacher can make his thought intelligible.

MODERN SPIRITUALISM.

Next to Emerson I am inclined to give to Modern Spiritualism credit of being the greatest factor in the evolution of New Thought.

Unitarianism gave it intellectual power, but the spiritual, the Soul recognition, came from Spiritualism. This widespread movement prepared the way among the masses for a practical work, based upon the recognition of man as Spirit. This work is now done by both Christian Science and New Thought. The phenomena at Hydeville awakened an interest unequalled by any other phenomena in modern times. It set in operation all the present methods of psychic investigation, and it may be said that all the theories of Man, held during the first half of last century, have been modified as the result of the Hydeville raps. Teachers of Spiritualism have gone into almost every school district; its literature has whitened the world like a winter's snow the landscape, while mediums with their words of comfort have been in every home. It would have been the mightiest of miracles if it had not met antagonism in conservative circles—did not disturb many old institutions and awaken many prejudices into active opposition. Seeing that it came to a common humanity, it would have also been a mighty miracle if it had not also operated, like all other phases of truth, upon the weaknesses of that common humanity and attracted to it much that has proven to be error, and some that is not in accord with good morals. But this is also necessarily true of every awakening. Truth must use the men and women it finds, and through expression unfold them to a higher plane. The theologian, the sectarian, and the moralist, have never been the friends of progress. "Nothing so good as the old," is their cry. But despite all that a calm judgment, after its fifty-eight , years progress, can find to condemn, the fact remains that it has proven itself to be the greatest movement for good of all the nineteenth century, and has given birth to two others destined to be still more powerful than itself. Rev. R. Heber Newton says that for many centuries the only ideas-that have modified human conceptions of the Hereafter have come from Swedenborg and Modern Spiritualism. It has compelled a change in the popular opinion of death, angels, heaven, hell, and the resurrection, and forced a rational philosophy into the pulpits. In the sensational spirit which the Hydeville raps awakened the grander and more beautiful, and the most practical side of this movement, has been overlooked, save by a few teachers, societies, journals, until the movement under the name Spiritualism is almost wholly given over to phenomenalism. By taking advantage of the credulity and ignorance of the masses many charlatans have stolen its livery, to serve the selfish propensities of man, using here, just as they have in all ages and times, the semblance of truth for selfish ends. For this reason the philosophical and practical side of the movement has separated itself from the merely phenomenal and become the inspiration of NEW THOUGHT.

ANDREW JACKSON DAVIS.

All New Thought ideas, save those that make man conscious that he IS spirit here and NOW, were born before the Hydeville raps, as noted before of Unitarianism. They have been repeated by Spiritualists during all the years of its existence. In 1845, three years before the Hydeville raps, in the person and Revelations of Andrew Jackson Davis, was Modern Spiritualism really born. And to him we may honestly date New Thought birth, though present "founders" of systems of" Healing' ' and teaching, and many teachers of various phases of New Thought, are not aware of the source from whence, by evolution, their ideas sprang. Davis was at that time a lad of fourteen years. While in mesmeric trance he gave those lectures which were later published under title of "Nature and her Divine Revelations." This book was followed up by twenty-nine others, which make a library that no student of the "Progress of Ideas" can ignore. In them can be traced the heredity of every New Thought proposition. Davis called his system " The Harmonial Philosophy."

The difference between this and New Thought lies principally in the emphasis which is now placed upon the individual soul in its independence from all external control, its unity with the One, and its power to build its body into health and keep its environments to its desire through right thinking. But Davis, in teaching the Divinity of Man and Nature, virtually taught all this. Later teachers have brought into clearer light the truth he proclaimed. Methods of application are many, but Truth is One. Davis started Philosophical Spiritualism and this is so near New Thought that I am not able to "Draw a line between the two where God has not." The Affirmation of Phenominal Spiritualism is: I live as Spirit after the death of my body. The Affirmation of New Thought is: Man is Spirit, here and now. The Affirmation of Soul Culture is: I live the Spiritual life, here and now. Davis writes and speaks in what he terms the "Superior condition" which is the condition of all inspired persons. Tennyson tells us that he reached this condition by repeating his own name till he passed into a state he termed "the perfection of individuality." New Thought people arrive at it by concentration under some Affirmation. It is termed, "Going into the Silence." A better term is, "Listening to the Silence." When present prejudices and sectarian feelings are lost in a love of Truth, the meed will be awarded to Ralph Waldo Emerson and Andrew Jackson Davis as the greatest prophets of the New Civilization which is a Brotherhood, or, as Davis termed it:—An Arabula.

CHRISTIAN SCIENCES

A very important Thought-movement, found at the beginning of this century, is named "Christian Science." To Mary Baker Eddy rightly belongs the credit of originating both the name and the interpretation of Scripture adopted by this sect. Long prior to her advent, others had used the same Principles for healing purposes. Emerson had, long before, taught the same truth and mesmerists of all names and grades, magnetic healers and faith curers, had all applied it. She instituted a method based upon a peculiar interpretation of the Bible. The Principle of Suggestion is the foundation. Most of her philosophy is the common stock of all liberal people, and, prior to her advent, had been much more clearly taught as spiritualism. Christian Scientists are restricted to a reading, and a study of the Bible, and Mrs. Eddy's interpretation of it in her book, "Science and Health," and to the official publications of the "Mother Church" in Boston. No latitude is allowed for individual opinion. Mrs. Eddy, in the Preface to the 48th edition of "Science and Health," printed in 1890, says: "The first edition of 'Science and Health' was published in 1875." In the first chapter of this edition, she says: "In the year 1866, I discovered metaphysical healing and named it, 'Christian Science.' " All who wish to know her system and her interpretation of Scripture, are referred to the publications of this sect. Most of the writings of these people are repellant from their dogmatism and authoritative manner of presentation. They are persist ant proselytes. All lectures and books are made to accord with the teachings of "Science and Health." That, in an age of freedom, so large a following can be obtained to so sectarian a movement, is a strange psychological fact which can be accounted for only upon the propensity men have to lean on authority, and by recognizing that the spirit which led men to follow a "Thus said the Lord,' in time of Moses, still controls the masses. Wise men do not submit to limitations. "Unchain Truth," is the cry of Col. Sabin who has come out from that sect to a broader field of thought. Christian Science is a necessary step in the evolution of the race. Through it many will pass from the tyranny of ecclesiastic dogma to that of "Science and Health," and finding this too narrow will pass, as thousands already have, into the freedom of New Thought.

Mrs. Eddy's basic proposition is pure Idealism. Mind is All. In Chapter X of her book she gives the "Platform of Christian Science." It consists of twenty planks none of which are original. Was there allowed a free interpretation they would not be obnoxious. But Mrs. Eddy is the Supreme Court and gives her own interpretation, thus imprisoning the intellect of her followers. This is the distinction between Christian Science and New Thought, for Christian Science is not New Thought, and is not to be classed among New Thought movements. Because the popular conception so places it, I devote this space to it.

Christian Science is fifteenth century in its methods. It follows the theologic tendency in its dominion over the human will. It limits, as did Moses, inspiration. The God of Mrs. Eddy is Mohammedan in its exclusiveness. The author of "Science and Health" claims to speak from the authority of "the Spirit," and her word is final. What she says must not even be discussed. The liberty of private judgment is the gift of the Reformation. Here it is denied with all the power of a Tetzel or a Diet of Worms. The Truth in Christian Science is the common inheritance of Humanity. Inspiration is still common. Well says Samuel Longfellow:—

Lord, thy Word abideth ever,

Inspiration is not sealed;

Answering unto man's endeavor,

Truth and Right are still revealed.

That which came to ancient sages,

Greek, Barbarian, Roman, Jew,

Written in the heart's deep pages,

Shines today forever new.

The power of Authority over the Soul is broken. Mrs. Eddy's proclamation looks like .another attempt to corner Truth, for she says, on page 12 of "Science and Health": "No human tongue or pen has suggested the contents of "Science and Health," or can tongue or pen overthrow it." Christian Scientists heal thousands. They cure a much larger proportion of their patients than do doctors of all schools. Their only mistake lies in denying the same power to others and in limiting the One Universal Life to one method and to one person's conception of Supreme Power. They have Truth but not all of truth. They have a method, but not all possible methods. They heal, but in no greater proportion than other Thought-Healers. All healing is one, for the origin of Life is One. Neither Life nor Healing depends upon our conceptions of Truth any more than our being hit with lightning depends upon our knowledge of electricity. All who are in the lightning's path are hit, be they wise or ignorant in electric lore. So all who obey •conditions of health have it, and heal, no matter what are their opinions of the power. Mind is one in all men. Thought is Power, Suggestion in the Law. Whenever in sincerity one thinks Health, he is healed.

These two streams, New Thought and Christian Science, will both continue. As long as man is weak and seeks for assistance outside himself Christian Science will endure in some form and under some name. As long as man is intellectually free New Thought will be his Philosophy and control his life. Freedom and authority are represented by the two systems and are now, as never before, brought face to face in a practical work in a scientific and inventive age and in a free land. Give them both a fair field. Between the two the Soul goes marching on. and never long submits to limitations. Truth finds a way of expression or makes one. New Thought will make ten thousand channels and will reach the sea. The other, like all organized power, must ultimately die. New Thought will never organize. Its genius is Freedom. There will come a unity of action. Under it all will come to a Realization of Truth, and societies of expression will naturally crystallize, not to think alike, but to work together for the good of all. Both movements are now disintegrating old institutions. The one whose watchword is " without limitations" will redeem the world.

MENTAL SCIENCE.

Mrs. Helen Wilmans of Sea Breeze, Florida, is rightly the founder of this branch of New Thought. She terms it Mental Science. It is based upon the principles of Idealism. She differs from many, and from myself, through the ignoring of psychic phenomena, rejecting all conception of spirit and claiming all phenomena to be mental. She recognizes no communication except between minds incarnate, and seems to limit the individual entirely to his own mentality. Man is Mind, is her Affirmation, and she consistently follows the Affirmation in all her writings, but seems to limit mind entirely to the thinking function. Her paper, Freedom, her books and lessons have been a most important factor in New Thought. She has laid a foundation broad and deep for future builders. She is a most successful healer by absent treatment and cures 90 per cent of her patients. Her two books of power are " Conquest of Poverty "and " Conquests of Death." She is a strenuous advocate of earthly immorality. These books will carry her name down to posterity. She has suffered, and at this writing is still suffering, civil persecution through antagonisms aroused by her absent treatments. All reformers have had similar persecutions, and Truth the more abounds because of it. Freedom, Mrs. Wilmans' paper, is a weekly, published at Sea Breeze at $2.00 a year. At present writing, owing to governmental interference, it is suspended, I trust but temporarily.

DIVINE SCIENCES

This phase of New Thought was instituted by Mrs. M. E. Cramer, of San Francisco. It is midway between Christian Science and New Thought. It has New Thought freedom with Christian Science reliance upon Bible. Yet Mrs. Cramer claims no authoritative interpretation. She has a rational, common-sense philosophy of life. This is her statement of Truth:—

There can be but one All. This All in All is God, and God manifest.

One is the number of Unity. Unity is forever the state or nature of one. God being Infinite, there can be no finite. He is all of Being, Creative action and Creation. "I and my Father are one!"

God is Spirit; all of Life, Love, Truth, Substance, Soul, and Intelligence; all of Knowledge, all of Power, all of Presence. Like expresses like; hence Man is Spirit, Life, Love, Truth, Substance, Soul, Knowledge, Power, and Presence, the exact image and likeness of Him, co-eternal and co-equal with Him.

Nothing can be manifest that is not before it is manifest. As God alone is, it is God who manifests in an ever-present creation.

That which is begotten of Spirit is Spirit. I am before I am manifest. Man is potential in God, and is expresser, co-worker, and capable of doing God's will demonstrating the Nature of Spirit.

Man is Being and Existence, created in the image of God's eternity and wholeness. There is one Spirit and one Body. Individually, we are inseparable. Evil, so-called, is simply falling short, or missing the mark of, this Truth. The organ of this movement is Harmony, now in its 17th year, published in San Francisco at $1 a year. Mrs. Cramer also publishes several books and holds meetings and classes at her College of Divine Science in this city.

TRUTH STUDENTS.

A class of sincere, intelligent and progressive people take this name. They establish "Homes of Truth" where teaching and healing is done and freewill offerings received. Their thought does not differ from that of Mental and Divine Scientists. Their methods are, however, more in harmony with Divine Science. They use the Bible, giving it a spiritual interpretation. They are in every way successful and form an important branch of the New Thought movement. Unity, $1 a year, of Kansas City, Mo., is their principal journal. It is ever fair and honorable in its treatment of all other phases of thought, and has at its head two of the clearest of teachers,—Charles and Myrtle Fillmore. Unity Company also publishes the only child's paper in New Thought, —Wee Wisdom. It is a beautiful little sheet,, filled with just the thought that will make the child who reads it, self-reliant, honorable and happy. It is 50c a year, and should be in every home as the child's companion.

SUGGESTIVE THERAPEUTICS.

One of the most important phases of New Thought is known as Suggestive Therapeutics or Healing by Suggestion. It is based upon the Law of Suggestion,—a Law which underlies all the methods of the various schools of Mental Healing. While other schools use silent methods alone, in this school every known method of conveying a Suggestion is used. Since the Law is: / am that which I think I am, it follows that all that any system can do is to bring the patient into a right mental attitude, then the Soul (or Mind) works the cure. * 'Magnetic Healing," and other forms of healing, are facts, but Suggestion is an ever-present factor in them all. That the Human body possesses something akin to radio-activity that will heal, is a well attested fact. That there are mental and psychic forces that can heal, is also a fact; but without Suggestion they can be neither conveyed nor received. A Suggestion, by word,, gesture or thought, is necessary. It is constantly becoming more widely recognized that Suggestion plays a more important part in healing, even when medicine is used, than most have been willing to allow. The underlying Principles of all schools of New Thought are: Mind controls all the manifestations of Human life, and disease is the result of mental conditions. Whatever, therefore, conduces to proper and healthful mental states, tends to cure. The success of practitioners in Suggestion in curing all manner of human ills, is making extensive demands upon its teachers, and schools, institutions and teachers of all grades of excellence, are plentiful.

The leading journal in this line is Suggestion, published in Chicago, $1 a year. The literature upon this subject is large. Any good author upon Hypnotism -will do to start with. Hudson's "Law of Psychic Phenomena" is good, providing one will not be misled by his special plea for a dual mind and his prejudice against Spiritualism. A. E. Carpenter's little book "Plain instructions in Hypnotism," and my two books, "How to Control Fate through Suggestion" and "Not Hypnotism but Suggestion," are especially recommended to be read before others are taken up. They will open the way to a more accurate judgment than can be formed from advertisements. A most essential knowledge in New Thought is that of Suggestion. Without it, one will fall into fads and impose limitations upon Truth. Suggestion, when used upon one's self, is termed Self-Suggestion—Auto-Suggestion—or better still, Affirmation. Through the use of Affirmation, one can cure all ills, including failure and poverty.

The popular name for this method of healing is Hypnotism, but this term convey s a wrong impression. It was coined from a misconception of the source of the power, and is now repudiated by all advanced thinkers in this field of thought. The power is that of the patient's own mind, directed by the wise Suggestion of the Healer. Suggestion here, as everywhere in life, is the potent factor.

PSYCHIC RESEARCH SOCIETY.

For twenty years or more a number of scientific gentlemen, under the name of "The Psychic Research Society," have been investigating psychic phenomena with a view of ascertaining first, "the truthfulness of the common tales;" next, to discover the origin of the phenomena. Among its more active members are included eminent psychologists, physicists and authoritative thinkers in many fields of activity. Among them are Sir William Crooks, Oliver Lodge, Balfour Stewart, W. F. Barrett, Arthur

Balflour, E. W. H. Myers, Andrew Lang, Lord Rayleigh, and many others of prominence in England, with Phillips Brooks, William James, J. H. Hyslop, R. Heber-Newton, Minot J. Savage, and others of equal power in the United States. Gladstone remarked to Professor Myers that the work of the Society "was the most important being done in the world—by far the most important." This society has published the results of its researches and many have been convinced, by the phenomena so carefully reported and studied, that Man lives after death and can, under right conditions, communicate with those still in the material form. Prof. Myers, the secretary, has given the world the results of these years of investigation in a work entitled, "Human Personality and its Survival of Bodily Death," which is one of the most important works since Darwin's promulgation of "The Origin of the Species."

What may be the opinion of other members of the committee, Prof. Myers in these words announces the results of the study upon himself—

It seems to me that a growing conception of the unity and the solidarity of the Human race is preparing the way for a world religion which expresses and rests upon that solidarity. * * * The new conception is neither of benefactors dead and done for, inspiring us from their dates in the almanac, nor of shadowy saints imagined to intercede for us at the tribunals more shadowy still; but rather of a human unity, close linked beneath an unknown sway, wherein every man who has been or now is, makes a living element, inalienable, incorporate, and imperishable cooperant, and joint inheritor of one Infinite hope.

From the evidence presented he draws this conclusion:—

Every element of individual wisdom, virtue and love, develops in infinite evolution towards an ever-nearing hope* towards "Him who is at once thine innermost Self and thine ever unattainable Desire."

In this outburst of faith he gives as the promise for the Twentieth century's zenith the realization of Immortality: — I have often felt as though the present age were ever unduly favored, as though no future revelation and calm could equal the joy of this great struggle from doubt into certainty; from materialism or agnosticism which accompanies the first advance of Science, into the deeper scientific conviction, that there is a deathless soul in man. I can imagine no other crises of such deep delight. End* less are the varieties of lofty joy. In the age of Thales, Greece knew the delight of the first dim notion of cosmic unity and law. In the age of Christ, Europe felt the authentic messages from a world beyond our own. In our own age, we reach the perception that such messages may become continuous and progressive; that between seen and unseen, there is a channel and fair way which future generations may learn to widen and clarify. Nay, in the Infinite Universe, man may now feel for the first time at home. The worst fear is over; the true security is won. The worst fear was the fear of spiritual extinction or spiritual solitude; the true security is in the telepathic law.

OSTEOPATHY.

While this school of medicine is a great advance upon the old schools, it cannot be properly classed with New Thought. It recognizes body, and adopts methods of bodily treatments and hygienic precautions while New Thought relies entirely upon Mental treatments. However, this school recognizes, to an ever-widening extent, the effect of mental conditions and adopts mental methods of healing. Its progressive practitioners are rapidly growing into Suggestive Therapeutics. This ally is heartily welcomed. They have secured legal recognition in many states, and are an important factor in securing Medical Liberty for all. This extract from the Health Magazine by Dr. W. P. Burk, of the College and Sanitarium in this city, reveals something of the position of Osteopathy:—

I have found that where the organs of the body are thrown down by reason of the mental part being out of adjustment, that in spite of all physical methods the mal-adjustment continues and will, until the psychic part is adjusted. Condemn no organ of the body, but agree with it and the victory is complete and lasting. Ignorance of the Laws of Life on the plane of man's existence is responsible for the great horde of physicians and nurses, drug stores, and drug-giving, the existence of sanitariums and all the different systems of cure in use at the present time.

LITERATURE OF NEW THOUGHT.

Students of New Thought will find an extensive literature from which to choose. Poems, essays, lessons, treatises, lectures, tracts, compends and journals are numerous. I can mention only the most widely known of these. Among authors I notice first Rev. F. W. Evans. He began to publish early in the sixties. His books are among the very best. "Mental Cure," "Mental Medicine," "Divine Law of Cure," " Primitive Mind Cure," "Soul and Body," and "Esoteric Christianity," -comprise a valuable library. Prentice Mulford was also one of the prolific and powerful Dearly authors.

P. P. Quimby of Portland, Maine, was probably the first to apply in its present form the principle of Mental Healing. The reader is referred to a book by Mrs. A. G. Dresser, entitled "Philosophy of P. P. Quimby," and " The True History of Mental Science," by J. A. Dresser, for an extended report of Dr. Quimby. Mrs. Eddy was a patient and pupil of Dr. Quimby, and later applied the Principle he discovered and the philosophy she obtained from her acquaintance with Spiritualism, to her system of Biblical interpretation and method of cure. Dr. Quimby was first a practitioner in "Animal Magnetism," and by experimentation came to the conclusion that disease was a belief. For several years he taught and treated from this Thought, which is now the foundation Principle of all mental healing.

Dr. J. H. Dewey of New York City has taught for many years a rational, but spiritual interpretation of the Bible, and his many works are a valuable contribution to New Thought.

Especially recommended are the works of Ralph Waldo Trine, H. S. Dresser, Chas. New-comb, Henry Wood, Paul Tyner, Horace Fletcher, Eugene Del Mar, R. Heber Newton, Anna McGowan, Lillian Whiting, Ella Wheeler Wilcox, F. B. Dowd, W. J. Colville, Lizzie Doten, Franz Hartman, Minot J. Savage, Charles Brodie Patterson, Thomas J. Hudson, Henry Frank, Eleanor Kirk, Emilie Cady, Ursula Gesterfield, James Allen, Hannah Moore Kohaus, Helen Van Anderson, Emma Curtis Hopkins, Fannie B. James, Thomas J. Shelton, Anna Rix Militz, Edmund Whipple, A. P. Call, Stanton Kirkham Davis, Helen Wilmans, Theodore F. Seward, Nancy McKay Gordan, Lida Churchill, Alfred Russell Wallace, Dr. J. R. Buchannan, Sir William Crookes, Margaret B.

Peak, Hudson Tuttle, Ernest Loomis, Andrew Jackson Davis, C. W. Close, S. A. Weltmer, Robert G. Ingersoll, Charles Dawbarn, F. N. Doud, Joseph Stewart, O. Kashnu Hara, and HENRY HARRISON BROWN. These authors cover all the many phases of New Thought. Each has his or her work in the great evolution of Thought, which the twentieth century is to manifest.

NEW THOUGHT JOURNALS.

No field of journalistic labor shows greater intellectual power than New Thought. In addition to this fact is this more important one: they show a moral power that is a saving grace to the nation. The spirit of the old martyrs is upon the editors of New Thought journals, but having up-to-date wisdom they do not invite martyrdom, or believe in it. In strong and convincing words they speak, and behind the word is that spirit of love, which recognizes mankind as one, and they all trust that common Father who moves upon the hearts and brains of His children. It is an honor to be a co-worker with such men and women. Here is a brief glance at the Journals:— Mind, New York City, $2.00 per year, monthly, edited by Charles Brodie Patterson, is the only magazine of its class devoted to New-Thought. It is the heavy artillery of the movement.

Metaphysical Magazine, N. Y., is a quarterly edited by Leander Whipple at $1. Realization, Washington, D. C., $1.50, edited by Joseph Stewart; bi-monthly. Christian, Denver, Colo., monthly, $1. Edited by Thomas J. Shelton. This is one of the oldest and most widely circulated of New Thought Journals. Mr. Shelton calls himself " Christian Science," but has nothing in common with Mrs. Eddy, being in all ways an individualist.

Freedom, Sea Breeze, Fla., weekly (see p. 43) Nautilus, Holyoke, Mass., monthly, 50c. Elizabeth Towne, editor. This is to be classed with the successful and outspoken of New Thought journals. Its philosophy is individualistic and free from all theological tendencies.

Eleanor Kirk's Monthly, Brooklyn, N. Y., $1. A progressive, clear-headed woman edits this and it is felt wherever read. Dominion, Brooklyn, N. Y., bi-monthly, $1. Edited by Francis Edgar Mason, who for years has been pastor of the " Dominion Church." A journal with clear statements of the Principles of Life. Radiant Centre, Washington, D. C., monthly $1. Kate Atkinson Boehme, editor. Fills an important place as it recognizes what many do not,— the reality of psychic phenomena.

Washington News Letter, Washington, D. C., monthly, $1. Col. Oliver C. Sabin, editor. This is the organ of " The Reformed Christian Church," of which Col. Sabin is Bishop. Aside from its close adhesion to Biblical terms and interpretations it has nothing that differentiates it from other phases of New Thought.

Unity and Wee Wisdom, of Kansas City, $1 and 50c, have been noticed. Both are doing noble service. They are welcome at "NOW" Home for the spiritual atmosphere they bring. Life, Kansas City, Mo., monthly, $1. A journal of Applied Metaphysics. A. P. and C. J. Barton, editors. One of the oldest and staunchest of independent metaphysical journals. Every word Mr. Barton pens for Life is fraught with a deep sense of the responsibility of his position as teacher. Ella Wheeler Wilcox's articles in the Hearst Syndicate are valuable contributions to New Thought.

The Higher Thought, Kalamazoo, Mich., monthly, 50c. Evelyn Arthur and Chester See, editors. A journal full of strong spiritual vibrations.

Worlds Advanced Thought, Portland, Ore., 50c monthly. Lucy A. Mallpry, editor. Mrs. Mallory has published this for many years. I am of the impression that it is the oldest New Thought journal. She is a very clear thinker and careful writer, her principles of the highest and her ideal the noblest. She is a great sower of seed thoughts, which are -widely quoted.

Fred Burfs Journal, monthly, Toronto, Can., $1. This is the only Canadian journal advocating New Thought. The editor publishes only his own articles and has no need to call assistance. He puts out a most helpful journal, free from the limitations of any authority but his own sense of right. It, San Antonio, Tex. Editor, G. Ralph West-on, M. D., $1. This is a comparatively new venture and evidently has come to stay for it claims quite a circulation. It is a fearless, outspoken journal along Mental Science lines. Mental Advocate, Chicago, 111. Organ of the Prentice Mulford Society. $1 a year. Common Sense Advocate, Denver, Colo. Eugene Del Mar, editor. $1.00. Is a meaty journal by a clear and forcible reasoner and Mental Science teacher.

New Thought Searchlight, Allegheny, Pa., $1.00. Edited by Virginia F. Sheppard. A clean little journal advocating Suggestion in healing and recognizing that psychic phenomena which demonstrates Man to be spirit now and eternally.

Now, A Journal of Affirmation, monthly, San Francisco, Cal. Henry Harrison Brown, editor. $1 a year. Its Fundamental Principle is: Man is Spirit here, and lives the spiritual life now. Its method of instruction is by Affirmation. It is in its 4th volume. Each number contains" A Lesson in Soul Culture;" a series of Affirmations; an editorial upon some phases of Life and its manifestation, besides report of Phenomena, selections from leading New Thought journals, book notices, and poem by the editor, and dialect poems by SamExton Foulds. It is a leading New Thought journal, carefully edited, outspoken and fearless, yet ever kindly. Its spirit is that of Emerson's admonition:

"Don't bark against the bad, but chant the beauties of the GOOD."

THE UNITARIAN JOURNALS ARE: Christian Register, Boston, Mass., $2. There is not in the U. S. a more carefully edited journal. It has contributions from the brightest writers and ministers, and while conservative, is free in expression. It has powerful influence in literary and theological fields. Unity, Chicago, $1. Is the organ of Western Unitarianism, edited by one of the most soulful of ministers, Jenkins Lloyd Jones. It is in the front rank of journals for its humanitarian and progressive ideas. Pacific Coast Unitarianism is represented by the Pacific Unitarian, published at San Francisco, Cal., at $1. This is a fine little paper much less known than it deserves. Our Best Words, Shelbyville, 111., at 50c., is a little journal in its 21st volume, edited by Jasper L. Douthit, Unitarian minister at that place.

SPIRITUALISM,

Among journals devoted to Spiritualism I recommend the Banner of Light, Boston, Mass., weekly, $2 a year. Light of Truth, Columbus, Ohio, weekly, $1. Philosophical Journal, San Francisco, Cal., $1. Sunflower, Lilly Dale, N. Y., $1.

MISCELLANEOUS.

Among journals devoted in part to New-Thought is noted:— Magazine of Mysteries, N. Y., monthly, $1. Medical Talk, Columbus, O.

Monthly, 50c a year. Ariel, monthly, 50c., West wood, Mass., $1. Riches, Ruskin, Tenn. 25c. Moments, New Denver, B. C., $1. Self-

Culture, Omaha, Neb., $1. P. Braun, editor. Reasoner, $1 a year, San Luis Obispo, Calif. Jacob Tulley, editor. A very progressive journal; two pages devoted to New Thought. New Life, Orfino, Ida., 75c a year. Occult Tiuth Seeker, Lawrence, Kan., $1. Naturopath, N. Y. City, devoted more especially to the Father Kneipp nature cure. $1.

TEACHERS AND SOCIETIES

Are numerous in every city. It would require quite a book to contain their names. Many have cards in the various journals. The reader is referred to them. Anyone desiring lessons is recommended to take advice in regard to teachers from those well posted in New Thought. All sorts of fads and personal idiosyncrasies are being palmed off upon the public as phases of New Thought. Astrology, Palmistry, Physical Culture, Vegetarianism, Fasting, Dieting, Graphology, Chromophathy, etc., are no more a part of New Thought than are Geology, Chemistry and Physiology. These may be truth, but they are not New Thought. They rest upon a recognition of the body. New Thought recognizes Mind alone, and cures alone through mental agencies. Hygiene, Dieting, etc., take cognizance of body—are the application of methods that recognize physical instrumentalities. It is not the author's business to decide what truth there may be in any system. It is his business to classify. Only those who teach and rely upon purely Mental Methods does he class as New Thought. Mind is all. Mind controls its manifestation, called body. Body is the creation of mind. All physical conditions are the reflection of mental conditions. Unpleasant conditions are to be removed by mental means. Thought is the instrumentality, and the only one, used by New Thought teachers. The axiom of the movement is—

MAN HAS POWER THROUGH RIGHT THINKING TO CONTROL HIS ENVIRONMENT.

SOCIETIES.

Many societies along each of the lines enumerated in preceding sections, have been formed all over the United States. It is estimated that those who accept some phase of New-Thought already number millions. This list of societies in Chicago sent out with the circulars for a New Thought Convention may be taken as a criterion for other cities: College of Freedom; Chicago Truth center; Exodus Society; Esoteric Extension;

Mental Science Institute; Prentice Mulford Club; Sara Wilder Pratt Rooms; Universal Truth Club; and Truth Students.

FOREIGN JOURNALS, AND PROGRESS.

The only foreign New Thought journals that come to NOW office are: The Light of Reason, edited by James Allen, London; the English Magazine of Mysteries, edited by O Hashnu Hara, the well-known English writer upon Occult themes; The Century, published at Adelaide, New South Wales, Australia; and one from Madras, India, printed in native tongue, entitled The Viveka Chintamani" That this Thought has penetrated every land is evidenced by the fact that NOW has subscribers, and "NOW" Folk correspondents, in every land where English is spoken.

SOUL CULTURE AND "NOW" PHILOSOPHY, EXPLAINED AND DEFINED.

Soul Culture is an attempt to systematically cultivate the spiritual faculties. Conscious of physical powers, man has learned to cultivate them; conscious of intellectual powers, he has learned to discipline them; conscious of esthetic powers, he has learned to develop them. He is now becoming conscious of himself as-Spirit, and in this consciousness is recognizing within himself spiritual faculties. Call them "psychic" if it please you, or name them with Paul, "Spiritual gifts." In this recognition, he is learning to develop them. I AM AN UNFOLDING SOUL, is the Affirmation of progressive persons. All New Thought schools are more or less imbued with this perception. But in the inception of so great a movement, there is necessarily much chaff with the wheat. No method, no Philosophy, should be too critically examined, but each should bestudied for the Truth there is in it, and not as an expected perfect expression of Truth. As the best that can be formulated under present knowledge, I put forth Soul Culture, which is an extended application of the present scientific method of investigation and practice, by carrying rational thought into spiritual fields.

I AM SPIRIT

Soul Culture is based upon the Affirmation: I AM SPIRIT ! which is the individual application of the larger Affirmation: ALL is SPIRIT! Let it be understood that no attempt is made to tell what this Universal Spirit is. It stands for that "power behind phenomena" which men in all ages have recognized and named by various names, among which are "God," "Brahma," "Allah," "Mind," "Force," "Intelligence," "Eternal Wisdom," "Omnipotence," "Energy." I prefer the term, Spirit.

AFFIRMATION.

"NOW Philosophy is based upon the Principle of Affirmation. This is the individual side of the Law of Suggestion:—I AM THAT WHICH I THINK I AM. It is also termed Auto-Suggestion and Self-Hypnotism. This is stating in the terms of today the thought of old as expressed in the words, "As a man thinketh in his heart, so is he," which is to be interpreted thus: A person is controlled by his convictions of Truth. Upon this Law, all the work of Soul Culture rests. Teach a person WHAT

TO THINK, and How TO THINK,, and you have done for him all you can. The Law of Suggestion is the Universal and Ever-present Law of Human life. Through a knowledge and application of it, one may control his fate.

UNITY.

This also is a fundamental Principle in "NOW" Philosophy. It is now fundamental all philosophic and scientific reasoning! But in this system it is carried to its full logical extent. Everywhere and in everything, nothing is seen but the manifestation of ONE SOMETHING, and that something is GOOD. This One, which I call indifferently Spirit or God, manifests in millions of ways, but no matter what the manifestation, that form of manifestation is known only as "A mode of Motion." The only way this One is known to us is through these modes of Motion. IT will not do to affirm that this One is Motion, but it is true, that all we can ever know of IT, is through Motion. This motion may be etheric, atomic, molecular, electric, or the action of ions, but in whatever form, it is manifest to the senses as Vibration, and consciously recognized as Sensation.

These Modes of Motion differ in the speed of Vibration. Both Vibration and the resulting Sensation are named alike. For instance: Heat is the name for waves of motion of a certain length and speed, and also for the sensation produced by them. So it is with light, sound, etc.

THE IDEA OF DUALITY.

The primitive man's, the child man's, idea of the Universe was that of two antagonistic forces ever at war. One was good and one was evil. This primitive idea still maintains its place among the masses, but has passed away from all who adopt New Thought. Science having demonstrated that there is but one Energy under various Modes of Motion, it follows that Philosophy and Ethics must also give up the idea of duality. The One Power cannot be both Good and Evil. To New Thought all is Good. Good and evil are not conditions of the One, but are the mental attitude the individual takes toward manifestations of the One. Evil is not in the circumstance; it is the way in which the circumstance is viewed. Evil is not in the manifestations of God, in the manifestations of Eternal Energy, but is the opinion one holds of that manifestation. The circumstances of life are non-ethical. Electricity, wind, rain, fire, flood, sun, night, etc., are in themselves without ethical significance. These, in lands where man is not, are neither good nor bad. When man comes among them e soon divides them into those he enjoys and those he fears. This distinction he makes from their effects upon himself. Thus, sun is good to the person who wishes it to ripen his grain; it is evil to him who falls under its stroke. But the ultimate of every human experience is knowledge and unfoldment. New Thought looks beyond present appearance, to the wisdom and goodness of the ONE and affirms:—

ALL IS GOOD

This is one of the principal Affirmations of Soul Culture. To affirm it and actualize it by living it is to make every circumstance good, easily endured, because it is a lesson. The recognition of the All Good makes the manifestations of life joyous.

TELEPATHY

Soul Culture is in harmony with the deductions of science, and through the phenomena of Telepathy, which is the transference of a thought or an emotion from one person to another without material means of contact. It is now a demonstrated fact that Thought and Emotion are also forms of Force," Modes of Motion," manifestations of Universal energy, and subject to investigation and intelligent control as are the ordinary forms of Energy. This fact is the connecting link between Physical and Spiritual science. It unites physics and metaphysics, making of the two one Science of Mind.

SPIRITUAL FACULTIES

Heretofore man has limited his perceptions of Modes of Motion (Vibrations) to those recognized by his five senses. The fact that Thought and Emotion are also Modes of Motion led to the discovery that man has means of recognizing these finer Vibrations, and to the five senses is added those spiritual means of recognition which we term: Intuition, Inspiration, Telepathy, Clairvoyance, and Psychometry. These are the conscious responses to the higher, as the five senses are to the lower, Vibrations.

CONTROL OF LIFE THROUGH KNOWLEDGE OF FINER FORCES

Understanding Thought as Force, man has it in his power, through the control of Thought, to control his life expression, and make of himself whatever he chooses. All possibilities lie latent within the Soul. Since Man is that which he is convinced he is, it is possible by the persistent holding of an Ideal to become in manifestation that Ideal. Only thus has any person accomplished anything in life. Soul culture teaches how to do this intelligently, and how to develop any faculty at will. Through choice, Man will in future avoid sickness, failure, pain, sorrow, and all unhappiness, since he can think what he chooses, and Thought, because it is Force, moulds his Ideal into material shape.

UNFOLDMENT OF SPIRITUAL FACULTIES

Through application of the knowledge of sound as Vibration, man has trained the ear so that where the uneducated will not notice discord, the trained ear will detect a false tone on any one of fifty instruments. The trained eye detects shades in colors the ordinary does not see. The tea taster has trained his tongue to detect slightest flavors, and the fingers of the blind are sensitive to slightest inequalities in surfaces. This sensitiveness is an extension of the recognition of Sensations. Thought and Love produce Sensations, not upon special organs, but upon the whole nervous system. For instance, we FEEL uncomfortable in the presence of certain persons or in certain rooms; we sense coming events; at times we feel depressed or elated without being able to find cause in the ordinary channels. A study of these sensations in the present recognition of Thought and Love as Power, has given rise to the many schools of New Thought, and the methods of healing noted in preceding pages. Soul Culture is the result of thirty-five years investigation on my part of all psychic phenomena under the Law of Suggestion.

EACH PERSON IS AN EGO.

Each person is an Ego, an individual Soul, a part of the Indivisible ONE, and possesses in the Real Self—also called the Sub-conscious— .all possibilities of Infinity. These possibilities lie in it, awaiting unfoldment into consciousness. All power and all wisdom are there. Life, Thought, and Love, are there in limitless quantity. Therefore, when one knows how to awaken into expression this sub-conscious self, he can call upon it for supply of Life, and thus ever manifest normally in that condition we call health; can call upon it for Intelligence, for Love, for Supply in any direction. Supply is Infinite, for the Soul is One with Infinity, and has the ALL for its reservoir. With right thought and emotion, body and environment can be made as desired. The secret of health, success and happiness lies in knowing what and how to think and then —THINKING.

THE PURPOSE OF SOUL CULTURE

Is to teach men and women so to think as to open to conscious manifestation this Infinite Supply; to help men and women to consciously control their destiny through right thinking; to help them, through conscious choice, to build life to desire. As a child of Infinite Energy, as "A son of God," as "The heir of all the ages," man is to become conscious that he possesses ' 'dominion over all things." Mankind has looked forward to a "Millennium," to the "Second Coming of Christ," to a "Day of Redemption," when all shall be blessed. All may consciously, by the Affirmation, ALL IS GOOD, make conditions to fulfill all these prophecies, longings and hopes of mankind. That time has come to thousands who have accepted New Thought. All should recognize it as being here now, for it comes to every one as soon as he recognizes that the Soul is one with Infinity arid he consciously lives in the Affirmations: I AM SPIRIT HERE AND NOW! I LIVE THE ETERNAL LIFE HERE AND NOW!

THE END.

Printed in Germany
by Amazon Distribution
GmbH, Leipzig